From Value to Uneven Development

Historical Materialism Book Series

VOLUME 312

The titles published in this series are listed at *brill.com/hm*

From Value to Uneven Development

Selected Writings by John Weeks in the Marxist Tradition

Edited by

Ben Fine
Simon Mohun
Alfredo Saad-Filho

BRILL

LEIDEN | BOSTON

Library of Congress Cataloging-in-Publication Data

Names: Fine, Ben, editor. | Mohun, Simon, editor. | Saad-Filho, Alfredo, editor.
Title: From value to uneven development : selected writings by John Weeks in the Marxist tradition / edited by Ben Fine, Simon Mohun, Alfredo Saad-Filho.
Description: Leiden ; Boston : Brill, [2024] | Series: Historical materialism book series, 1570-1522 ; volume 312 | Includes bibliographical references and index.
Identifiers: LCCN 2024019829 (print) | LCCN 2024019830 (ebook) | ISBN 9789004703186 (hardback) | ISBN 9789004703193 (ebook)
Subjects: LCSH: Weeks, John, 1941- | Marxian economics.
Classification: LCC HB97.5 .F54 2024 (print) | LCC HB97.5 (ebook) | DDC 335.4/2–dc23/eng/20240522
LC record available at https://lccn.loc.gov/2024019829
LC ebook record available at https://lccn.loc.gov/2024019830

Typeface for the Latin, Greek, and Cyrillic scripts: "Brill". See and download: brill.com/brill-typeface.

ISSN 1570-1522
ISBN 978-90-04-70318-6 (hardback)
ISBN 978-90-04-70319-3 (e-book)
DOI 10.1163/9789004703193

This book is printed on acid-free paper and produced in a sustainable manner.

Contents

Acknowledgements

We are grateful to the editors of *Capital & Class, Latin American Perspectives, Historical Materialism* and *Science & Society* for their permission to include the articles listed below in this Volume.

John Weeks 1977, 'The Sphere of Production and the Analysis of Crisis in Capitalism', *Science & Society*, 41, 3: 281–302.

John Weeks 1983, 'On the Issue of Capitalist Circulation and the Concepts Appropriate to its Analysis', *Science & Society*, 47, 2: 214–25.

John Weeks 1979, 'The Process of Accumulation and the "Profit-Squeeze" Hypothesis', *Science & Society*, 43, 3: 259–80.

John Weeks 1982, 'A Note on Underconsumptionist Theory and the Labour Theory of Value', *Science & Society*, 46, 1: 60–76.

John Weeks 1997, 'The Law of Value and the Analysis of Underdevelopment', *Historical Materialism*, 1, 1: 91–112.

John Weeks 1985, 'Epochs of Capitalism and the Progressiveness of Capital's Expansion', *Science & Society*, 49, 4: 414–36.

John Weeks 1982, 'Equilibrium, Uneven Development and the Tendency of the Rate of Profit to Fall', *Capital & Class*, 6, 1: 62–77.

John Weeks 2001, 'The Expansion of Capital and Uneven Development on a World Scale', *Capital & Class*, 25, 2: 9–30.

Elizabeth Dore and John Weeks 1979, 'International Exchange and the Causes of Backwardness', *Latin American Perspectives*, 6, 2: 62–87.

Elizabeth Dore and John Weeks 1977, 'Class Alliances and Class Struggle in Peru', *Latin American Perspectives* 4, 3: 4–17.

John Weeks 1977, 'Backwardness, Foreign Capital, and Accumulation in the Manufacturing Sector of Peru, 1954–1975', *Latin American Perspectives*, 4, 3: 124–45.

Figures and Tables

Figures

Tables

Introduction

Ben Fine, Simon Mohun and Alfredo Saad-Filho

This book brings together a selection of the theoretical writings of the Marxist economist John Weeks. They were mostly written in the decade following 1975, two of them with his lifelong partner Elizabeth Dore.

1 A Brief Biography

John (Johnny) Weeks was born in Texas in 1941, and spent his undergraduate years at the University of Texas (Austin). There he became active in the civil rights movement, participating for example in sit-ins to de-segregate Woolworths' lunch counters. But by and large in these years he regarded Austin as benignly tolerant, and only later did he come to see the years of his youth in the context of the subjugation of black Americans, with whom he had had little contact because of segregation.

He graduated in 1963, and went north to the University of Michigan (Ann Arbor) for postgraduate studies in economics. In Michigan he was active in the anti-war movement, and in 1968 participated in founding the Union of Radical Political Economics, promoting heterodox ideas within economics whilst attempting to forge links with broader non-academic social movements. His academic specialism was in development economics, focusing on Nigerian industrialisation. After gaining his PhD in 1969, he taught at Ahmadu Bello University in northern Nigeria before moving to the UK to take a position at the University of Sussex and, subsequently, at the newly-established Economics Department at Birkbeck College, London.

In 1974, en route to a consultancy in Jamaica, Johnny stopped over in New York, meeting Elizabeth (Liz) Dore, his future wife. Liz was leaving for Peru for fieldwork, and after his consultancy they spent the summer backpacking in the Andes. Subsequently Johnny left Birkbeck and joined Liz in Lima, learning Spanish in order to collect data for what would become his book on Peruvian industrialisation (Weeks 1985a). He then found a position at American University in Washington, D.C., whose economics department was welcoming to heterodoxy, and he spent the late 1970s there teaching and writing up his positions on Marxist economics (Weeks 1981).

His students were drawn from all over the world, and were often involved in revolutionary movements in their home countries. Amongst these, Nicara-

 DOI:10.1163/9789004703193_002

guans discussed with him the policies and prospects of the Sandinista government that had gained power in July 1979, and, stimulated by these discussions, Johnny took leave from American University to work in Nicaragua initially as an advisor in the Nicaraguan Planning Ministry. But there was little tolerance for critical advice, and he began to work instead for a Sandinista think-tank with a mandate to develop industrial policy. On his return to American University in 1983, he used his experience to write a survey of the economies of Central America.[1]

Moving to Middlebury College in Vermont in 1986, Johnny had a growing profile as a Marxist theorist. As such, he came to the attention of 'Accuracy in Academia (AIA)', an American organisation committed to driving left-leaning scholars out of teaching, and was placed on its list of 'dangerous' academics. During a spell of research leave in London in 1990, the School of Oriental and African Studies (now SOAS University of London) asked Johnny to create an MSc programme in Development Studies. He accepted enthusiastically, remaining at SOAS until retirement in 2006, holding appointments in the Departments of Development Studies and Economics, chairing each at various times, and founding the Centre for Development Policy and Research.

During his retirement, Johnny continued research, writing, speaking and consulting. He even started his own weekly radio programme. He fully embraced the resurgence of political economy and activism in the wake of the Financial Crisis, actively participating in the Occupy Wall Street movement in both New York and London, and publishing two further books.[2] From 2018 to his death in 2020, Johnny devoted his time to the Progressive Economy Forum, whose aim was to coordinate the development of a radical new UK macroeconomic programme.

Johnny wanted his writings to be accessible to non-economists as guides to public understanding and political action. By nature a radical contrarian, he questioned conventional wisdoms, and in his extensive consultancy work (across Asia, Africa and Latin America) advocated pragmatic and politically feasible alternatives to the myths around 'fiscal austerity' and the reactionary orthodoxies of the World Bank and the IMF. In his later years, he increasingly focused on macroeconomic performance, growth and inequality, and devoted strenuous efforts both to exposing the disastrous policies of neoliberal governments, and to formulating the more radical economic policies he saw as essential. These efforts continued Johnny's prodigious output of papers critically

1 Weeks 1985b.

2 Weeks 2014, 2020.

assessing mainstream economic theory and the impact of conventional (Washington Consensus-type) stabilisation, structural adjustment and 'fiscal austerity' programmes on distribution, welfare, and the development prospects in Latin America, sub-Saharan Africa, Asia, the 'transition economies' in Eastern Europe and the UK. These papers examine in great detail and in a wide variety of contexts the inconsistencies and perversities of mainstream macroeconomic policies, and their damage to the economic and social fabric of both the richest and the poorest regions in the world.

The counterpart to this engaged activity in both less and more developed economies was his theoretical work on the basic concepts of the theory of value, and its applications to developed capitalism, transitions to capitalism, the dynamics of uneven and combined development, dependency theory and unequal exchange. It is this theoretical work that is reproduced here, and the remainder of this introduction tries to set the intellectual context within which the articles collected in this volume were written.

2 The Framework for the Analysis of Developed Capitalism

During the 1970s, especially in the wake of (student) radicalism inherited from the 1960s and the collapse of the post-war boom, there was a notable revival of Marxist political economy, with fierce debates over the 'correct' interpretations of Marx's own contributions, over their precise meaning, validity, and application to contemporary capitalism (in particular the stagflation of the 1970s).

At that time, there were two broad schools within the field, the neo-Ricardian (Sraffian) and the Fundamentalist. The first school rejected Marx's value theory and associated arguments about movements in the rate of profit; the key text was Ian Steedman's book *Marx After Sraffa*.[3] The second school accepted Marx's value theory, and presumed the rate of profit must fall within capitalism, leading more or less automatically to crises; in the UK the key texts were two articles by David Yaffe, 'Value and Price in Marx's *Capital*' and 'The State and the Capitalist Crisis'.[4] In this era of stagflation, sharply falling profitability (at least in the first half of the 1970s), industrial struggle (in particular a UK-wide miners' strike), a Labour government with a tiny majority but seemingly committed to radical policies it then rowed back upon, subordination to IMF supervision of tax and spend, and a social contract of wage restraint,

3 Steedman 1977.

4 Yaffe 1976, 1978.

seemingly academic differences were often translated into direct political differences in campaigning interventions. Academic debates were therefore politically charged in a way that some fifty years later is hard to comprehend and remember, although there was no direct relationship between theoretical and political positions.

In this contested context, Fine and Harris (1979) developed an approach to Marxist political economy at Birkbeck in the 1970s, subsequently continued by Fine and others after Fine's move to SOAS in the early 1990s.[5] Johnny encountered this approach when he was at Birkbeck, maintained contact with Fine when at American University, and re-encountered it upon his own move to SOAS.

Fine and Harris were regarded as Fundamentalist by the neo-Ricardian school for their enthusiastic promotion of Marx's value theory, but their position was more nuanced than Yaffe's, partly due to their methodological approach to the layering of abstractions, and partly because of their emphasis on the dynamics of accumulation in the production of relative surplus value. As regards the latter, Fine and Harris made a careful distinction between the composition of capital (the ratio of constant to variable capital) at the general level of prices prevailing at the time of the innovation (the organic composition of capital), and the composition of capital at the prices prevailing once the technical innovation had been generalised through the relevant industries (the value composition of capital). Clearly, if prices were held at their initial level, the rate of surplus value was held constant. Under these circumstances capital-using-labour-saving technical change must raise the organic composition of capital, and at a constant rate of surplus value the rate of profit must fall. This was Marx's law of the tendency of the rate of profit to fall (LTRPF) 'as such'. The subsequent changes in prices generated the counteracting tendencies (in particular a changing rate of surplus value, and the re-computation of the composition of capital as the value composition), but this was part and parcel of the same process of the production of relative surplus value. The overall outcome on profitability depended upon the interaction of the law as such with the counteracting tendencies, and no general prediction of changes in the rate of profit would be possible, because there were just too many possible contingencies.

Since the LTRPF and the counteracting tendencies were part of the same process, Fine and Harris' separation of them was a typical example of their adoption of a general methodological position on how to analyse complex

5 For an overview, see, for example, Fine and Saad-Filho 2016.

phenomena. Marx had generally pursued a structured sequential approach in his analysis, concentrating on what he thought were the elements (abstractions) of primary importance, and only subsequently (if at all) dealing with less abstract or more contextual issues that both reflect and, to some degree, modify the concrete effects of the primary elements. The advantage of this sequential procedure is that it allows a clear focus on causation and explanation. The disadvantage is the danger that it might miss explanatory factors that turn out to be important. For this latter reason, the neo-Ricardian approach favoured a simultaneous rather than a sequential approach. While the advantage of this is that all factors are, at least in principle, taken into account, the disadvantage of a framework in which everything depends upon everything else is that causation and explanation become very difficult, if not impossible.

Johnny was heavily influenced by the Fine-Harris approach and its subsequent development, and integrated large elements of it into his own perspective. This is evident in his work on the rate of profit, his insistence on the centrality of class relations and his focus on the restructuring of capital. It also informed his critical work on underconsumptionism and his wide-ranging critique of the neo-Ricardian school.

3 Underconsumptionism and Distributional Struggle

Underconsumptionist approaches to the post-war development and crisis of capitalism, while weak in a UK context, dominated Marxist political economy in the USA through the works of Baran and Sweezy.[6] For them, the problem for capitalism was not that it could not *produce* sufficient surplus but rather that it was incapable of *realising* it, due primarily to the suppression of wages through distributional struggle generating deficient levels of demand. Through this prism, many economic and social phenomena were seen as attempts to sustain the realisation of surplus, especially through state expenditure.

That sufficient state expenditure in particular could restore growth and profitability is of course also suggested by Keynesian perspectives on aggregate demand, with which underconsumptionism has strong affinities. But for Johnny crises acted as a restorative mechanism for profitability through the destruction of weaker capitals, which laid the basis for renewed accumulation. In the context of the 1970s, he regarded Keynesian attempts to sustain accumulation through state expenditure as at best postponing the crisis for weaker

6 Sweezy 1942, Baran 1957, Baran and Sweezy 1966.

capitals, and as leading to inflation in the meantime. In Johnny's work in this area, such theoretical observations are tied to the historical specificity of capitalism after 1945, in which US dominance coming out of the war had been eroded by more successful accumulation in other countries (West Germany and Japan to the fore), with catch-up and intensified competition underpinning crisis.

Johnny's earlier work was also characterised by a rejection of an approach based on the net rather than the gross product. There were two main reasons for this. First, whenever wages might be paid in practice, they remained a logical precondition of production under capitalism, and they had to be reproduced as new value along with surplus value (in the form of profit) at the end of the circuit of capital. But the creation of surplus value always depended upon the effectivity of exploitation, and this could not be taken as given. So net output could not exist before it was distributed, and this further problematised the neo-Ricardian focus on distributional struggle between wages and profits. Second, Johnny thought that a focus upon gross rather than net product to be realised enabled a move away from macroeconomics as a sequence of equilibria to the consequences of the contradictions of the accumulation of capital. In this, elements of constant capital were subject to devalorisation (due to increased productivity) from one production cycle to another.

Johnny also offered a detailed critique of the wage-increasing, 'profit-squeeze' (neo-Ricardian) approach to the falling rate of profit and crisis. Along with his critique of underconsumptionism, this marked his rejection of two of the most influential Marxist framings of crisis theory at that time. For, in the case of underconsumptionism, the argument was that wages were too *low* to sustain sufficient demand to realise the potential surplus value produced, primarily because wages were squeezed by the corporate sector (ably supported by the state) in order to sustain profitability. But, from the profit-squeeze perspective, wages (deriving from workers' struggles and full employment) had been pushed too *high* to sustain profitability, so the rate of profit fell, precipitating a crisis.

For Johnny, analysis of the accumulation of capital in developed capitalism had to focus on the competitive processes involved, whether between capitals themselves, in labour markets, and in the roles played by the state and finance. He considered that accumulation through pursuit of productivity increases allowed for both an increase in wages and the capacity to sustain profitability. In such a pursuit, both the supply of and demand for labour, and the latter's capacity to press for higher wages, were conditioned by the accumulation processes themselves, and could not be taken to be independent forces in their own right. Clearly, if wages increased disproportionately relative to productivity increases, then the rate of profit must fall. But rather than focus on this arithmetic, Johnny thought it more important to focus on how capital was being restructured, both within and between sectors, creating push and pull factors (supply and demand) on labour markets, in which increasing wages might be a consequence.

Further, if the restructuring of capital created pressures on profitability through wage increases, then the pace of accumulation could slacken without necessarily giving rise to a crisis as such. Johnny questioned any simplistic relationship between some numerical level of, or movement in, the rate of profit and the automatic collapse into crisis. Because some profit was always better than none, the focus should rather be on whether the competitive processes of accumulation can be sustained.

In short, whilst underconsumptionism viewed the capitalist economy as driven by the levels of macroeconomic expenditures (to realise the potential surplus that can be produced), and neo-Ricardianism viewed it through the levels of wages and their effects on profitability, Johnny considered these variables as outcomes to be explained. He also thought that taking them as starting points fell prey to the illusions of exchange, thereby mis-specifying both the structures and the dynamics of a capitalist economy. The same positions underpinned his extensive work on the economies of poorer or less developed countries.

4 Uneven and Combined Development

In a piece written for the first issue of *Historical Materialism*,[7] Johnny reviewed the methodological and other insufficiencies of mainstream economics, and outlined the alternative provided by Marx's theory of value, focusing on the role of competition, technical change, and the LTRPF. He then neatly moved into the analysis of the progressiveness of capitalism, and how it could inform our understanding of processes of 'development'. He applied these insights to the analysis of the counter-tendencies to the LTRPF as they emerged in advanced capitalist economies and in developing countries, focusing on the role of agriculture supporting the accumulation of industrial capital and the extraction of surplus value in the economy as a whole. Finally, Johnny summarised the implications of the expansion of capital on pre-capitalist social relations, focusing on the form of capital (whether commodity, productive

7 Weeks 1997.

or money-capital), and the broader context of the mode of production. This showed that the penetration of capital(ism) was both creative and destructive at the same time, implying that simplistic views attributing inevitable 'good' or 'bad' outcomes to the capitalist transition were misguided. Outcomes depended on the historical context, economic forces at play and, crucially, the form and intensity of the class struggle.

Johnny's analysis of capitalist development drew upon the notion of uneven and combined development (UCD) under capitalism. UCD was originally developed in the early twentieth century, to try to explain the perceived divergence of Russian social and economic development from the trajectory followed by more developed economies such as the UK, Germany and France, and to suggest the possibility of a socialist revolution despite the comparative low level of capitalist development in Russia and other 'backward' (in the vocabulary commonly used at that time) regions. Back then, orthodox Marxist views in the highly influential German social-democratic party as well as among Russian Narodniks ('left-populist') and Mensheviks argued for a 'linear' trajectory for the historical development of countries, including a fixed sequence of modes of production driven by the development of technology. This implied that a transition to socialism was only possible when capitalism was sufficiently advanced.

Such a mechanistic interpretation of history found justification in Marx's famous remarks from the Preface to the *Contribution to the Critique of Political Economy*:

> In broad outline, the Asiatic, ancient, feudal and modern bourgeois modes of production may be designated as epochs marking progress in the economic development of society. The bourgeois mode of production is the last antagonistic form of the social process of production … but the productive forces developing within bourgeois society create also the material conditions for a solution of this antagonism.

Yet, in his 1877 Letter to the Editor of the *Otecestvenniye Zapisky*, Marx was concerned with:

> the question whether, as her liberal economists maintain, Russia must begin by destroying *la commune rurale* (the village commune) in order to pass to the capitalist regime, or whether, on the contrary, she can without experiencing the tortures of this regime appropriate all its fruits by developing *ses propres donnees historiques* [the particular historic conditions already given her]. … In order that I might be qualified to estimate the economic development in Russia to-day, I learnt Russian and then for many

> years studied the official publications and others bearing on this subject. I have arrived at this conclusion: If Russia continues to pursue the path she has followed since 1861, she will lose the finest chance ever offered by history to a nation, in order to undergo all the fatal vicissitudes of the capitalist regime.

In the same letter, he pointed to the contingency rather than the necessity of a fixed sequence of modes of production, referring to his own work as a 'historical sketch of the genesis of capitalism in Western Europe', rather than 'the general path imposed by fate upon every people'.[8] Four years later, when Vera Zasulich wrote to him querying the possibility of Russia bypassing the pains of the primitive accumulation as it was described in *Capital* Volume I, and using the traditional peasant commune as the springboard for a socialist revolution, Marx replied that:

> At the heart of the capitalist system is a complete separation of … the producer from the means of production … Only in England has it been accomplished in a radical manner … But all the other countries of Western Europe are following the same course … The 'historical inevitability' of this course is … expressly restricted to the countries of Western Europe … In the case of the Russian peasants, however, their communal property would have to be transformed into private property … The analysis in *Capital* therefore provides no reasons either for or against the vitality of the Russian commune.[9]

This non-linear interpretation of history and acknowledgement of the co-existence of different modes of production at different stages of development, in contrast to the abstract logical sequencing of modes of production, opened the way for a richer understanding of the spread of capitalism: rather than creating an homogeneous world, capitalism generated complex and historically specific patterns of UCD. In such an understanding, relative poverty, limited industrialisation and large peasant populations did not preclude revolutionary politics; instead, they could ground a new type of politics, which was different from that in developed countries but had just as much revolutionary potential.

Johnny drew upon these debates and on Marx's theory of competition to suggest an interpretation of UCD that distinguished primary and secondary

8 Marx 1877.
9 Marx 1881.

elements. For him, the emergence and early diffusion of capitalist relations of production in Europe and North America produced a *primary* manifestation of UCD: the division of the world into a 'core' of integrated and economically dynamic capitalist countries, and a non-capitalist and economically less dynamic 'periphery'. Primary UCD generated a pattern of global divergence that was very difficult to overcome: after the 'first wave' of capitalist development in Western Europe, the following 'wave' included only four European settler states (USA, Canada, Australia and New Zealand), plus Italy and Japan.

The *secondary* pattern of UCD was due to competition and technical change among all capitalist countries, in both the core and the periphery. Secondary UCD generated a cyclical pattern of convergence and divergence among these economies as new industries, employment and wage levels rose and fell depending on the forces of competition.

The interaction between primary and secondary UCD suggested that there was a strong tendency towards convergence among capitalist regions (primarily but not exclusively in the global 'core'), while they tended to diverge from non-capitalist regions (primarily located in the global 'periphery'). In periods of rapid accumulation the capitalist regions converged faster, while in times of crisis they converged more slowly or even diverged. In contrast, the developing capitalist areas might or might not converge even in periods of rapid global growth. Recognition of these complex relationships, driven by the forces of competition and accumulation, could help to overcome the limitations of 'linear' views of history that suggested that capitalism drives an unrelenting process of global convergence.

5 Dependency Theory and Unequal Exchange

In the 1970s, dependency theory offered a radical critique of capitalism in the periphery in general and in Latin America in particular, in the context of the exhaustion of the post-war boom in the centre and, in the periphery, the crisis of import-substituting industrialisation, the collapse of populism, and the decline of the structuralist theory associated with the UN Economic Commission for Latin America. This critique derived from Paul Baran's book *The Political Economy of Growth*,[10] which outlined an explanation of the relationship between developed and underdeveloped countries in which countries in the periphery were systematically exploited by those in the centre. While not a

10 Baran 1957.

unified school, the various approaches to dependency theory focused on the economic relations between centre and periphery, especially the forms and mechanisms of extraction and transfer of the economic surplus.

Dependency approaches generally shared three features. First, they were historically grounded and conceptualised a world economy integrated by commercial and financial exchanges, in which centre and periphery fulfilled distinct roles. The separation between them derived from the incorporation of the periphery into the world economic system originally created by European commercial capitalism from the fifteenth century. Since then, the periphery had been subjected to three types of relations of dependence: mercantile during the colonial era; industrial-financial from the late nineteenth century; and technological-industrial since the mid-twentieth century. Across these phases, colonial domination, imperialist subordination, and unequal trade and financial relations have extracted surplus from the periphery to benefit the centre. The systematic extraction of surplus was the main factor responsible for the 'backwardness' of the periphery.

Second, relations of dependence between core and periphery had created a peculiar social structure in the periphery. A parasitic *comprador* ruling class managed the exploitation of peripheral workers and peasants on behalf of the core, exported the commodities they produced (and the surplus contained in them), and thereby obtained the foreign currency needed to purchase the imports which allowed it to live in luxury. The transfers of surplus and the high living standards of the *comprador* class were possible only because of the extremely high rates of exploitation in the periphery. Inevitably, this expropriation of surplus implied that the periphery lacked both resources and markets for autonomous development.

Third, the surplus generated in the periphery was transferred to the core through unequal commercial exchanges, profit remittances by transnational companies and financial transactions, especially debt repayment and capital flight. These transfers depressed incomes, welfare standards and investment in the periphery, and produced a distorted growth pattern favouring the production of primary products for export (and hence the consumption of imported luxury goods by the *comprador* class).

Dependency writers have offered different arguments to explain unequal exchange. The most rigorous model was proposed by Emmanuel,[11] drawing on David Ricardo's theory of commodity prices, Sraffian solutions to the transformation of money values into prices of production, and the (Latin Amer-

11 Emmanuel 1972, 1975.

ican structuralist) Prebisch-Singer hypothesis of deterioration of the terms of trade of the periphery vis-à-vis the core. Emmanuel assumed that capital was mobile, profit rates were equalised globally, labour was immobile, and wages were higher in the core than in the periphery. In this case, commodities produced with the same quantum of labour time would have higher prices in the core than in the periphery; consequently, the low-wage (peripheral) country would export goods produced in more labour-time than the goods it received from the high wage (core) country. Emmanuel called 'unequal exchange' this transfer of labour-hours (and surplus value), hidden by the price system.

Johnny pointed to the inconsistency that, on the one hand, capital flowed to the periphery presumably because of higher rates of return there, and on the other hand that profits were remitted rather than re-invested in the periphery, implying higher rates of return in the core: the periphery could not be both an outlet for the surplus generated in the core and a source of surplus to be pumped away. He also drew on his perspective of UCD to suggest that the combination of a single 'global' capitalist class and separate 'national' working classes competing for resources in circulation was neither realistic nor helpful.

In a different literature, the assumption that the core exploited the periphery (by whatever means) led André Gunder Frank to claim that underdevelopment was not a transitional stage through which countries must pass *en route* to development; rather, underdevelopment was a *condition* that plagued subordinate regions of the world economy, and the more countries participated in these unequal relations the more underdeveloped they would become ('the development of underdevelopment').[12]

Johnny was very critical of attempts to attribute the relations of exploitation in any mode of production to unequal exchange. He considered, instead, that the class relations of capital created systematic inequalities in the sphere of production which might appear, in different ways, in the sphere of exchange. For him, dependency theory could not explain historically how one group of countries came to extract surpluses from other countries, and could not deliver a consistent explanation of how surplus was extracted in one part of the world and transferred to another. Moreover, dependency theory was generally associated with the underconsumptionist argument that capitalist accumulation must rely on a non-capitalist periphery in order to avoid realisation crises, an argument with which Johnny disagreed. Finally, he saw dependency theory as over-reliant on a demobilising functionalism: for that school of

12 Frank 1966.

thought, a dependent country that remained tied to the world market *could not* develop, which was disabling both for the subordinate subjects and for the theory itself, since it could not readily explain late development under capitalism (for example, in Scandinavia, the first- and second-generation Asian 'Tigers', Eastern Europe, and elsewhere). From this point of view, if underdevelopment was due to international integration, the logical solution was a 'delinked' (autarkic) strategy of national development in which all peripheral classes can express a common interest, and in the pursuit of such national interest, socialist strategies could only suffer.

Rather than the international relations between core and periphery, Johnny proposed an account of development in which class relations and the mode of production took centre stage. For him, earlier capitalist development in the core was not predicated primarily and essentially upon the extraction of a surplus from outside the core, but upon internal class exploitation. International transfers of value were the consequence of exploitation between classes, not countries, and patterns of exploitation in the periphery were reproduced by imperialism.

6 Following the Financial Crisis

In the years after 2007, Johnny took a more nuanced view of the state and its role in capital accumulation. He had always recognised that the state had an impact upon accumulation through channels other than demand as such. This implied that state expenditure was never neutral in relation to competitive processes – it must favour some relative to others, however indirectly, and this was important in thinking about restructuring consequent upon economic crisis. But he also knew that the state could also thereby influence the pace and rhythm of the accumulation of capital (if not necessarily sustain it indefinitely). So for Johnny restructuring entailed demand management, and demand management entailed restructuring.

But the disastrous austerity policies pursued by the UK after 2010 led him to place much more emphasis on the absolute necessity of demand expansion. In that sense, Johnny's later policy work represented an implicit rejection of the more simplistic theory of state expenditure found in his earlier work reproduced in this volume. Indeed, he strategically adopted positions that he had earlier criticised in order to combat, in the short run, what he thought of as the catastrophic consequences of neoliberal policies. Yet he was always mindful that expansionary demand management required a perspective on restructuring, and he was an enthusiast advocate of the UK Labour Party's plan for a

National Investment Bank and an associated green 'new deal'. He also believed that although improvements could be won, they would be both limited and precarious in the absence of a more fundamental shift to socialism, to which he had always remained committed.

References

Baran, Paul A. and Paul M. Sweezy 1966, *Monopoly Capital*, London and New York: Monthly Review Press.

Baran, Paul A. 1957, *The Political Economy of Growth*, London and New York: Monthly Review Press.

Emmanuel, Arghiri 1972, *Unequal Exchange: A Study of the Imperialism of Trade*, London and New York, The Monthly Review Press, 1972.

Emmanuel, Arghiri 1975, "Unequal Exchange Revisited", *IDS Discussion Paper* No. 77 (August), Institute of Development Studies, University of Sussex.

Fine, Ben and Laurence Harris 1979, *Rereading "Capital"*, London and Basingstoke: Macmillan, and New York: Columbia University Press.

Fine, Ben and Alfredo Saad-Filho 2016, *Marx's "Capital"*, Sixth Edition, London: Pluto Press.

Frank, Andre Gunder 1966, *The Development of Underdevelopment*, London and New York: Monthly Review Press.

Marx, Karl 1859, *Preface to A Contribution to the Critique of Political Economy*, in Karl Marx and Frederick Engels, *Collected Works*, Volume 29, Moscow: Progress Publishers 1987. Also at https://www.marxists.org/archive/marx/works/1859/critique-pol-economy/preface.htm

Marx, Karl 1877, *Letter to Editor of the Otecestvenniye Zapisky*. Available at https://www.marxists.org/archive/marx/works/1877/11/russia.htm

Marx, Karl 1881, *Reply to Zasulich*. Available at https://www.marxists.org/archive/marx/works/1881/zasulich/reply.htm

Steedman, Ian 1977, *Marx After Sraffa*, London: New Left Books.

Sweezy, Paul M. 1942, *The Theory of Capitalist Development*, New York: Monthly Review Press.

Weeks, John 1981, *Capital and Exploitation*, Princeton: Princeton University Press.

Weeks, John 1985a, *The Limits to Capitalist Development: The Industrialisation of Peru, 1950–1980*, Boulder: Westview.

Weeks, John 1985b, *The Economies of Central America*, New York: Holmes & Meier Publishers Inc.

Weeks, John 2014, *Economics of the 1%: How Mainstream Economics Serves the Rich, Obscures Reality and Distorts Policy*, London and New York: Anthem Press.

Weeks, John 2020, *The Debt Delusion: Living Within Our Means and Other Fallacies*, Cambridge UK: Polity Press.

Yaffe, David 1976, "Value & Price in Marx's Capital", *Revolutionary Communist* No. 1 (Second Edition), May. Also available at https://davidyaffe.org.uk/marxism/critique-of-political-economy/68-value-price-in-marx-s-capital.

Yaffe, David 1978, "The State and the Capitalist Crisis". First published in February 1976. 2nd Edition, September 1978. Available at https://davidyaffe.org.uk/marxism/critique-of-political-economy/25-the-state-and-the-capitalist-crisis

PART 1

Essays on the Theory of Value

CHAPTER 1

The Sphere of Production and the Analysis of Crisis in Capitalism

The current economic crisis which has swept the capitalist world caught most bourgeois and some Marxist analysts largely unawares. The apparent economic stability of the post-war period – the absence of deep depressions such as occurred during the inter-war period – generated a myth of permanent economic stability, and a faith among the bourgeoisie that capitalist economies could expand without limit, with only minor crises. It became fashionable to talk of the 'obsolescence of the business cycle'. Some of the radical and Marxist literature on the expanded postwar role of the state (particularly the work of Kidron in England),[1] while providing valuable insights, has suggested that the source of post-war stability can be found in the growth of state expenditure.

This paper argues that the attempt to explain the stability of capitalism in the post-war period by the role of state expenditure derives from a fundamental misunderstanding of the nature of crises in the development of capitalism; in particular, from the error of underconsumptionism, which mistakes the *form* of crisis for its cause. But the underconsumptionist theory of crisis is quite widespread; indeed, in the United States underconsumption is a generally accepted doctrine among those on the left. The first section of this paper deals with this doctrine, and the subsequent sections suggest an alternative analysis of the post-war period derived from the basic contradictions of capitalism arising out of the law of value.

1 The Error of Underconsumptionism

The underconsumptionist thesis sees the cause of crises to be the unequal distribution of income which creates a tendency to over-production.[2] The 'disproportionality' thesis is closely related and will not be considered separately.[3]

1 For example, Kidron 1970. This position is examined critically in Purdy 1973.

2 Rosa Luxemburg provided the first major statement of the underconsumptionist thesis (Luxemburg 1968). Sweezy 1968 devotes most of its discussion of crises to underconsumptionist causes.

3 For a critique of disproportionality explanations of crisis, see Yaffe 1973, pp. 209–11.

 | DOI:10.1163/9789004703193_003

The argument is that the low income of the masses in capitalist society is the obstacle to the expansion of capital; i.e., the low income of the masses results in a lack of 'effective demand', to use the Keynesian phrase, for the commodities produced by expanding capital.[4] Thus, the *cause* of crisis is seen as the inability to *realise* surplus value in the sphere of circulation, the inability to sell what is produced. The role of the state is to alleviate this crisis of over-production through increased expenditure on goods and services. This analysis is in the tradition of Hobson[5] and Keynes, not Marx.[6]

The major figures in the development of Marxian theory – Marx himself, Engels, and Lenin – all rejected underconsumptionism as the explanation of crises in capitalism. The error of underconsumptionism can be demonstrated at various levels of abstraction. Most fundamentally, ascribing the cause of crises in capitalism to the inability of capitalists to realise surplus value is tantamount to rejecting the concept of the mode of production:

> ... the underconsumption of the masses, the restriction to what is necessary for their maintenance and reproduction, is not a new phenomenon. It has existed as long as there have been exploiting and exploited classes ... The underconsumption of the masses is a necessary condition of all forms of society based on exploitation, consequently also of the capitalist form of production *which first gives rise to crises*. The underconsumption of the masses is therefore also a requisite condition for crises, and plays in them a role which has long been recognized. But it tells us just as little why crises exist today as why they did not exist before.[7]

That is, all societies divided into classes have been and remain characterised by the poverty of the masses of the working people relative to the wealth of the

---

4 This view can be found in such diverse publications on the left as *The Guardian*, *Class Struggle*, and the *Monthly Review*.

5 'Whatever is produced in England can be consumed in England, provided that the "income", or power to demand commodities, is properly distributed' (Hobson 1938, p. 88); and, 'My contention is that the system prevailing in all developed countries for the production and distribution of wealth has reached a stage in which its productive powers are held in leash by its inequalities of distribution ...' ('Introduction' to Hobson 1938, p. xii).

6 Marxist underconsumptionists frequently cite the following from *Capital* to support their thesis: 'The ultimate reason for all real crises always remains the poverty and restricted consumption of the masses as opposed to the drive of capitalist production to develop the productive forces as though only the absolute consuming power of society constituted their limit' (Marx 1972a, p. 347). As we shall see below, this quotation offers no support to an underconsumptionist interpretation of crises.

7 Engels 1962, pp. 393–4.

ruling classes. This only *describes* class societies, explaining nothing. Capitalism as a social system is not unique in this regard. But only under capitalism are crises, taking the form of over-production and widespread unemployment, inherent in the economic system. While it is certainly true that the poverty of the masses is necessary for economic crises, this poverty cannot explain why they occur only under capitalism and not under pre-capitalist modes of production.[8]

At this level of abstraction, the error of underconsumptionism is the confusion of the form of crisis for its cause; this is clearly shown in the crisis of the second half of the 1960s, and the failure to make the distinction between *form* and *essence* of social phenomena.[9]

At another level, underconsumptionism results from a profound misunderstanding of the nature of capitalist accumulation. Implicit in the underconsumptionist thesis is the proposition that the engine of accumulation is the growth of individual consumption.[10] In this view, investment by capitalists is derived from, or prompted by, the growth of this consumption demand. That is, it is the growth of the market for 'consumer goods' (individual consumption) which determines the rate of accumulation. This line of argument turns the process of accumulation on its head; it is the rate of accumulation itself which determines the growth of individual consumption through determining the level of employment and the value of labour-power. Similarly, the size of the market for all types of goods is a *consequence*, not a determinant, of the rate of accumulation. Fundamentally, the problem of 'demand' under the capitalist mode of production is resolved through the demand among capitalists

---

8 Capitalism can be analysed scientifically only by recognising and investigating its historical uniqueness. Marx epitomises this in his critique of bourgeois political economy of his time: 'If then we treat this mode of production [capitalism] as one eternally fixed by Nature for every state of society, we necessarily overlook that which is the differentia specifica of the value-form, and consequently of the commodity-form and of its further developments, money-form, capital-form, etc' (Marx 1972b, p. 58). It is precisely this historical understanding of the uniqueness of capitalism that enables us to understand crises.

9 This distinction appears in the first chapter of *Capital*. Marx is making this distinction when he writes: 'Political economy has indeed analysed, however incompletely, value and its magnitude, and has discovered what lies beneath these forms. But it has never once asked the question why labour is represented by the value of its product and labour-time by the magnitude of that value' (Marx 1972b, p. 52).

10 Consumption of use values by workers and capitalists for personal needs is 'unproductive' in the sense that it does not directly produce surplus value, but in the case of workers, produces the ability to supply the means by which surplus value is later produced (labour-power).

for the means of production.[11] This is the sense in which the rate of accumulation can be treated as an independent variable, determined by the state of the class struggle, the degree of centralisation of capital, the quality and size of the labour force, and the technical conditions of production.

It must be stressed that we have not argued that crises of realisation are not inherent in capitalism. That all crises eventually take the form of a realisation crisis is a necessary consequence of the dialectical role which crises play in the capitalist system (discussed below). But to see realisation as the cause, or even as the *signal* that the crisis has arrived, is either, in the first case (confusion of cause with form) never to move beyond the sphere of circulation in the analysis; or, in the second case (believing that all crises are heralded by a failure to realise surplus value) to fail to see that the contradictions of capitalism are always resolved to a higher level, only to reappear in more acute and altered form. These points will be explained at length in the next section; but as a final comment on the underconsumptionist thesis, one can do no better than Marx's criticism:

> It is sheer tautology to say that crises are caused by the scarcity of effective consumption, or of effective consumers. The capitalist system does not know any other modes of consumption than effective ones, except that of *subforma pauperis* or of the swindler ... But if one were to attempt to give this tautology the semblance of a profounder justification by saying that the working-class receives too small a portion of its own product and the evil would be remedied as soon as it receives a larger share of it and its wages increase in consequence, one could only remark that crises are always prepared by precisely a period in which wages rise generally, and the working-class actually gets a larger share of that part of the annual product which is intended for consumption.[12]

Marx showed that the possibility of crisis is inherent in the capitalist mode of production *on the assumption* that there are no interruptions in the process of circulation; i.e., that surplus value is realised as profit. Surplus value must be realised as profit, and increased wages cannot aid in this realisation prob-

11 In his critique of the Narodniks, Lenin wrote: '... the problem of the home market as a separate, self-sufficient problem not depending on that of the degree of capitalist development does not exist at all. This is why Marx's theory does not anywhere or ever raise this problem separately ... The "home market" for capitalism is created by capitalism itself' (see Lenin 1972b, p. 69). The first chapter of this book has perhaps the clearest theoretical exposition of the nature of capitalist accumulation outside of *Capital* itself.

12 Marx 1956, pp. 414–15.

lem.[13] Here lies the contradiction: if capitalists cannot sell all that they produce, a rise in wages, far from ameliorating the crisis, intensifies it, for this reduces the profit which capitalists could realise were they to sell all they produced. For the system as a whole, the problem of the capitalist class is to realise profit; this problem cannot be reduced by diminishing that portion of the product which capitalists receive.

The role of the underconsumption thesis as an explanation of crises is practical and immediate. Reformism and the doctrines of social democracy are its logical extension: if crises are caused by insufficient demand, then there is no reason in principle why crises cannot be eliminated or drastically curtailed by either income redistribution (the cure offered by social democrats) or by more reactionary measures such as military spending. On the other hand, if crises are the result of the process of production itself under the capitalist mode of production, as we argue below, they can be eliminated only by the overthrow of capitalism and the building of socialism.

2 The Dialectical Role of Crisis

Equating a failure to realise surplus value with the cause of crisis arises from misperceiving the role of economic crises in capitalism, and, more fundamentally, the nature of capital itself.

Capital is self-expanding value. For the system as a whole, stagnation, except in the short run, is not possible. Further, the longer capitalism goes without a major crisis, the more necessary a crisis becomes. These points represent a summary of the argument to which we now turn.

Crises in capitalism arise from the tendency of the rate of profit to fall – changes in values.[14] This tendency is not a *trend*, but a pressure inherent in the self-expansion of capital, which necessitates steps on the part of individual capitalists to counteract the tendency. One of the most important counteracting forces for the system as a whole is the crisis itself. Thus a crisis plays a dialectical role – it is both the *consequence* of the internal contradictions of

---

13 See Yaffe 1973, pp. 208 ff., for a clear explanation. This point is also made in Kemp 1967, pp. 130–1.

14 'Involuntary interruptions of an individual circuit [of capital] presuppose a force or disturbance external to the circuit itself. This could be due to the intervention of some influence from outside the spheres of exchange and production, or must otherwise depend upon a previous break in one of these spheres. This is important because it shows that, within the movement of total social capital, crises can only be generated by changes in values, not by the process of circulation itself'. Fine 1975, p. BF6.

capital as a social relation, *and* a measure to resolve those contradictions to a higher level.

Before proceeding further, it is necessary to deal briefly with the question of the tendency of the organic composition of capital to rise in the process of accumulation. Throughout the hundred years since the publication of *Capital*, both sympathetic and hostile critics have seized upon this tendency as the focus of their revision of Marx.[15] The critics, whether using bourgeois or Marxian terminology, base their 'refutation' upon one apparently telling argument:[16] They point out that technical progress (the revolutionising of the means of production) can, in principle, reduce the constant capital necessary in production as well as reducing the variable capital (necessary labour time) in production. Often the argument stresses the possibility of technical change increasing the durability of machinery, thus making 'capital-saving' possible. The conclusion seems to follow that the direction of change of the organic composition of capital is solely an empirical question.[17]

This line of argument, as Yaffe, and Bullock and Yaffe have shown,[18] involves a rejection or misunderstanding of Marx's analysis. Implicitly, the critics ignore circulating constant capital, and treat only fixed constant capital as such.[19] It is certainly possible for the amount of fixed capital to be economised in production, but fixed capital is only a portion of constant capital. Once it is recognised that raw materials and intermediate goods are important portions of constant capital, a rising organic composition of capital is a self-evident tendency when productivity of labour rises. An increase in the productivity of labour implies that a given amount of labour produces more commodities in a given period of time. In order to do so, labour must process more raw materials and intermediate goods in a given amount of time. This reflects a contradiction of capitalism: increases in the productivity of labour always result in a greater mass of the

15 For a recent statement of the major points of the critique, see Hodgson 1974.

16 Gough, for example, takes it as established that there is no inherent tendency for the rate of profit to fall as accumulation proceeds. Gough 1975, p. 57.

17 A detailed critique of this literature is beyond the scope of this paper. Hodgson summarises the position well and draws the usual conclusion, '… we must bury the last iron law of Marxian political economy – the law of the falling tendency of the rate of profit' (Hodgson 1974, p. 80).

18 Yaffe 1973; and Bullock and Yaffe 1975.

19 Hodgson is explicit, defining the organic composition of capital as the ratio of *fixed* capital (k) to 'net product' (variable capital plus surplus value, y). (See pp. 60 and 80.) The organic composition of capital was defined by Marx as the ratio of (circulating) constant capital to variable capital (c/v), where the former includes only that part of fixed capital used up in one production period (depreciation).

means of production being set in motion over the production period. This is the *immediate impact* of an increase in the productivity of labour. Certainly there are counteracting tendencies: namely, a) the possibility of the value of the means of production falling relatively, so that the technical composition of capital rises, but the organic composition of capital does not rise as quickly, b) greater durability of fixed capital, so that the value it adds to each commodity falls, and c) revolutions in the means of production which reduce the *mass* of raw materials and intermediate goods consumed in the production process.

But we are not left with an 'agnostic' position (to use Hodgson's term). It is a *necessity* that increases in productivity involve a tendency to put in motion more constant capital. It is a *possibility* that this necessity will be offset by one of the three counteracting tendencies listed above. This relationship between the necessity inherent in accumulation and the possibility of it being counteracted at a particular moment yields a tendency for the organic composition of capital to rise.

With this in mind, we turn to the analysis of crises. In the period of uninterrupted expansion of capitals, several forces are acting to undermine that expansion. The technical composition of capital is rising with the increases in productivity, and with it, eventually, the organic composition of capital in terms of exchange value, which actualises the latent tendency of the rate of profit to fall. But this rising technical composition of capital proceeds unevenly, so some capitals fall behind in the growth of labour productivity. Thus, in the expanding period the uneven development that characterises capitalism is accentuated. If no particular forces, such as a sudden rise in raw material prices or state action, trigger the crisis, it will be brought about by the reduction of the reserve army and a general rise in wages.[20] This general rise in wages makes the fall in the rate of profit more acute. The actual impulse which turns the crisis into the form of a realisation crisis is of incidental importance, though it is the obsession of Keynesians who mistake the starter-switch for the engine. The important point is that once there is a general rise in wages (or even before), a trigger-mechanism for altering the form of the crisis becomes a necessity. For with the reserve army reduced to a low level, individual capitals compete directly over the distribution of the now limited amount of profit; that is, with the reduction of the reserve army, the mass of surplus value which can be created approaches its limit.

20 Crises can, and usually do, occur before the reserve army is eliminated. The argument here takes the case of its virtual elimination to demonstrate clearly that crisis arises from the contradictions within the expansionary process.

It is now inevitable that the crisis must take the form at some point of a crisis of realisation, a 'recession'. For at this point, capitals momentarily reach their maximum expansion, and must turn upon one another for further expansion. This intra-class conflict over surplus value takes the form of a failure to realise surplus value and, therefore, profit. For out of this form of crisis will emerge the potential to produce a greater mass of surplus value and realise this as profit than before. The purpose of the crisis is two-fold: first, to drive down the cost of labour-power to the capitalists; but more important in the long run, to eliminate other capitalists and to restructure capital in the system as a whole.[21] The realisation crisis leads to the cheapening of individual capitals, and the more efficient capitals seize the moment to 'absorb' their less efficient brothers. What is being absorbed, in essence, is the power to purchase labour-power in the market.

What is gained in this process of fratricidal conflict is what was denied to the capitalist class before the crisis took the form of an inability to realise surplus value – the possibility of further expansion. Thus the role of the crisis is to raise the average rate of profit (the social productivity of labour) by the elimination of less efficient capitals, which once the limit of the reserve army is approached represent only a dead-weight drag on the rate of profit. It must be emphasized that the necessity to eliminate capitals *results in* the manifestation of the crisis in the form of an inability to realise surplus value. It is not the failure to realise surplus value that is the impulse for the elimination of relatively inefficient capitals, but the contrary – the successful production of the mass of surplus value inherent in the labour force, and its realisation as profit, brings about the necessity to eliminate inefficient capitals. At the moment of success the weaker capitals are the barrier to further expansion.

It might be thought that as capitalism passes through crisis after crisis the process of centralisation and concentration would so advance that at some stage the contradictions and, thus, conflicts, arising from the competition among capitals would be eliminated. This is the implication of the 'monopoly capitalism' school, and from that analysis derives a new interpretation of Marx which stresses that the tendency towards crisis is much less pronounced now than in capitalism's competitive stage.

Below it is argued that the present world crisis refutes such an interpretation. But on a theoretical level it is interesting to note the similarity between the theory of monopoly capitalism, in particular its conclusions about the absence of competition, and Kautsky's analysis of imperialism. Kautsky argued that there was a trend toward a single world cartel, or monopoly, and this trend would

21 See Fine and Harris 1975.

eliminate the warring among factions of the capitalist class and end imperialist rivalry.[22] Lenin's reply is an excellent statement on the importance of the dialectical method:

> There is no doubt that the development is going *in the direction* of a single world trust that will swallow up all enterprises and all states without exception. But the development in this direction is proceeding under such stress, with such a tempo, with such contradictions, conflicts, and convulsions – not only economical, but also political, national, etc., etc. – that before a single world trust will be reached, before the respective national finance capitals will have formed a world union of 'ultra-imperialism', imperialism will inevitably explode, capitalism will turn into its opposite.[23]

The culmination of the centralising trend in capitalism toward a single, integrated production system without competition will be reached, of course, but under socialism, when capitalism has turned into its opposite through a convulsive revolutionary upheaval.

3 The Genesis of the Current Crisis

We are now in a position to analyse the current crisis and explain its particular form. This form, which differs from that of previous crises (that is, the high rate of inflation accompanying mass unemployment), is the result of the resolution of the contradictions of capital through previous crises. These resolutions to a higher and more intense level have resulted in the state assuming a more prominent and altered form, and have generated in the working class greater strength to defend its material conditions. These two factors, one superstructural (the form and role of the state), the other inherent in the contradictions in the sphere of production (the strength of the working class), are fundamental to the current epoch.

Marxist commentators have tended to explain the period of expansion from the end of World War II to the late 1960s in terms of an alteration in the fundamental laws of capitalism. In particular, it has been argued that the decline of competition has resulted in a suspension of the law of value; that is, the emer-

22 See the discussion in Kemp 1967.

23 Lenin's introduction to Bukharin 1972, p. 14.

gence of monopoly capitalism eliminates the inherent tendency of the rate of profit to fall, and as a consequence, sustained expansion of capital or stagnation of the system as a whole (without breakdown) is possible. The essence of this argument is that the tendency for crises and the potential for breakdown have receded.

One need not question that capitalism in each developed capitalist country is in a monopoly stage. But, as Lenin argued in his work on imperialism, it does not follow that competition has been eliminated at an international level. The crisis of the 1930s, and the world war which followed, led to a profound restructuring of capital. During the inter-war years, the process of centralisation advanced for capital as a whole. On an international level, however, the competition among large capitals was keen. Indeed, it was this process of centralisation which generated the intensified competition among capitals. The much more rapid accumulation of capital in the United States and the emergence of Germany and Japan as capitalist powers laid the material base for the political necessity of a redistribution of world markets, which before World War II were largely dominated by weak capitalist states – Great Britain and France.

Thus, the Great Depression was the vehicle for the restructuring of capital, and the Second World War was the vehicle for the redistribution of markets. The consequence of the war was the temporary elimination of North American capital's rising capitalist competitors (Japan and Germany), and the subordination of the older national capitals (the United Kingdom and France) to secondary status.

This monopoly position of U.S. capital provided the basis for a new phase of accumulation, but inherent in this accumulation was *the re-emergence of competition*. As always, capitalism advanced in the grip of dialectical forces in the post-war period – the hegemony of the United States made further accumulation possible, but the recreation of competition was a *necessary* consequence. And the re-emergence of competition among capitals on a world scale brought about the current crisis.

In the restructuring of capital, the bourgeois state took on a new and vastly expanded role. This new role had first emerged in the inter-war period, but during the war the tendency towards a stronger state was accelerated tremendously. The new role of the state arose out of the needs of capital, but more profoundly, it represents the political form which contradictions within capitalism assume at their higher and more intensified level.

It is important to understand that it was not the crisis of the 1930s which gave rise to the new role of the state. Such an interpretation derives from a bourgeois 'pragmatic' interpretation, and does not explain why previous crises, such as that in the 1890s, did not bring about a 'New Deal'-type government in the United States. The growing centralisation of capitals in the United States provided the material basis for the expanded state and thus its possibility. The crisis of the 1930s was the historical mechanism for transforming this abstract possibility into actuality. The centralisation of capital had two consequences. First, it generated a tendency towards the concentration of the power of the capitalist class into the hands of finance capital, so that the conflicts within the class were repressed in the interests of the advance of capital as a whole.[24] Second, inherent in the centralisation of capital is imperialism, characterised by the division of world markets and the export of capital. This development, which counteracts the tendency of the rate of profit to fall, places extended demands for military expenditure upon the state. This is clear in the case of the United States. But, again, we do not explain the expanded role of the state in terms of the growth of the military alone. This expanded role must be understood in terms of the total needs of capital in monopoly form.

The growing harmony of interests within the capitalist class, due to fratricidal centralisation, made it possible for the class as a whole to transfer more surplus value to the state. The necessity of this transfer arose from the growing instability of capitalism, part of the same process which generated centralisation, and the rising strength of the working class. As capital becomes more centralised, the seriousness of a crisis necessary to restructure capital, and to enable it to emerge from the crisis with a higher social rate of profit, increases. This is because the fratricidal struggle during the crisis tends to be among giant financial capitals, which possess great power to endure the crisis of realisation and to take advantage of the devaluation of capital through the elimination of their weaker brothers. But as the crisis becomes more profound, the fact that large capitals gain relatively in the crisis is tempered by the possibility that capitalism itself may be destroyed. In other words, each crisis tends to be more severe than the previous, in order to achieve the necessary restructuring of capital, but the same tendency threatens to turn capitalism into its opposite. The role of the bourgeois state is to counteract this tendency.

Out of this dialectic, the state emerges as a rationaliser of competition, acting to lessen the violence of crisis and to try to bring about the restructuring of capital without crisis. In the United States, this second function of the state, restructuring of capital, has played a much less important role than in European capitalist countries.[25]

---

24 'Repressed', because the conflicts are eliminated by the destruction of, say, smaller capitals, at the level of production; i.e., by absorption into larger capitals.

25 In the United Kingdom, for example, the restructuring of capital has played a more import-

Integral to the new role of the state was the development of working class consciousness. The severe crisis of the 1930s, while not generating a revolutionary proletariat in the United States, did cause an important leap forward in class consciousness. Growing class consciousness strengthened the resolve of the working class to defend itself through mass action against the return of unemployment rates of the level of the 1930s. The strength of the working class has been an important impetus to reforms like those of the 1930s and the post-war Full Employment Act. Obviously, these measures were taken in the interests of capital, but the strength of the working class forced the interests of capital to take these forms.

Thus, we see the *possibility* of the expanded state to be the result of centralisation. Its *necessity* derives from the increased severity of crisis inherent in national capitalism in monopoly form and the emergence of a more militant proletariat. But this new form of the state, arising out of the contradictions of capitalism, does not *resolve* the contradictions, but brings them to a higher level. These contradictions have re-emerged in the present crisis in their altered and more severe form.

We have argued that one of the major functions of the expanded state is to temper the severity of crisis inherent in the monopoly form of capitalism. However, this gain is a limited one, for the crisis itself is one of the counteracting tendencies to the tendency of the rate of profit to fall. Without crises, or with only minor ones, the wage may tend to rise above the value of labour-power; but more important, the necessary restructuring of capital does not occur unless achieved in some other manner. Thus, the tempering of crises (reducing the swings of the 'business cycle') is a mixed blessing. It not only represses the *symptoms*, but precludes one form of the cure.

The symptoms of the contradictions within the expansion of capital could be repressed so long (from 1945 to the middle 1960s)[26] because World War II had virtually eliminated international capitalist competition. United States capital emerged from the war in a monopoly position in the capitalist world. This absence of competition temporarily postponed the necessity of restructuring capital and allowed accumulation to proceed in the absence of major

ant role than 'demand management', particularly under Labour Governments, beginning with the nationalisations of the 1945–52 period. For the last two Labour Governments (1964–70 and 1974–9), this has become an obsession – the selective employment tax, the nationalisation of strategic industries in crisis, and the National Enterprise Board. See Fine and Harris (1979).

26 It is not being argued that the expansion of US capital was continuous and uninterrupted, but that the tendency for each crisis to become more severe (culminating in the Great Depression) was arrested.

crises. But the underlying contradictions remained. The tendency of the rate of profit to fall lay dormant, but as accumulation proceeded, American capitalism developed in an increasingly fragile manner. Relatively inefficient capitals maintained an artificial hold on life, and larger capitals, in the absence of competition, were not forced to revolutionise the means of production. This is the sense in which monopoly capitalism tends to stagnation, in the social productivity of labour.[27] Thus, United States capital expanded in the post-war period, with a rot at its core, requiring only the re-emergence of competition to turn the possibility of crisis into actuality.

The re-emergence of competition was *inherent* in the world monopoly position of US capital. Like all synthetic resolutions of contradictory forces in capitalism, within the early post-war monopoly position lay the seeds of its antithesis – competition. The expansion of US capital in the post-war period, in the face of a catastrophically changed Europe, required the reconstruction of capitalism in these countries. The dialectical situation is clear in retrospect: the destruction of the productive power of the other major capitalist countries (particularly Japan and Germany) was the basis of the US monopoly position; yet, the expansion of US capital and the repression of socialist tendencies in the working classes of the war-ravaged countries required the reconstruction of capitalism in Europe and Japan. Thus the very expansion of US capital progressively eroded the US monopoly position, rebuilding capitalism in Europe and Japan. The only alternative to direct US rule in perpetuity was the fostering of eventual competitors, the local capitalist class.[28]

In the countries of reconstruction it was inevitable that the technical relations of production would develop at a more rapid rate than in the United States. If the re-emerging capitals were to exist at all, they had to develop and utilise more progressive production methods. This is because the first *form* of the re-emergence of competition was, and had to be, in the internal markets of the economies under reconstruction. The growing national capitals faced markets dominated by US consumer and producer goods. In this early stage of the growth of the war-ravaged economies, the pressure of competition was hardly felt by US monopoly capital, with its predominant world position. But for the national capitals in each capitalist country, this competition was the major determining factor in accumulation.

---

27 And *not* in the sense of stagnation in accumulation; see Monthly Review Editors 1975.

28 Why this local capitalist class emerged as *competitive* to US capital and not *complementary* in the war-ravaged countries lies beyond the scope of this article, but the answer lies in the high level of the development of the *social relations of production*. This is in contrast to the development of the national bourgeoisie in backward countries in the imperialist epoch. On the last, see Dore, Weeks and Bollinger 1975.

In a study of eight industrial capitalist countries and one backward country, Christensen, Cummings, and Jorgenson write:

> The ranking of the United States in international comparisons of growth in real output, man-hour productivity, and total factor productivity is always near the bottom. Our study is no exception ... During the period 1960–73, the United States ranked eighth of nine countries in growth of real output, ninth in growth of man-hour productivity, and ninth in growth of total factor productivity.[29]

These bourgeois economists find that man-hour productivity in the US grew at 2.8% per annum from 1960 to 1973 (ninth of the nine countries), compared to 8.9% in Japan (the highest) and 3.6% in Canada (the next lowest). Further, in the early post-war years (1947–60), the US performance was better (3.7% per annum), but ranked next to last, with Germany (Federal Republic) having the highest rate of growth of labour productivity (6.7% per annum). While we must be cautious in using measures derived from bourgeois ideology, the same study finds that the average rate of profit in the United States was falling in the post-war years; and relevant to the present argument, it began a sharp fall in 1967 (after a rise from 1959 to 1966), *before* the US crisis took the form of a crisis of realisation, and fell continuously to 1970, when it began to rise very slightly, but from a level well below 1961–6.

Thus, we can see that the 1950s, the period of the Japanese and German economic 'miracles', was a period in which US capital was continually falling behind in the process by which the means of production are revolutionised, and this tendency accelerated in the 1960s. The possibility of crisis is inherent in capitalism. With the re-emergence of competition, the necessity for crisis returned. Only absent was the impulse which would transform possibility into actuality.

We have argued that the *cause* of the current crisis was the activation of the latent tendency of the rate of profit to fall, brought on by the re-emergence of competition on a world scale. For the United States, the first symptoms of this crisis were a deterioration in the balance of payments and a pressure on the dollar in international markets. But these symptoms were only the concrete manifestation of the declining relative efficiency of US capital. While the crisis

29 Their study covers Canada, France, Germany (Federal Republic), Italy, Japan, the Netherlands, the United Kingdom, the United States and Korea. 'Total factor productivity' represents a bourgeois attempt to simultaneously account for the productivity of the two 'factors', 'capital' and 'labour'. See Christensen, Cummings and Jorgenson 1975, p. 2.

of 1929–40 first manifested itself in the domestic markets of each country and later in international markets, in the era of capital in monopoly form and state demand-management, the crisis first manifested itself in international markets.

The expanded role of the state, whose material base is national capital in monopoly form, dictated that the crisis would assume the form of accelerating price inflation.[30] The declining competitive position of US capital turned the tendency for the rate of profit to fall into actuality. The fall in the rate of profit reduced the rate of accumulation, and, thus, the rate at which value expanded. In a previous, non-monopolistic epoch, this would have quickly brought the crisis to its form of a failure to realise surplus value. However, in the monopolistic epoch, state fiscal and monetary policy in the years 1962–8 maintained the expansion of the economy counter to the underlying contradictions which were operating to necessitate a crisis.[31] The action of the state could only postpone the crisis, not eliminate its necessity. State expenditure, while ensuring that the circuit of capital continued unbroken, could not increase the mass of surplus value produced, and the essence of the crisis was (and is) that the mass of surplus value was (and is) too small in relation to capital advanced. In other words, the problem for US capital in the 1960s was not the *realisation* of surplus value, but the *production* of it, due to US capital's declining competitive position.

The contradictions go even deeper. Not only could the state not increase the mass of surplus value, but also its growing expenditure,[32] which was aimed at maintaining the rate of accumulation, actually aggravated the problem by dir-

30 From 1962–5 the US GNP price deflator rose at an annual rate of less than 2.0%; from 1965–7, at about 3%; and after 1967, over 4% and rising annually. Department of Commerce, Bureau of Economic Analysis, *Survey of Current Business 1972*.

31 From 1962–8, GNP grew at 4–6.5% per annum in real terms (except for 1966–7, when it grew at slightly over 2%). Ibid.

32 The proportion of state expenditure in GNP for the second half of the 1960s was:

	All	Federal	Percentage change in GNP
1965	20.0%	9.8%	-
1966	20.9	10.4	6.5%
1967	22.7	11.4	2.3
1968	23.1	11.4	4.7
1969	22.6	10.4	2.7
1970	22.4	9.9	0.5

SOURCE: IBID.

ecting a larger proportion of surplus value to unproductive expenditure. This is the dialectical contradiction in Keynesian 'counter-cyclical' policy: crises are the result of the underproduction of surplus value in the future. Such 'counter-cyclical' fiscal policy can be successful only when a crisis is the result of accidental or occasional causes,[33] or when the restructuring of capital has been accomplished and only the impetus to expansion is wanting. When the crisis is a result of *changes in values* (the underproduction of surplus value), 'counter-cyclical' policies aggravate the crisis.

This aggravation takes the form of price inflation. The state, through its expenditure, attempts to maintain the rate of accumulation, following the interests of capital; but capitalists in each successive unbroken circuit of capital discover that their realised surplus value is less (absolutely or relatively) and the rate of accumulation declines. After a point, the new value created in each successive reproductive circuit is less. Inflation is the consequence of the state attempting to maintain the rate of accumulation when the mass of surplus value is contracting relatively or absolutely.

This explains the failure of Keynesian policies in the present crisis and the disarray in which bourgeois economics finds itself as it seeks to account for the present form of the crisis. The disarray is so complete that the capitalist class was even prepared to flirt briefly with the morbid monetary metaphysics of Milton Friedman. The failure of Keynesianism was a result of the absence of a theory of value in this analysis. With its analysis completely in the sphere of circulation, it interprets symptoms (failure to realise surplus value) as causes. Keynesian policies could be effective in the Great Depression (to the extent they were used), because they were employed after the crisis had performed its function of re-establishing the basis of accumulation by driving down the cost of reproducing labour-power and restructuring capital. Similarly, in the period of US monopoly, when the law of the tendency of the rate of profit to fall lay dormant, Keynesianism had its 'golden age'. But such 'counter-cyclical' policies can never re-establish the basis of profitability. On the contrary, by 'smoothing out the business cycle' they postpone the necessary cure, and by draining off surplus value the policies aggravate the crisis.

In the pursuit of its interests, sections of the US capitalist class recognized the impotence of Keynesianism to alleviate the crisis, and in the United States (and other capitalist countries) pressures developed for the reduction of state expenditure.[34] The effect of this is to transform the crisis to its form of an inability to realize surplus value as profit.

---

33 For example, changes in 'expectations', inventory cycles, etc.

34 In current prices US federal government expenditure was 98.8 billion dollars in 1968,

This assault upon state expenditure is necessarily an assault upon the working class. While a large proportion of state expenditure may be unproductive (in that it does not produce surplus value),[35] it is nonetheless necessary for the expansion of capital.

Military expenditure is only the most obvious example. Thus, the capitalist class seeks on all levels of government to reduce state expenditure which is least essential to its interests in the short run – expenditure which goes to the working class – 'welfare', education, medical care, etc. As in all crises, it is the proletariat, the possessors of the source of value, labour-power, which must bear the burden of crisis.

4 Conclusion

This paper has offered an approach to the current crisis, and makes a sharp break with the underconsumptionist thesis. It is in agreement with the position that seeks to shift Marxian analysis in the United States to an emphasis on contradictions of capitalism which arise in the sphere of production. By stressing the central role that contradictions in the sphere of production play, we have consciously played down the sphere of circulation. We have done this, not because we do not see the sphere of circulation as important – indeed, Marx devoted an entire volume of *Capital* to its analysis (a volume sorely neglected).

The analysis of the sphere of circulation has been given little space because it is necessary at the present state of Marxist and radical thought in the United States starkly and unambiguously to differentiate underconsumptionist theories of crisis from the Marxian materialist analysis of crisis. At the risk of oversimplification it is necessary to initiate and advance a debate concerning the nature of crises, with the aim of revealing and isolating the underconsumptionist thesis for demolition. The position that crises are the result of changes in values, the tendency of the rate of profit to fall, requires much more theoretical work. However, its unresolved analytical difficulties can be of no solace to underconsumptionists. As we showed in Section I, the underconsumptionist thesis fails in its own terms; i.e., it cannot explain why economic crises are pecu-

---

the same in 1969, and 96.5 billion in 1970. With inflation, this represented substantial decreases. While federal government purchases of goods and services was in the range of 10.5 to 11.5% of GNP during l. 96tH59, subsequently it fell to 9 to 10%. Department of Commerce, op. cit.

35 Yaffe 1975, pp. 225ff. This is a controversial point. Productive labour is defined carefully by Bullock and Yaffe 1975. For the contrary view, see Gough 1972.

liar to the capitalist mode of production. Marxists must discard this analytical framework and leave it to the Keynesians and neo-Ricardian social democrats. No analysis that incorporates it can break out of the bounds of reformism.

Once underconsumptionism is left behind, the possibility of theoretical advances in the analysis of the laws of motion of capitalism is again before us. One of the most important areas where theoretical work is necessary is in the analysis of the competition among capitals, a subject dealt with here only in general terms. The idea that the centralisation of capital has led to the virtual destruction of competition in the United States is another ideological weapon in the reformist arsenal. It suggests that the ills of capitalism lie in the form which capital takes – monopoly enterprises – not in capital as a social relation, whatever its form. The materialist theory of competition follows from the theory of crisis,[36] and is the extension of contradictions in the sphere of production into the sphere of circulation.

Second, with underconsumptionism behind us, progress can be made on the theory of wages. Once the erroneous idea is discarded, that the importance of wages lies in their relation to 'effective demand', the fundamental importance of variable capital can be explored: namely, its function of providing the means of reproducing the commodity labour-power, the source of value. From this insight, one can explore the motor of capitalist accumulation – the driving down of the value of labour-power in order to raise the rate of surplus value (the extraction of relative surplus value).[37]

And third, by rejecting underconsumptionism, we can open up the theory of imperialism for theoretical advances along a revolutionary line. The analysis of imperialism has too long been mired in the sphere of circulation,[38] and a clean break must be made with the 'search for markets' explanation. The direction along which investigation must go is clear: crises in capitalism are the result of the tendency of the rate of profit to fall, and imperialism in the form of the export of productive capital (as opposed to commodities) represents a counteracting tendency to the pressure on profitability.[39] From this perspective, the

36 See Marx 1972a, Vol. III, Chapter XV.

37 The use values bought by the wage may rise, of course, as the *value* of the means of consumption fall relatively to the *value* of other commodities. A step in the analysis of this process is made in Weeks 1975.

38 Most clearly seen in the work of the neo-Ricardian Emmanuel 1972, which has been influential on the left.

39 Or as Lenin wrote, imperialism is the manifestation of a capitalism 'over-ripe'. Lenin 1974. Bukharin's critique of the underconsumptionist explanation of imperialism is excellent. See Luxemburg and Bukharin 1972, particularly Bukharin's chapter 4 ('The Economic Roots of Imperialism').

excellent work of Bettelheim can be built upon to avoid the errors of the 'super-exploitation' and 'surplus extraction' thesis of imperialism.[40]

The present economic crisis in the United States is the most severe in thirty years. US capital in the post-war period built up a weight of inefficiency which requires a major restructuring of capital. It remains to be seen if the present crisis has been sufficient to bring about this restructuring. To understand the developments out of the crisis and the subsequent recovery, the materialist method must be applied, with the analysis proceeding from contradictions in the sphere of production. It is in understanding these contradictions that we understand the antagonistic struggle between capital and labour and the revolutionary possibilities inherent in that struggle.

---

40 Bettelheim, in Emmanuel 1972.

CHAPTER 2

On the Issue of Capitalist Circulation and the Concepts Appropriate to Its Analysis

In an article published in the Spring 1982 issue of this journal, I argued that the underconsumptionist hypothesis is inconsistent with the labour theory of value if the latter is *based upon the distinction between concrete and abstract labour*.[1] At the same time I argued that the underconsumptionist view is perfectly consistent *with the labour-embodied view* of the labour theory of value (which I identified as 'Neo Ricardian').[2] Thus, I do not argue that the underconsumptionist arguments are inconsistent with 'value theory' in general, but inconsistent with the *particular* value theory based on the distinction between abstract and concrete labour (the two-fold nature of commodities). Now Sherman takes me to task, arguing that underconsumptionism is consistent with value theory. I note in passing that Howard Sherman objects to my identifying him as an underconsumptionist, and for alleging that he does not use value theory and that he considers profit and surplus value to be the same thing; he is quite right in these objections, and I apologize for having made these statements. However, he at no point uses the terms *abstract* and *concrete* labour. Therefore, my argument, right or wrong, has not been challenged.

1 Question of Concepts

I do not mean to suggest that the issues Sherman raises are not important ones. They are, though they are not the issues I dealt with. Our two contributions are

1 If I may quote myself: 'If we follow Marx *and make the distinction between concrete and abstract labour* … the consequence of systematic and endemic incomplete realisation is quite serious … *In this line of argument*, the determining role of value disappears if, in general, there is incomplete realisation of commodity capital' (Weeks 1982a, p. 70 [emphasis added]). I was remiss here in invoking the authority of Marx, since the argument is about a theoretical method, not about who used that method (Weeks 1982a).

2 I make myself clear on this point also: 'If one has the Neo-Ricardian, labour-embodied view [of the labour theory of value], incomplete realisation does not affect the value calculations … If one thinks that use values can be aggregated directly on the basis of *concrete labour*, then "value" is determined independently of the interaction of capitals, one aspect of which is realisation' (ibid., pp. 69–70 [emphasis added]).

 | DOI:10.1163/9789004703193_004

like ships that pass in the night. I would like now to try to make contact with the other vessel, send out a launch, and try a non-belligerent boarding of the other vessel for the purpose of analysing the cargo stowed therein. Specifically, I am interested in considering the concepts relevant to the analysis of the process of capitalist circulation.

The central issue to which Sherman addresses himself is that of the process by which commodity capital is transformed into money-capital, or, less precisely (but still correct), the realisation of commodities as money. On the basis of Sherman's note on my article and another of his works,[3] I shall attempt rendering of the concepts he uses to consider this process.

In Sherman's formulation of the circulation of commodities, the key concepts are 'aggregate demand' and 'aggregate supply', and these concepts are measured in monetary units.[4] He notes that while it is the case that the price (and value, though not necessarily being the same) of a product includes the cost of intermediate commodities (constant capital), for purposes of analysis of social production as a whole intermediate costs should be subtracted out, leaving one with what bourgeois economists call 'value-added', or the value created by living labour during the period in question. This net value (or new value) can be viewed on the one hand as wages plus profits, in which case it is 'the total revenue flow (per period) of net product',[5] or *aggregate supply*. Obviously these money incomes must derive from the sale of commodities. Thus, on the other hand, the national product corresponds to the sum of individual consumption expenditures and investment expenditure by capitalists, with this sum being *aggregate demand*. This two-sided[6] nature of the net product corresponds to what bourgeois textbooks call the 'income approach' and 'expenditure approach' to national income accounting.

3 Just as I could not in a brief article present fully my framework for analysing circulation, so Sherman's comments are specific to his immediate purpose. The summary which follows is based upon his comment on my article in this issue: Sherman 1979.

4 '... cycles must be understood in price terms, not value terms' (Sherman 1979, pp. 1–2).

5 'If constant capital is subtracted from both sides of [the gross value of output], the remainder is ... the value-added in each enterprise. In Marx's terms, it is the living labour .... In terms of measurable prices and quantities, Marx's value of net national product becomes the total revenue flow (per period) of net product ...'. (Ibid, p. 3).

6 Sherman makes a slight slip by suggesting that 'consumption' plus 'investment' (C + I = Y) corresponds to Marx's division of material production into two departments – that which produces the means of consumption and that which produces the means of production. However one may define investment and consumption, it should be clear that the aggregate demand equation represents the division of *expenditure* on the two types of commodities, not, in general, the division of *production*. I point this out in anticipation of the next section.

Using these two concepts, one can proceed to analyse social production: if aggregate supply exceeds aggregate demand, then commodities go unsold and the level of the net product falls; if aggregate demand exceeds aggregate supply, the level of net product rises. Taking the former case, net product falls because by definition aggregate supply is both the value of net production and the income flow generated by that production. If aggregate demand (consumption plus investment) is less than the net product, then commodities go unsold and capitalists reduce their level of production. This, in turn, reduces income generated, and since aggregate demand derives in part from income, aggregate demand falls more, inducing capitalists to further cut back production, etc. This feedback is what is called the 'multiplier process', well-known to anyone who has taken introductory college economics.

The contraction process (or expansion process) does not go on forever, even in theory, because of the particular theoretical formulation of the determinants of personal consumption expenditure and expenditure on fixed means of production. Personal consumption expenditure is explained in the simplest case as determined by personal income flow. Analytically, personal consumption expenditure is determined simultaneously with the level of the net product, *via* the 'consumption function', whose most important parameter is called the 'marginal propensity to consume'.[7] Since personal consumption expenditure is derivative from the net product (and *vice versa*), the process of contraction or expansion would go on to zero or infinity without the inclusion of an element of aggregate demand which is independent of the level of the net product. This 'autonomous' element (autonomous with regard to the current level of the net product) is investment in fixed means of production.[8] 'Investment functions' come in many varieties, and Sherman argues for one in which the level of investment in fixed means of production is determined by profit expectations, with those expectations approximated by past profit levels and profit rates ('distributed lag' function).

With these conceptual elements in mind, one can summarise the process by which the net product is determined. The 'initial conditions' are the past his-

7 There are many specifications of the consumption function. Sherman argues in favor of one which explicitly divides wage and profit incomes, with the 'marginal propensity to consume' out of wages being not significantly different from unity, while the marginal propensity to consume out of profits is significantly less than unity. Neo-Keynesians also tend to favor this treatment.

8 Investment in fixed means of production can be rendered 'endogenous' (determined by the level or changes in the level of the net product). In this case, 'explosive cycles' can result from the model. Such a possibility was first elaborated in detail by John Hicks. Samuelson, of course, first formulated the accelerator algebraically.

tory of profit performance. These determine the level of investment. The level of investment, *via* the multiplier (whose value is implied by the consumption function), determines the level of the net product, and the latter determines the level of personal consumption expenditure. Expansion or contraction proceed until personal non-spending ('savings') equals the autonomously determined investment.[9] Cycles in this model are the result of the volatility of investment. The causes of this volatility within the framework so far described are discussed in some detail by Sherman, and there is no need to go into them since they play no part in what follows.

All of this is, of course, quite familiar. The reason for the elaboration here will soon become clear. In order to facilitate discussion, I need a term to describe the analytical approach so far presented. Since it is not my purpose to identify anyone as a Marxist or not a Marxist, I shall describe the foregoing as the 'net product framework'; i.e., it considers the circulation of commodities in terms of the product of living labour only ('value added').

I can now clarify my theoretical difference with Howard Sherman. I reject the 'net product framework' in its entirety, from start to finish, and all of the concepts it encompasses, without exception.[10] To be specific and in order to avoid misunderstanding:

1. I reject as invalid the analysis of the circulation of commodities[11] in terms of the net product, whether this net product is called (or defined as) aggregate demand, aggregate supply, value added, the product of living labour, the net national product, the total revenue flow of net product, or simply income; in other words, I reject analysing circulation of commodities ('realisation') in net terms, be the net product defined in Keynesian, Neo-Ricardian, or Marxian language;
2. I reject the concept of the consumption function and, therefore, the concept of multiplier process, and the analytical category 'consumption' itself; and
3. I reject the concept of an investment function, be it endogenous or exogenous, and the analytical category 'investment'.[12]

9 In this simple model. I have assumed that all profits are distributed as personal income to capitalists, so all 'saving' is by individuals. This is a common simplification and is, I think, consistent with Sherman's model in the article cited above.

10 I do not mean that the concepts are 'wrong' or necessarily invalid. Precisely what I mean by 'reject' is expounded in the following section. At the moment, 'reject' can be taken in the dictionary definition of refusing to credit or adopt a thesis.

11 I use the term 'circulation of commodities' to include what is frequently called 'realisation', but I view it to be broader. See the next section.

12 This implies also a rejection of the terms 'capital stock', 'physical capital', 'capital output

The three points above can be summarised by saying that I reject *in toto* and all its parts Keynes's formulation of 'macroeconomics'. I argue that one understands the aggregate functioning of the capitalist economy, the movement of capital-as-a-whole, by making a complete and total methodological break with the 'net product framework'. Marx made precisely such a break and made it explicitly.

2 Net versus Gross Product

A reader at this point (particularly an economist) might justifiably ask, what depth of ignorance or mind-affecting drug would lead anyone to reject the basic concepts of macroeconomics, which are obviously real and measurable? To justify rejecting these cornerstones of contemporary economic analysis, I first outline the argument, then elaborate it. The production of wealth in capitalist society takes the form of the production of commodities. These commodities are *capital*; they are produced as capital and circulate as capital. Therefore, the circulation of commodities is part of the process of the reproduction of capital and must be analysed as such. When we analyse circulation as the circulation of capital, the relevant *aggregate* is the *gross* product and the *gross* value of commodities. Further, the reproduction of capital has two aspects, as do commodities: the reproduction of capital in the abstract (reproduction of value), and the reproduction of capital in the concrete (material replacement). When one considers these two aspects and their interrelationship, the relevant *time period* of analysis is the turnover period of capital, not a year, quarter, or some other arbitrary segment of time.

It goes without saying that the central concept of the analysis of capitalist society is 'capital'. Capital is not means of production, nor is it commodities or money, though it assumes the form of all three in its reproductive life-cycle.[13] Capital is the social relation in which money serves as a general claim on society's wealth and elements of production. Capital is the historically specific relationship based upon the monopoly of the means of production by the bourgeoisie, which itself is predicated upon the dispossession of labour from those means of production. This separation of labour from the means of production (proletarianization) necessitates that labour and the means of

ratio', and, of course, 'capital-intensity' and 'labour intensity'. These concepts have also been called into question by Neo-Keynesians and Neo-Ricardians. See Harcourt 1973.

13 Marx's definition of capital is found in Marx 1906, Chapter IV ('The General Formula for Capital').

production be reunited by the medium of money. The circuit of capital begins with the exchange of value in abstract form, money, for the use values by which the material process of production is made possible. Marx called this step the advance of *money-capital*, and when the exchange is realised, capital has transformed itself into *productive capital*, from capital in the abstract to capital in the concrete. At this moment, capital exists in the form of labour-power and the means of production, or as the potential to produce use values.

Within the sphere of capitalist production, all of the ingredients of the labour process are capital – the buildings, land, machines, raw materials, and, of course, the labour to be set in motion. In this context Marx repeatedly uses the phrase 'investment in wages',[14] a phrase which strikes the eye as quaint and old-fashioned if one has been trained to the neoclassical framework in which 'labour' and 'capital' are defined ahistorically and divorced from the social relations of production. Labour-power in use or marshalled in anticipation of use is as much capital as the machines that labour-power is combined with. It is for this reason that money exchanged against labour-power is called 'variable *capital*' (and money exchanged against raw materials, intermediate commodities and machinery, 'constant *capital*').[15] Once production has occurred, a new set of use values results, and these, too, are a form of capital, commodity capital. This commodity capital is the material carrier of the surplus value created in production. It then remains for the commodity capital to be exchanged against money, which returns the capital to its initial form of money-capital, and the process begins again.[16]

The process of reproduction in capitalist society is the circuit of capital. Fundamental to understanding this circuit is the two-fold nature of commodit-

14 The phrase is repeatedly used through all three volumes of *Capital*. See, for example, Marx 1956.

15 Because all of the elements of production are capital, including labour-power, the term 'capital-intensity of production', however measured, has no meaning within Marx's framework. The 'capital-intensity' of capitalist production is always unity for all production processes. That is, both the 'inputs' and the 'outputs' are 100% capital. To quote Marx, 'The following general proposition applies to capital production: All products reach the market as commodities and therefore circulate for the capitalist as the commodity-form of his capital, regardless of whether these products must or can function in their bodily form, in accordance with their use values, as elements of production and therefore fixed or circulating elements of productive capital; or whether they can serve only as means of individual, not of productive, consumption' (Marx 1993, p. 213).

16 The expansion of capital (which is the expansion of value) appears as the expansion of money-capital, a never-ending repetition. This repetitive character of the circuit of capital promoted Marx to characterise capital as 'self-expanding value', or 'value in motion'. See Marx 1906, p. 171.

ies, for the reproduction involves both the reproduction of value relations and the reproduction of material wealth. That is, capital must be reproduced both in money form and in material form. On the material side, labour-power and means of production must be reunited in each successive circuit. On the value side, capital must achieve its metamorphosis into money in order that it be exchanged against use values and assume its productive role. Marx's analysis of circulation was precisely the study of this opposition and interaction of the abstract (value) and the concrete (use value).[17] This approach is not an obscure theoretical one, but a quite practical one: since value must have a material form (be objectified in a commodity), the real nature of circulation requires that we consider both the circulation of value and the circulation of use values. If one considers only the circulation of value, as Neoclassicists and Neo-Keynesians do, the concrete process of production is ignored or subsumed. If only material circulation is treated, as the Sraffians do, the capitalist nature of circulation is lost.

A moment's reflection should make it clear that one cannot understand the two-fold nature of circulation by using the net product to represent society's currently produced commodity wealth.[18] This is for two reasons. First, the net product, or the product of living labour, excludes on the value side the consumption of means of production in the production process. If one uses the net product, then the material *and value* reproduction of part of the capital value in commodities is presupposed. The second problem with the net product derives from its being defined over a time period other than the turnover period of capital. Net national product, for example, is defined for a year or a quarter. In consequence, the two components of net capital value (variable capital and surplus value) are aggregated over several turnovers, and conceptually one loses sight of the fundamental aspect of circulation, which is the recapture

17 'For our present purpose this process of reproduction must be studied from the point of view of the replacement of the value as well as the substance of the individual component parts of C′ (commodity capital). We cannot rest content any longer … with the assumption that the individual capitalist can first convert the component parts of his capital into money by the sale of his commodities, and then reconvert them into productive capital … In as much as these elements of production are by their nature material, they represent as much a constituent of the social capital as the individual finished product' (Marx 1993, p. 397).

18 Marx wrote: 'Even on the basis of simple reproduction there takes place not merely a production of wages (variable capital) and surplus value [*i.e.*, W + *n*, where n is profits], but direct production of new constant capital-value …' (Marx 1993, p. 373). Since Marx says 'simple reproduction', he is clearly referring to raw materials and intermediate commodities as 'new constant capital' (Marx 1993).

of capital advanced through sale of commodities and the replacement of the material components of production.

With regard to the limited consideration of the conversion of commodity capital into money-capital, the use of the net product is quite misleading. Because it treats the product of living labour as income or revenue to workers and capitalists on the 'supply side', the character of the product of living labour as capital is lost.[19] But the net product also proves unsatisfactory on the 'demand side', for it misrepresents the relationship between the production of use values and the production of value. In the simple Keynesian model, wages plus profits equal expenditure on the articles of personal consumption plus expenditure on fixed means of production. That is, the value created by living labour must be equal to the value of the articles of consumption plus the value of fixed means of production.[20] In fact, this equality can hold only under simple reproduction; that is, when the level of gross production (and, thus, net production) does not change. In this case of no expansion, the sum of all variable capital and surplus value equals the total value of the articles of consumption (the sum of constant capital, variable capital and surplus value in Department II).[21] If there is expansion, then part of the surplus value must be transformed into additional capital. This additional capital has three parts: the increment in fixed constant capital (if existing fixed means of production cannot accommodate the expansion), the increment in circulating constant capital (since all commodities require raw materials or intermediate commodities), and the increment in variable capital. The material form of the increment in fixed constant capital is fixed means of production, or what the net product approach calls 'investment' (contrary to Marx's broader use of the term). The increment in variable capital becomes additional wage income and has as its material form articles of consumption. This appears in the net product model as 'induced' consumption. The increment in circulating constant capital exchanges against raw materials and intermediate commodities, which by definition are excluded in the net product model, because constant

19 Sherman refers to the nineteenth-century writer J.B. Say, and it is noteworthy that Marx takes Say to task for considering only the net product, and, further, for treating this net product as revenue (income), not capital. Marx comments: '… [A] part of the annual consumption of values consists of values that are used not as the stock for consumption, but as means of production, and which are returned to production … just as they originated in production' (Marx 1969).

20 This is the 'equilibrium' condition in the net product framework. See previous section.

21 The point which follows is made by Marx in Chapter XXI of Volume II of *Capital*. Paul Sweezy also demonstrates it, and Tarbuck shows it in a numerical example. See Sweezy 1968, p. 164; Luxemburg and Bukharin 1972, pp. 271–4; Tarbuck 1972.

capital has been 'subtracted from both sides'.[22] There is an inconsistency here, which is an inconsistency not only in theoretical modelling, but in the concrete: to produce commodities, material inputs as well as labour-power are required. Surely no one would contest this obvious fact. To produce *more* commodities than before, more inputs are required and the value equivalent of these is part of the net product. Therefore, except in the case of simple reproduction (no expansion or contraction of material and value production), the net value product cannot be equal to the value of the articles of consumption and net increase in fixed means of production. In other words, wages plus profits cannot equal 'consumption' plus 'investment' in equilibrium as Keynes maintained.[23]

3 The Circuit of Capital

A capitalist society reproduces itself through the circuit of capital, and it is the circuit of capital that provides the appropriate model of analysis for capitalist society. As we consider this circuit, the categories of the net product framework present themselves, but as distorted forms of the metamorphosis of capital. The circuit of capital takes the form of two moments of circulation around the moment of production; that is,[24]

$$M(CC + VC){-}C \ldots P \ldots C'{-}M'$$

The moment of production (P) is the pivot around which the moments of circulation turn and interact; it is the hub, from which the moments of circulation radiate like spokes. In the net product models, production is presupposed, viewed as a step in a linear sequential process, in which commodities are produced, then must be sold, with sale being a separate and discrete process predicated upon production, but analytically separate. In reality, production both

22 See footnote 5. I do not single out Sherman for this, since it is the practice of a generation of 'macro-economists', a practice found in every introductory economics text book.

23 Thus when one writes the Keynesian equilibrium condition, C + I = C + S, or the Neo-Keynesian equivalent, C + I = W + n (W = wages, n = profits), there is a logical (and real) inconsistency. Either 1) the increment in circulating constant capital has been left out of 'aggregate demand' (C + I), in which case W + n understates the net product; or 2) W + n is correct, but C + I includes in part expenditure on circulating constant capital, which the model should exclude by its definition of the net product for 'final goods' only.

24 See Weeks 1982a, p. 62, for a complete explanation of the symbols.

creates the commodities to be circulated and determines their realisation, so that the categories of production must be the basis of the categories of circulation. This is what Marx meant when he said, 'production determines circulation and distribution',[25] not merely that commodities must be produced before they circulate, but also that the actual relations of circulation derive from the actual relations of production. It is not valid to construct circulation relationships such as the 'consumption function' (a relationship between revenue and individual or group motivation) which are divorced from production.

We can demonstrate this by following the circuit of capital. Capital marshals the ingredients of production by the exchange of money-capital for productive capital, M(CC + VC)–C. This is followed by the productive consumption of labour-power and the means of production, from which a new set of commodities results (C ... P ... C′). These commodities, commodity capital, are then transformed into money-capital (C′–M′). The net product framework considers circulation in the context of the post-production moment, C′–M′, but in reality this conversion of commodities into money is purely derivative from the earlier circulation moment, M–C, and the relationship between this moment and production.

One must be quite clear here in order to transcend the confusion created by the circulation process. It *appears* that the following three discrete and sequential steps occur: first, the elements of production are purchased; second, production occurs; and third, the final commodities are sold. And it is the third step which the net product models treat as an independent process, analysed in terms of their own particular concepts which are based in this step ('consumption' and 'investment' and their functional forms, based on the revenue or income received by individuals or classes). In reality, there are only two steps or phases, circulation and production, for *the first and the third (M–C and C′–M′) are the same*. Put another way, the sale of commodities, step three (C′–M′), is merely the way the first step (M–C) appears to the seller of commodities, while phase one is the same set of transactions to the seller in his necessary role as a buyer.

When capital first purchases the means of production (fixed and circulating) with the exchange M–C, this is simultaneously the final step, C′–M′, for the producers of the means of production (Department I). Thus, what serves as the first step of one circuit of capital is the last step for the previous circuit, so

25 '... the intensity of exchange, its extent and nature, are determined by the development and structure of production' (Marx 1973, p. 32). Marx gave emphasis to this entire phrase in the original. See also Marx 1970a, p. 204.

the end-phases cannot be viewed separately. Similarly, the exchange of money for labour-power uniquely determines the personal consumption expenditure of workers, so the part of C′–M′ which refers to the articles of consumption is merely the direct extension of the advance of variable capital.

In a comment often quoted, Marx observed that all relationships appear *as their opposite* in the circulation process,[26] and this is no better demonstrated than in the aggregate movement of social capital: the advance of capital determines the personal consumption of workers, but it appears that the consumption expenditures of the masses set in motion the advance of capital; it appears that profit calls forth the advance of capital, but in reality, it is the advance of capital that allows surplus value to be produced and realized in money form. In the analysis of aggregate circulation, as in all other areas of capital's reproduction, Marx's fundamental insights, based on the distinction between value and use value, the abstract and the concrete, reveal the appearance of things to be an inversion of the actual operation of capitalist society.

4 Summing Up

Among contemporary Marxists in the United States there are two major schools of interpretation of Marx's work and contribution. One of these views the work of Keynes as a complementary addition to Marx, incomplete since it incorporates neither value theory based on labour time nor a concept of exploitation, but essentially correct in its conceptualisation of the circulation process. This view, presented coherently by contemporary writers such as Sherman and Thomas Weisskopf, sees Keynes as 'following' Marx,[27] with less insight and profundity, certainly, but providing a more modern set of concepts, at least for the analysis of circulation.

Other writers, Anwar Shaikh and myself in the United States, Ben Fine, Simon Mohun and Susan Himmelweit in the United Kingdom, take a different view.[28] This view takes literally and incorporates Marx's critique of Adam Smith in Chapter XIX of Volume II of *Capital*.[29] In this chapter Marx unequivocally rejects the procedure of analysing circulation in terms of the product of living

26 Marx 1973, p. 657

27 Sherman 1979, p. 2.

28 I am not here trying to share responsibility, but to identify a general approach to the analysis of the aggregate behaviour of the capitalist economy, which the mentioned people seem, in my view, to share, while perhaps disagreeing on other theoretical points.

29 The chapter immediately precedes Marx's treatment of simple reproduction and expanded reproduction, and is entitled, 'Former Presentations of the Subject'.

labour ('value added' or the net product). Whether he is right or wrong, there can be no doubt that he argues that one must analyse the circulation process in terms of the *gross* product, or what he calls the 'total annual product'. He refers to the procedure of resolving the total product to the net product (subtracting out circulating constant capital) as 'Adam Smith's first mistake', at another point as an 'absurd formula'.[30] Marx argues that the reduction of the gross product to a net product not only should not be made, but cannot be made. Indeed, Marx specifically takes Smith to task for trying to resolve production into wages plus surplus value.[31] This critique is astoundingly modern, applying equally to the definition of the 'value added' measure of national income found in basic economics textbooks. After ridiculing Adam Smith rather unkindly, Marx relents a bit and concedes that Smith's 'first mistake' has a real basis; namely, in the obfuscation of the concrete (use value) by the abstract (value).[32] After criticising Adam Smith, Marx adds, as a final comment (somewhat disgustedly, no doubt):

---

30 Marx 1993, pp. 383, 389. To complete the first reference, Marx writes, 'Now Adam Smith's first mistake consists in equating the *value* of the annual *product* to *the newly produced annual value*' (emphasis in original).

31 Commenting on Adam Smith's reduction of the total product to the net product, Marx writes: 'His proof consists simply in the repetition of the same assertion. He admits, for instance, that the price of commodity does not only consist of V + S, but also of the price of the means of production consumed in the production of commodity, hence of a capital-value not invested in labour-power by the farmer. But, he says, the prices of all these means of production resolve themselves into V + S, the same as the price of corn ... He refers us from one branch of production to another, and from that to a third. The contention that the entire price of commodities resolves itself 'immediately' or 'ultimately' into V + S would not be a hollow subterfuge only if he were able to demonstrate that the commodities whose price resolves itself immediately into C (price of consumed means of production) + V + S, are ultimately compensated by commodities which completely replace those 'consumed means of production', and which are themselves produced by the mere outlay of variable-capital ...' (Marx 1993, p. 378). A Keynesian would ask, where was Marx on the day his economics lecturer explained national income accounts and 'double-counting'?

32 Marx comments: 'Although the social capital is only equal to the sum of the individual capitals and for this reason the annual commodity-product (or commodity-capital) of society is equal to the sum of commodity-products of these individual capitals; and although therefore the analysis of value *for every individual commodity-capital must also be valid for the commodity-capital for all society – and actually proves valid in the end* [emphasis added] – the form of appearance which these component parts assume-in the aggregate social process of reproduction is *different* [emphasis in original]' (Marx 1993, p. 373). It is beyond the scope of this note to pursue this specific example of the changes in the appearance of relationships at different levels of analysis.

> John Stuart Mill likewise reproduces … the doctrine handed down by Smith to his followers. As a result, the Smithian confusion of thought persists to this hour and his dogma [of the net product] is one of the orthodox articles of faith of Political Economy.[33]

And in 1983, a century after Marx's death, the faith is stronger than ever.

33 Marx 1993, p. 395.

CHAPTER 3

The Process of Accumulation and the 'Profit-Squeeze' Hypothesis

For decades underconsumptionism dominated the thinking of American Marxists, and while it still has some currency, the revival of interest in Marx's work has weakened its ideological hold as a new generation of Marxists have rediscovered the criticisms of this position by Engels, Lenin and other writers of the nineteenth and early twentieth century.[1] As underconsumptionism has waned, profit-squeeze theories have waxed. This hypothesis – that rising wages result in falling profits – is generally considered an 'advance' on underconsumptionism, by bringing to centre stage 'the class struggle', even if commentators do not completely agree with it.[2] The purpose of this paper is to demonstrate that the profit-squeeze hypothesis not only is not an advance, but is a great leap backwards, for it rejects *in toto* Marx's contribution to political economy in favour of Ricardo's. Specifically, it will be argued that 1) to the extent that the profit-squeeze hypothesis is offered as a theory of crisis, it is wrong; 2) to the more modest extent that it is presented as a theory of the timing of crisis or of state fiscal policy, it is also wrong; and 3) insofar as it seeks only to analyse the role of wages in the cycle of accumulation, it is still wrong. In short, under close examination, the profit-squeeze hypothesis is satisfactory neither as theory nor as description.

1 The Hypothesis as Such

The essence of the profit-squeeze hypothesis is disarmingly simple: in the process of accumulation, the reserve army of the unemployed declines, which leads to rising 'real wages' (a term whose ambiguous use is considered below), which reduces profits. At this point, a higher level of unemployment becomes an objective necessity for capital in order to re-establish normal profitability; this inevitably drives down 'real wages'. Whether this is a general theory of

1 Engels 1976, and Lenin 1972a, Lenin 1972b.

2 'The theory of the profit squeeze has the considerable merit of bringing the class struggle into the very heart of a theory of accumulation and crisis' (Wright 1977, p. 217).

 | DOI:10.1163/9789004703193_005

crisis or of 'fiscal policy' is largely semantic, for all writers in this school agree that rising 'real wages' eventually require an interruption in the normal circuit of capital, whether brought about automatically or by the conscious design of the bourgeoisie through the state. The hypothesis presents itself in many forms, from the very simplistic, with virtually no use of Marxian categories,[3] to the sophisticated.[4] Here, we shall deal first with the very simple form of the hypothesis and briefly consider criticisms that have been made of it. We shall see that the criticisms of the simple profit-squeeze hypothesis do not get to the heart of the matter, because, like those they are criticizing, the critics fail clearly to distinguish between expanded reproduction and accumulation. By expanded reproduction we mean the purely quantitative expansion of the circuits of capital, and by accumulation we mean the expansionary process that incorporates the development of the forces of production, concentration and centralisation, and the establishment of new values.[5]

Boddy and Crotty summarise their position as follows:

> We view the erosion of profits as the result of successful class struggle waged by labour against capital – struggle that is confined and ultimately reversed by the relaxation of demand and the rise in unemployment engineered by the capitalists and acquiesced in and abetted by the state.[6]

In the view of these authors, the expansion of capital provides the demand for labour-power, and demographic and other social factors determine the supply of labour. As capital expands, the industrial reserve army is reduced. This tightening of labour markets strengthens the economic power of the working class, and wages rise. Rising wages reduce profits, and the reduction of profits requires a response on the part of capitalists to eliminate the cause of rising wages, which is a low level of unemployment. The authors consider this to be consistent with 'the Marxian concept of cycle', which presumably means consistent with Marx's theory of crisis.[7] The foregoing summary of the Boddy and

3 Boddy and Crotty 1975.

4 Itoh 1978.

5 Wright fails to make this distinction when he writes, 'the *rate* of accumulation can be expressed as $(\Delta C + \Delta V)/(C + V)$'. This formula could equally apply to expanded reproduction (Wright 1977).

6 Boddy and Crotty 1975, p. 1. It is beyond the scope of this paper to analyse the implicit view of class struggle in this quotation, but it should be noted that the class struggle is here equated with the wage struggle.

7 While the phrase, "the Marxian concept of cycle" is ambiguous, Boddy and Crotty seem to

Crotty profit-squeeze hypothesis involves a number of implicit theoretical positions, and it is useful to make these explicit. First, the supply of labour-power is treated as determined independently of the demand for labour-power. Second, and related to the first, accumulation is treated in a purely quantitative way, and is seen as demand-generated. Third, a 'tight' labour market generates a *general* rise in 'real' wages, which implies that wages themselves are determined in circulation. And fourth, the wage-profit relationship is treated statically, implicitly in terms of the Sraffian wage-rate-profit-rate frontier.[8] In our critique, we will take issue with each of these positions.

Criticism of the profit-squeeze hypothesis, particularly as put forward by Boddy and Crotty, has generally focused on one or another of these four implicit positions. Wright bases his criticism on the second, when he argues that 'the level of productivity ... plays almost no role in the view of the rate of exploitation'.[9] While this is certainly correct, and a promising line of departure, its theoretical implications are lost in Wright's own eclectic treatment of crises. In effect, he accepts the profit-rate-wage-rate frontier analysis, which places distributional struggles as key, and only calls for a more complex treatment of them in relation to underconsumptionist theory and his own particular view of the tendency of the rate of profit to fall. He criticizes the profit-squeeze thesis for being mono-causal, not for being incorrect.[10] Bell takes a similar position, arguing that 'although class struggle certainly occurs around the distribution of national product in the sphere of circulation, it must first be analysed in terms of value relations in the sphere of production ...'[11] He does not pursue this as

suggest that Marx thought "the cycle" to be caused by rising wages which reduce profits. Marx did comment on this view: "The tendency of the rate of profit to fall is bound up with a tendency of the rate of exploitation to *rise*, hence with a tendency for the rate of labor exploitation to *rise*. Nothing is more absurd, for this reason, than to explain the fall in the rate of profit by a rise in the rate of wages, although this may be the case by way of an exception." Karl Marx, *Capital* (London and Moscow, 1972), Vol. III, p. 240. This would seem to identify Marx fairly conclusively with a position contrary to what Crotty call "the Marxian concept of cycle." This does not of itself make their position wrong.

8 See Broome 1973.

9 Because of the great theoretical similarity between Boddy and Crotty and Glyn and Sutcliffe, I do not discuss the latter authors. See Glyn and Sutcliffe 1972.

10 To quote Wright, 'The same class struggle over wages will have very different consequences depending upon whether the accumulation process is dominated by the dynamics described in the rising organic composition of capital/falling rate of profit view of crisis or in the underconsumptionist view' (Wright 1977, p. 217). His view of the 'organic composition of capital/falling rate of profit' explanation is similar to that of Dobb. See discussion of Bell's work, below.

11 Bell 1977.

a critique, however, but incorporates it into the profit-squeeze hypothesis, as Dobb does.[12] He also feels that Boddy and Crotty have committed the sin of mono-causality and, with Wright, applauds the profit-squeeze for delivering 'class struggle' from the wilderness.[13]

By far the most serious recent critique of the profit-squeeze hypothesis is that of Shaikh, who rejects the hypothesis out of hand as theoretically invalid and concerned only with the appearance of things.[14] To individual capitalists, a fall in profitability can appear in only two forms – failure to sell what is produced, or failure to sell it at a sufficient profit rate. The latter must involve a rise in costs relative to price. The profit-squeeze hypothesis is merely the generalisation of this perception to capital as a whole. To demonstrate the error of this reasoning, Shaikh analyses the relationship between the abstract concepts surplus value and variable capital, on the one hand, and the empirical concepts net corporate income ('profits' as they appear) and wage income.[15] He argues that the profit-squeeze theorists equate S/V with P/W, and in doing so confuse the manifestation of the underlying causal variables with those variables themselves. This is an extremely important point, for if it were possible to understand the accumulation process from the appearance of economic phenomena, there would be no need to utilize concepts like value, surplus value, variable capital, etc. However, as important as Shaikh's point is, it does not seriously damage the profit-squeeze hypothesis unless it is pursued *further*. What must be demonstrated is that the failure to distinguish between surplus value and variable capital, on the one hand, and wages and profit, on the other, makes a scientific consideration of the latter impossible. Put another way, the profit-squeeze theorists could accept Shaikh's criticism and reply that it in no way

12 In Dobb's view the value composition of capital rises as a consequence of wage increases, which stimulates capitalists to substitute dead for living labour. Dobb 1973, pp. 157 ff. For a critique, see Shaikh 1978b, pp. 233–51.

13 These analyses are an important advance in that they deal with actual social processes and place class struggle at the center of the explanation of the crises of capitalism. Bell 1977.

14 Shaikh 1978a, pp. 219–41.

15 We take issue with a point in Shaikh's analysis, where he refers to surplus value as 'this complex and powerful Marxian category' and by implication suggests that the bourgeois category of profit is less complex. As a point of method, we would argue that surplus value is the simple concept, because it is *abstract*, and the empirical category is more complex. For example, surplus value can be conceptualised and analysed without considering the competition among capitals, or even the existence of many capitals. Profit, on the other hand, can be conceptualised only subsequent to an analysis of the complexities of competition. For a discussion of this general methodological point, see Fine and Harris 1979, Chap. 1. This point does not affect Shaikh's conclusion.

affects their contention that rising wages lead to falling profits, a proposition which is presented as essentially empirical.

We seek to demonstrate that the analysis implied by Shaikh's critique implies that all of the four basic positions of the profit squeeze hypothesis are wrong. To do this, we first consider the work of Itoh, which integrates the hypothesis with what appears at first glance to be a Marxian method, and in which the basic theoretical elements of the hypothesis become explicit.

2 Itoh's Theory of the 'Over-production of Capital'

Itoh's work draws heavily upon the writings of Marx, something largely absent in the writings of Boddy and Crotty, and as a result is analytically richer than other profit-squeeze theories. Thus while it is virtually impossible to oversimplify the Boddy and Crotty and Glyn and Sutcliffe theories, this is a danger in the case of Itoh. The author distinguishes between his theory of crisis and underconsumptionism with the descriptive labels 'over-production of capital in relation to the labouring population' and 'the excess commodity theory'.[16] There is imprecision here, since in a capitalist society commodities are also capital, *commodity capital*, one of the forms assumed by capital in its circuit M–C ... P ... C′–M′, where M and C stand for money-capital and commodity-capital and P the moment of production. With this circuit in mind, we can identify the underconsumptionist hypothesis as 'overproduction of capital with respect to the capacity to consume'.[17] Neither of these is Marx's theory, which we can call 'the over-production of capital in relation to surplus value produced'.[18]

Itoh's theory can be summarised as follows. The existence of fixed capital discourages the introduction of new plants and machinery, which occurs on a large scale only when economic conditions create favourable conditions for widespread revolutionising of the means of production. Here, Itoh seizes upon Marx's analysis of fixed capital in Vol. II.[19] What makes fixed capital 'fixed' is

16 Itoh 1978, p. 130. We shall not deal here with another article by Itoh, which makes the same analysis (Itoh 1977).

17 This is not merely a semantic difference, but provides the basis for the critique of underconsumptionism. Once it is recognised that commodities are capital, consumption demand is revealed as secondary to the demand among capitalists for commodities. Shaikh demonstrates this well (Shaikh 1978a, pp. 226–31).

18 An analysis of the falling rate of profit and the counteracting tendencies to it lies outside the scope of this paper. See Fine and Harris 1979, Chap. 4.

19 Marx 1956, Chaps. VIII and IX.

that its value is 'fixated' in material objects which have a lifespan beyond a single circuit of capital. The argument of Itoh is that capitalists will resist replacing fixed capital until its value is exhausted. This exhaustion can occur by depreciation (the transfer of value to commodities), or by a sudden fall in the exchange value of fixed capital due to market conditions. The latter will tend to occur in dramatic fashion during a crisis, when the inability to realise commodities renders fixed capital in part redundant. From this line of argument, it follows that new machinery will be introduced – and productivity raised – during a crisis, while during the expansion phase this will occur only as an exception. In other words, accumulation proceeds without the 'relative overpopulation' generated by the expelling of living labour.

Itoh begins his analysis with the process of expansion and proceeds to crisis. To understand his theory, it is useful to proceed first from crisis and then to see how one returns to a crisis situation. With the crisis, fictitious capital values fall, drastically cheapening fixed capital.[20] This allows old fixed capital to be eliminated and new to be installed, and is purely a *price* phenomenon. That is, the older means of production are not replaced because of a competitive struggle between more and less efficient capitals, but because it becomes relatively cheap to do so.[21] Were competition the impetus to revolutionizing the forces of production, it would be arbitrary to restrict this revolutionizing to the period of crisis. The process of replacement sets off a quantitative expansion of capital and revival is under way. In the crisis, the limit to the future expansion of capital is set. Since the revolutionizing of the means of production occurs only in the crisis, accumulation proceeds quantitatively – at a given ratio of constant to variable capital – and reaches its limit when the industrial reserve army is eliminated. The potential size of the reserve army is determined in the crisis by the extent to which living labour is expelled from production. If the introduction of machinery is fragmentary and limited, the resultant expansion will be correspondingly brief, because of the limited

20 Itoh makes no distinction between fictitious capital and fixed capital, though this distinction is crucial to the process he describes. See *Capital*, vol. III, Chaps. XXIX–XXXII; and Fine 1982.

21 '... in contrast with the prosperity period, the existing fixed capitals [*sic*] are in general no longer profitable, and so there is pressure to depreciate them in order that they may be renewed as soon as possible. When most capitals in the main branches of production come to depreciate a large proportion of the value of their fixed capitals [*sic*] and amass their own money-capital sufficient to invest in new equipment, then they adopt new methods of production through renewals of fixed capitals [*sic*]'. Itoh 1980 p. 153. Itoh presumably means the *fixed capital* of individual capitals.

extent to which labour-power has been rendered redundant. Speaking very simply, we can summarize by saying that in the crisis all the qualitative changes occur and lay a strict basis for a predetermined quantitative expansion of capital.

This analysis is certainly an improvement on the Boddy and Crotty view, since it explains how each period of accumulation involves a higher level of total production and production per worker. Once the 'initial conditions' are given by the qualitative changes during the crisis, accumulation proceeds. As accumulation advances, the reserve army contracts and there is a *general* upward pressure on wages; this is what Itoh calls 'the over-production of capital in relation to the labouring population'.[22] Here, again, his analysis is more sophisticated than that of other profit-squeeze writers, for he does not directly argue that rising wages cause profits to fall. Rather, rising wages increase the demand for money-capital, for capitalists require more money to advance as variable capital. This pushes up the market rate of interest and 'the net profits of industrial and commercial capitalists are dramatically squeezed by a rise of both wages and interest'.[23] This sets off a credit crisis, which transforms itself into a full-blown crisis. It should be noted, in anticipation of our critique, that this consideration of the contradictions between industrial and finance capital is Itoh's only reference to competition.

We can now summarise the cyclical nature of capitalist production according to Itoh. Crisis creates an absolute and relative surplus population through the depreciation of fixed capital and its replacement. Expansion occurs quantitatively on the basis of this surplus population and reaches a new peak. 'Over-production of capital' generates a general rise in wages, which sets off a credit crisis, which initiates a general crisis. In the theory, a *general* rise in wages is introduced explicitly and accumulation is explicitly seen as quantitative. However, it does appear that the supply of labour-power is no longer exogenous, and that the Sraffian wage-rate-profit-rate relationship is rejected in favour of a wage-profit-interest mechanism. Below, we will show that in fact all four of the basic profit-squeeze positions are retained in essence.

---

22 He argues that this is Marx's theory. '... [I]n section III of Chapter XV of the third volume of *Capital* Marx tries to show that 'a steep and sudden fall in the general rate of profit' due to 'absolute over-production of capital ... in a ratio to the labouring population' brings forth cyclical crises' (Itoh 1980, p. 130). We dispute that Marx attempted to show this in Volume I or any other place (Itoh 1988).

23 The problem of over-production of capital in relation to labouring population is expressed in a shortage of loanable money-capital. Ibid., p. 151.

3 Accumulation, Wages, and the Profit-Squeeze Hypothesis

3.1 *Nature of the Accumulation Process*

Since the product of living labour presents itself in capitalist society as profit and wages, it is superficial and obvious to ask whether accumulation can be *systematically* affected adversely by an increase in wages. It is precisely this question that Marx addresses in Vol. I of *Capital*, in the chapter called 'The General Law of Capitalist Accumulation'. In the first section of this chapter, he lays out the conclusion to which his subsequent analysis will bring him:

> The rise of wages therefore is confined within limits that not only leave intact the foundations of the capitalist system, but also secure its reproduction on a progressive scale. The law of capitalistic accumulation, metamorphosed by economists into a pretended Law of Nature, in reality merely states that the very nature of accumulation excludes every diminution in the degree of exploitation of labour, and every rise in the price of labour, which could seriously imperil the continual reproduction, on an ever-enlarging scale, of the capitalistic relation.[24]

First, it should be noted that Marx is unambiguously clear in his opinion. Here, in Marx's most mature work, in the only volume of that work which he himself rendered in final form for publication, he categorically and without qualification rejects the idea that accumulation can be 'seriously imperiled' by rising wages. However, more important than the conclusion itself, which he repeats elsewhere,[25] is how he reached it. In the quotation above we are told that accumulation *itself* 'excludes every diminution in the degree of exploitation …'. We now turn to an analysis of accumulation. In doing so, we seek to analyse the conditions under which the process of accumulation leads to a rise in the value of labour-power, for such a rise is crucial to the profit-squeeze hypothesis. If the value of labour-power does not rise, the rate of surplus value does not fall, and profits are not 'squeezed'.

Accumulation is both the expansion of capital-as-a-whole and the interaction of individual capitals in that expansion. If we consider only the possibility of expanded reproduction, as Marx does in Volume II of *Capital*, we can abstract from the interaction of capitals, from competition. But the process of accumulation is more complex than this and must incorporate the compet-

24 *Capital*, Vol. I, p. 582.

25 See Marx's comment from Vol. III, quoted in footnote 7 of this chapter.

itive contradiction.[26] That is, accumulation as a concept seeks to encompass the actual process of the expansion of capital, as opposed to merely the formal possibility of capital's reproduction on an expanding scale. In the actual process of accumulation, as each capital grows (the *concentration* of production), it comes into conflict with other capitals, and 'the battle of competition is fought by cheapening of commodities'.[27] The discipline of competition forces upon capitals the necessity to raise the productivity of labour, which by definition involves the expelling of living labour from the production process. Productivity increase can only mean that a given number of workers transforms a growing mass of products per unit of time.[28] Thus, the process of accumulation involves the values of commodities falling. This process of productivity increase is achieved both by the concentration of capital (accumulation by individual capitals) and centralisation (the redistribution of existing capital). At the level of appearances, centralisation takes the form of mergers, takeovers, and the actual elimination of smaller capitals. In this process, the larger, more efficient capitals gain access to the labour-power and the means of production of smaller capitals.[29]

This characterisation of the process of accumulation – reproduction on an expanded scale accompanied by productivity change and the centralisation of capital – is basic to Marx's analysis and would seem unexceptionable. To argue that productivity increases and centralisation are not part of the accumulation process is theoretically in error since it ignores the pressure of competition, as well as empirically absurd. Yet this is exactly the position of those who hold the profit-squeeze hypothesis.

3.2 *The General Law of Capitalist Accumulation*

The profit-squeeze theorists, and Itoh most explicitly, treat Marx's discussion of expanded reproduction (Vol. II, Chapter XXI) as if it were a system of accumulation. In this discussion, where Marx is refuting the underconsumptionist position that capital is incapable of self-reproduction, expanded reproduction occurs at a given technical composition of capital. In effect, this is Itoh's view of accumulation. From the previous discussion of accumulation, it should

26 For a discussion of why competition is inherent in capital, see Weeks 1981.

27 *Capital*, vol. I, p. 586.

28 This results in what Marx called the 'law of the progressive increase in constant capital, in proportion to the variable' (Marx 1906, p. 682), but whether or not the value composition of capital actually increases is immaterial to the present discussion. Here we consider productivity change alone.

29 Ibid., pp. 586–8.

be clear that nothing meaningful can be concluded about the dynamics of capital's expansion from such a view, for it only establishes the formal possibility of expansion; it is only a consideration of realisation for capital as a whole.

The process of accumulation, as opposed to expanded reproduction, involves the expulsion of living labour from production, and in this process capital affects both the demand for and the supply of labour-power. Each mode of production produces its own characteristic law of population, and under capitalist relations of production the supply of labour-power is in part determined by *capital*, not by the absolute size of the labour force alone or its natural rate of increase.[30] This theoretical insight is one of the most important which Marx developed, breaking completely with the bourgeois view that the supply and demand for labour are determined independently of each other. In the accumulation process, capital increases the demand for labour with one hand (through the expansion of total capital), and *simultaneously* increases the supply with the other hand (by expelling living labour). The actual size of the reserve army, so crucial to the profit-squeeze hypothesis, is the consequence of the balance of the demand-and-supply-creating tendencies in the accumulation process, given demographic factors, which are parameters in the short term. All of the profit-squeeze theorists treat accumulation in a mature capitalist society as if it were occurring in the stage of 'manufacture' (to use Marx's term), when the production of absolute surplus value is dominant.[31] This is explicitly Itoh's position, for in his characterization of accumulation, relative surplus value is raised only during the crisis itself, and subsequent expansion is on the basis of absolute surplus value. Such a dichotomy is totally arbitrary, conforming only to the mechanistic needs of his theory, not to reality.

The expelling of living labour during accumulation does not ensure that labour-power will be always in adequate supply. It is not a magic wand, by

30 'The labouring population therefore produces, *along with the accumulation of capital produced by it*, the means by which it itself is made relatively superfluous, is turned into a relative surplus-population; and it does this to an always increasing extent. *This is a law of population peculiar to the capitalist mode of production*; and in fact every special historic mode of production has its own special laws of population, historically valid within its limits alone' (Marx 1906, p. 692, emphasis added).

31 Describing this early period when capital 'takes the production process as it finds it', Marx writes: 'The composition of capital changed but very slowly. With [capital's] accumulation, therefore, there kept pace, on the whole, a corresponding growth in the demand for labour. Slow as was the advance of accumulation. *compared with that of more modern times*, it found a check in the natural limits of the exploitable labouring population …' (Ibid., p. 694, emphasis added).

means of which productivity increases always conjure up the labour-power capital needs. But 'the general law of capitalist accumulation' (or 'the law of surplus population') implies that any serious discussion of what happens to the reserve army during accumulation must consider technical change and its relation to accumulation. By this basic standard, all profit-squeeze theories fail. To put the matter simply: the heart of their argument is the relationship between the reserve army and accumulation, and they fail to analyse this relation except at the most superficial level. In particular, they must demonstrate that there is a *systematic* tendency for productivity change to occur at a rate insufficient to replenish the reserve army, but do not do so. If this cannot be established, then, as Marx wrote, a declining reserve army raises wages and lowers the rate of profit 'by way of an exception'.[32]

We can summarise our first criticism of the profit-squeeze hypothesis: while seeking to analyse the supply and demand for labour-power in the process of accumulation, it ignores what makes capitalist accumulation different from all previous modes of the accumulation of wealth; namely, that capitalist accumulation is based upon the continual revolutionising of the means of production. In Marx's words:

> Capitalist production can by no means content itself with the quality of disposable labour-power which the natural increase of population yields. It requires for its free play an industrial reserve army independent of these natural limits ...

The production of a relative surplus-population, or the setting free of labourers, goes on therefore yet more rapidly than the technical revolution of the process of production that accompanies, and is accelerated by, the advance of accumulation.[33]

At the beginning of Part 3 of this paper, we quoted Marx as saying that the rise of wages during accumulation 'is confined within limits ... that secure capital's reproduction'. The first reason for this is that accumulation *itself* provides a supply of labour independently of the size or growth of the labouring population. The second reason is that the same process which replenishes the reserve army cheapens labour-power, which we now consider.

32 Marx 1971, p. 169, quoted in footnote 7 of this chapter.

33 Marx 1906, p. 697.

3.3 *Accumulation and the Value of Labour-Power*

To individual capitals, or the capitalists who personify those capitals, the introduction of new and more advanced machinery is motivated by the necessity to keep pace with other capitals; in short, to produce that commodity at a lower cost, and in doing so, to maintain or expand a particular capital's share of the market. However, for capital as a whole, this is the means by which relative surplus value is extracted. What for individual capitals is the means for competition with one another is, for capital as a whole, the means to intensify the exploitation of labour. To quote Marx:

> Like every other increase in the productiveness of labour, machinery is intended to cheapen commodities, and, by shortening that portion of the working day in which the labourer works for himself, to lengthen the other portion he gives, without an equivalent, to the capitalist. In short, it is a means for producing surplus-value.[34]

Productivity increases raise relative surplus value for capital as a whole as long as they occur in branches of industry which produce the means of consumption of workers, or the means of production employed to produce those means of consumption, i.e., when they occur in non-luxury commodities.[35] That profit derives from surplus value is the basis of Marx's theory, presumably accepted by the profit-squeeze theorists. Surplus value is valorised surplus labour time – the difference between total working time and necessary labour time. Productivity increases, which by definition reduce the *value* of commodities, reduce necessary labour time (the value of labour-power) unless confined to the production of luxury commodities. For the means of consumption, this is obvious and direct: productivity increases in this case directly reduce the value of the commodities workers consume. In the case of the means of production, productivity increases reduce the value of the constant capital advanced for the production of the means of consumption. The *value of labour-power*, which determines the wage, can be written as

$W = \mathrm{VX}$

Where W = value of labour-power, a number;

---

34 Marx 1906, p. 405.

35 'Hence, a fall in the value of labour-power is ... brought about by an increase in the productiveness of labour, and by a corresponding cheapening of commodities in those industries which supply the instruments of labour and the raw materials, that form the material elements of the constant capital required for producing the necessities of life' (Ibid., p. 346).

V = the vector of the values of all commodities which workers consume; and

X = a vector of the physical quantities of the commodities workers consume.

When profit-squeeze theorists speak of the 'real wage' rising, they confuse W and X. The vector X reflects the *standard of living* of the working class, as it is a vector of *use values*. It is a 'real wage' in that it measures the material consumption of the working class. However, W is also a 'real wage', in that it measures in abstract necessary labour time the cost of a unit of labour-power to the capitalist, though perhaps the term 'the exchange value of labour-power' would be more precise. The profit-squeeze theorists proceed as if the two were identical, as if workers' wage demands were aimed at raising W, while in fact they are aimed at raising X. This confusion is serious, because the standard of living can *rise*, while the labour time necessary to produce that standard of living can *fall*, i.e., workers can become better off, while the value of labour-power falls. Indeed, this is precisely what happens in the process of accumulation.

One might think that this relationship can be epitomised by saying that profits will fall if 'real wages' (X) rise faster than productivity (which causes V to fall). This formulation is imprecise, however, since it confuses two processes, the decline of V and the rise of X. While it is true that the value of labour-power will rise if X ('real wages') rises faster than V (the values of wage commodities) falls, this algebraic definitional statement does not explain the conditions under which X would rise faster than V falls. Indeed, it implies that the two are independent of each other, while, *in fact*, the rise in the 'real wage' is negatively related to the fall in values. As productivity increases, simultaneous processes occur: values decline, which tends to reduce the value of labour-power (W), and *the reserve army is replenished*, which tends to weaken the ability of the working class to raise its standard of living. Thus, to the extent that profit-squeeze theorists consider productivity increases, they ignore the second process. With these two processes operating simultaneously, the accumulation of capital will lead to a rise in the value of labour-power (and a fall in surplus value) only if it is sufficiently rapid to offset both the continual replenishing of the reserve army by productivity change, which would lead to X rising ('real wages'), *and* the continuous fall in values, which counteracts the rise in X. Speaking mechanically, we have here two parameters: the parameter which relates the rate of productivity change to the rate of accumulation (which determines the rate at which the reserve army is replenished and the rate at which values fall), and the parameter which relates the growth of labour demand to increases in real wages. It is simple to demonstrate that there exists a range of values for these two parameters for which no rate of accumulation, no matter how high, will give a rising value of labour-power.[36]

The point here is not to degenerate into a mathematical specification of the conditions under which necessary labour time will rise in relation to surplus labour time, but to demonstrate theoretically that the accumulation process itself generates tendencies to counteract the tendency for surplus value to be squeezed, and as a tendency 'the rise of wages therefore is confined within limits that not only leave intact the foundations of the capitalist system, but also secure its reproduction on a progressive scale'.[37] This statement of Marx's is thus not an opinion, but a scientifically derived conclusion, based on the analysis of the accumulation process. Accumulation generates, *through its internal operation*, the solution to the potential problem of rising wages, without necessarily requiring interruption of that accumulation. This is not mere theory, but enables us to understand how a capitalist economy, like that of Japan, could accumulate at rates of eight to ten percent per year for over a decade, an empirical fact incomprehensible to the profit-squeeze hypothesis. Here it must be made clear what has been demonstrated. We have not shown that the process of accumulation cannot give rise to a momentary fall in the rate of surplus value; rather, we have shown that the profit-squeeze theory does not demonstrate why and the circumstances under which this *would* occur.

We can go farther, and on the basis of Marx's analysis, consider what would happen if it were the case, 'by way of exception', that the value of labour-power were to rise during accumulation, and surplus value were reduced in consequence.[38] This would occur if the process of accumulation generated a rate of productivity growth which was insufficient to replenish the reserve army, setting off rising real wages, which it was inadequate to offset by the cheapening of commodities. Marx considered this case, and had a simple answer: when the accumulation of capital is such that surplus value is reduced by rising wages, the rate of accumulation slows its pace, then accelerates again when the reserve army has been sufficiently replenished. But this *does not* lead to crisis, only to the adjustment of the tempo of accumulation.[39]

---

36 An earlier version of this paper provides a numerical example of this relationship between accumulation and the value of labour-power.

37 Marx 1906, p. 680.

38 Since the working day is divided between necessary and surplus labour time, and living labour is the source of surplus value, a rise in the former must imply a fall in the latter.

39 Marx 1906, pp. 596–8.

3.4 *Why Is a Crisis Necessary?*

Up to this point we have been demonstrating that a fall in surplus value as a result of rising 'real wages' occurs as an exception. We can ask a further question: when this exception occurs, why is a major contraction of capital necessary – either induced by the state or otherwise – to rectify the situation? Another way to pose this question is to ask, what is the mechanism which transforms a squeeze on surplus value into a crisis?

Boddy and Crotty argue that the state intervenes – an intervention 'engineered by the capitalists' – to arrest the accumulation process and generate unemployment. This, of course, presupposes that a major, or at least significant, downturn is necessary. Thus they are quite correct in their modest claim that they do not have a theory of crisis, but they also do not have a 'theory of fiscal policy', since the fiscal policy they consider to be in the objective interests of the capitalists presupposes the need for a crisis.

Itoh, as we have seen, does provide a mechanism which transforms rising wages into a crisis, namely through a credit squeeze. He argues that rising wages increase the demand for money to be used as variable capital advanced, and this pushes up interest rates. This, like other aspects of the profit-squeeze hypothesis, is an old argument, current in even Marx's time. It is merely a special case of the view that accumulation is at times constrained by the amount of the means of circulation available. In effect, Itoh is arguing that the rise in price of a particular commodity – in this case labour-power – results in insufficient money to circulate all commodities (or value) produced, and this insufficiency manifests itself in a rise in the rate of interest. It is beyond the scope of this paper to develop Marx's theory of money except for what is necessary to consider Itoh's crisis mechanism, but it should be noted that the scientific analysis of money developed by Marx demonstrates the purely *passive* role of the means of circulation in the accumulation process, revealing that it is accumulation which determines the amount of money in circulation.[40]

40 Shaikh summarises Marx's analysis well in 'On the Laws of International Exchange' (Shaikh 1980). Marx wrote: 'The velocity of circulation, hence the number of repetitions of the same function as means of purchase and means of payment by the same pieces of money in a given term, the mass of simultaneous purchases and sales, as payments, the sum of the prices of circulating commodities, and finally the balances of payments to be settled in the same period, *determine in either case the mass of circulating money* ...' (Marx 1971, p. 321, emphasis added). And even more explicitly: 'Prices are thus high or low not because more or less money is in circulation, but there is more or less money in circulation because prices are high or low. This is one of the principal economic laws ...' (Marx 1970b, pp. 105–6.).

A detailed analysis of the theory of money is not necessary to refute Itoh's crisis mechanism, however, for it can easily be demonstrated that a rise in money wages has no net impact on the demand for money. At any moment, circuits of capital overlap during accumulation, and the money-capital for constant and variable capital to reinitiate production is simultaneously money-capital for the realisation of commodities. The advance of capital for the reinitiation of production is the impetus to realisation, since capital advanced for the means of production realises Department I commodities (means of production) in sales between capitalists, and capital advanced as variable capital leads to the realisation of Department II commodities through workers' expenditure. If accumulation is proceeding smoothly, surplus value is realised through the advance of both categories of capital, constant and variable, by virtue of these advances increasing in each circuit. Given the mass of value produced, a rise in wages affects neither the value to be realised (by assumption), *nor* the money available to realise it. The only consequence is that the amount of money exchanged for commodities is exchanged against less surplus value and more variable capital. There is a shift in the value categories within the total value (constant capital, variable capital, and surplus value), but no change in the money necessary for their realisation. We have sought to avoid long quotations from Marx in the text of this paper, but here it is difficult to improve on the clarity of his argument:

> Let us consider particularly *the case in which there is a general rise in wages*, so that, under assumptions made, *there will be a general fall in the rate of surplus value*, but besides this, also according to our assumptions, there will be no change in the value of the circulating mass of commodities.[41]

This is precisely Itoh's case, and Marx proceeds:

> In this case there naturally is an increase in the money-capital which must be advanced as variable capital, hence in the amount of money which performs this function. But the surplus value, and therefore also the amount of money required for its realisation, decreases by exactly the same amount by which the amount of money required for the function of variable capital increases. The amount of money required for the realisation of the commodity-value is not affected thereby, any more than this commodity-value itself.[42]

41 Marx 1956, p. 207.

42 Ibid. Discussing the determination of the interest rate, Marx writes: 'The rising demand

Thus, Itoh's basic mistake is that he fails to see that the *entire* value of commodities circulates as capital, not merely the constant and variable capital advanced. As a consequence, a rise in wages does not represent an increase in the requirement of money for the circulation of capital, but only a shift in the relative weights of the component parts of total value. There is a kernel of truth in Itoh's crisis mechanism, in that crises always *appear* as credit crises, but this has nothing to do with rising wages, or even the demand for money as a means of the circulation of commodities.[43]

3.5 *The Role of Wages in the Accumulation Process*[44]

To this point, we have used the analysis of the accumulation process to carry out a largely negative task – to show that in every important aspect of its treatment of wages and accumulation, the profit-squeeze hypothesis is wrong. On the basis of our analysis of accumulation we can now consider the actual role of rising wages during accumulation. The profit-squeeze hypothesis not only incorrectly analyses the relationship between wages and accumulation, but directs attention away from the correct relationship. From the profit-squeeze hypothesis, one would believe that rising wages represent an unqualified problem for, and eventually a barrier to, accumulation. In reality, the opposite is the case: sustained accumulation would be *impossible* without rising wages. In saying this, we are not referring to the naive underconsumptionist view that realisation requires rising wages to ensure sufficient 'demand', but to the processes of centralisation and movement of capital between branches of industry.

As argued above, accumulation is a process of qualitative change, in which the means of production are revolutionized and capital is redistributed. In the earliest moments of the expansionary process, individual capitals cannot attract labour-power at more or less constant wages, because of the size of the reserve army. But as the reserve army contracts, rising wages become the mechanism by which the existing labour-power is redistributed (centralized) toward more efficient capitals. In a capitalist economy, based as it is on free wage labour, rising wages are the only mechanism available to capital to make the division of society's labour-power among branches of industry conform to

for labour-power can never by itself be a cause for a rising rate of interest, in so far as the latter is determined by the rate of profit' (Marx 1971, p. 369).

43 'In a system of production, where the entire continuity of the reproduction process rests upon credit, a crisis must obviously occur – a tremendous rush for means of payment – when credit suddenly ceases and only cash payments have validity. At first glance, therefore, the whole crisis seems to be merely a credit and money crisis' (Marx 1971, p. 351).

44 This section is based on ideas stimulated by Ben Fine of Birkbeck College.

the changing pattern of production within and between branches of industry. To effect this redistribution, rising wages must accompany the rapid expansion of capital. This reflects the unique role of the means of subsistence under capitalism. Under feudalism, the subsistence needs of the masses are merely the means by which labour-power is reproduced. Under capitalism, subsistence needs take the wage form and serve not only to reproduce labour-power, but also to regulate its social division.

Thus, it is incorrect to see all wage increases as a result of the distributional struggle between capital and labour, as the profit-squeeze hypothesis does. This treats capitalism as if it were feudalism, where the means of subsistence have no allocative function. In capitalism, rising wages during accumulation primarily reflect the distributional struggle *among* capitals – i.e., the struggle to redistribute *capital*. This struggle has two aspects. One is the redistribution among branches of industry, as capital flows to branches where the rate of profit is higher, which affects the social division of labour. The second aspect is the removal of labour from low-wage capitals, or centralisation proper. Both of these processes would be impossible within capitalist relations were wages somehow prevented from rising. Were wages successfully controlled, capital would have to turn to pre-capitalist methods of labour control, such as in South Africa, in order to achieve the necessary redistribution of labour-power during accumulation.

Perhaps the superficiality of the profit-squeeze hypothesis is nowhere more striking than in its failure to consider the role of wages in the social division of labour. It considers the *appearance* of things – a rise in the general wage level – and never considers the disaggregated movement of wages by branch of industry which makes up this general wage increase.

4 Summary

Overall, we can summarize as follows: in general, the accumulation process need not so reduce the reserve army that an acute shortage of labour results; when the reserve army does decline and 'real wages' rise as a consequence, this need not imply that surplus value per worker declines; should this be the case, a slow-down in accumulation, and not a crisis, is sufficient to correct the problem for capital; and, finally, the accumulation process, far from being checked by rising real wages, requires them as the necessary condition for the social redivision of labour and the process of centralisation. When inspected under the microscope of Marxian theory, the profit-squeeze hypothesis is found to be without substance.

Thus, the profit-squeeze hypothesis is a 'step forward' analytically as Wright and Bell suggest, to the extent that one thinks the analysis of capitalism is advanced by treating it purely quantitatively. While it is a somewhat idle exercise to make judgments as to which errors are better or worse, certainly the more sophisticated brands of underconsumptionism must receive better marks than the profit-squeeze hypothesis.[45]

Capitalism is a mode of production in which the reproduction of class relations involves a dynamic process of qualitative changes. These qualitative changes are not an aspect of the accumulation process, but the component parts of it. Centralisation, concentration, the development of the productive forces, and uneven development – the manifestation of these in the competitive struggle – are the essence of accumulation. To reduce the dynamism of accumulation to the question of a wage-profit trade-off is to relegate Marx to the status of a 'minor post-Ricardian', to use Samuelson's phrase. Such an analytical reduction may appear 'to get to the heart of the matter – class struggle'. In fact, it does not, but rather leads one away from precisely those aspects of the class struggle which uniquely characterise capitalism. We find the conflict over the distribution of the social product throughout the history of class struggle, long before the emergence of capitalism. The understanding of capitalism, and the class struggle within it, is moved back by failing to see that under the rule of capital, this distributional struggle is mediated and qualitatively transformed by the *value form*, and, in particular, the *wage form*. We have not here developed a crisis theory, but have sought to demonstrate the specific inadequacies of a particular school of crisis theory. An adequate crisis theory must incorporate in its analysis the qualitative changes we have considered, as is done in Volume III of *Capital* (particularly Chapters XIII–XV). Economic crises are unquestionably the most complex moments in the life-cycle of capitalism, moments during which the contradictions inherent in the value form manifest themselves starkly. To understand crises, analytical simplification is required; but this should not be bought at the price of treating accumulation as something which it is not.

45 Luxemburg, for example, and for all her mistakes, incorporates the development of the productive forces as central to her theory, and there is no doubt that she is dealing with capitalism (Luxemburg 1968).

CHAPTER 4

A Note on Underconsumption Theory and the Labour Theory of Value

1 The Issue at Hand

Since the 1930s the Marxist tradition has been dominated by a particular crisis theory – underconsumption. This theory of the cause of capitalist crisis is much older, of course, going back to the work of Sismondi, which Lenin analysed so acutely. Among American writers, Paul Sweezy[1] was particularly influential in making this theory the generally accepted 'Marxist' theory of crises. In recent years underconsumptionism has come under sharp criticism,[2] but it remains extremely influential among radicals and Marxists, with the 'profit squeeze' hypothesis as a rather distant second.[3]

The purpose of this article is not to rebut the underconsumptionist hypothesis, which has been done elsewhere.[4] Rather, I intend to demonstrate the relationship between underconsumptionist theory and the labour theory of value. In general, underconsumptionists, even when identifying themselves as Marxists, make little use of the labour theory of value in their analysis. Baran and Sweezy[5] have been criticised for their rejection of the concept of 'surplus value' in favour of the concept 'economic surplus'.[6] My purpose is to show that this criticism is somewhat misplaced (though theoretically correct), for *the underconsumptionist hypothesis is inconsistent with the labour theory of value.* To be explicit, if one postulates that a 'pure' capitalist system is endemically afflicted by the inability to sell all that is produced, then the Marxian concept of value *must* be rejected. Thus, Baran and Sweezy (and more recent underconsumptionists such as Sherman)[7] are quite correct in not using value in their analysis, and they are more logically consistent than writers such as Amin,[8]

1 Sweezy 1968.
2 Critiques of underconsumptionism are many. For one of the least technical, see Shaikh 1978a.
3 Itoh 1978, pp. 129–55.
4 See Weeks 1977b.
5 Baran and Sweezy 1966.
6 Barclay and Stengel 1975.
7 Sherman 1979.
8 See Amin 1976.

 | DOI:10.1163/9789004703193_006

who try to maintain the labour theory of value as part of their underconsumptionist theory.

If this argument is correct – that underconsumptionism and the labour theory of value are inconsistent – it implies that the critique of underconsumptionism is not only a critique of a particular crisis theory, but also a defence of the labour theory of value itself. This point is developed further in the final section.

The central concept in value theory is that of socially necessary abstract labour, and the elaboration of this concept will be the basis of my analysis. This concept operates at two levels of abstraction: at the level of capital as a whole, and at the level of many capitals. Marx's general method is to first establish concepts at the aggregate level (for capital as a whole), then to move to the more complex level of many capitals. In the case of socially necessary abstract labour, this method involves first resolving the 'realisation' problem theoretically, which determines social labour in the aggregate. Then, the value (socially necessary abstract labour time) which can be realised by each individual capital is treated. My exposition of this method demonstrates the theoretical inconsistency between the underconsumptionist hypothesis and value theory.

To make the procedure absolutely clear, it must be stressed that the argument is not that general over-production does not occur, which would be an absurdity. Rather, it is that the analysis of general over-production follows from first considering the value concept for capital as a whole.

2 Two Presentations of the Labour Theory of Value

In capitalist society social reproduction has its basis in the circulation of capital. In its circuit capital undergoes three transformations. Capitalists begin with money-capital, which they exchange for labour-power and the necessary means of production, which then represent productive capital. In the production process the means of production undergo a physical transformation into a new set of commodities, and capital momentarily is held as commodity capital. The circuit is repeated by the realisation of commodity capital in money form – a return to money-capital and the initial point of departure. This circuit can be represented by symbols.

M–C(CC + VC) … P … C′–M′;

where M′ less M is surplus value;

M is money-capital;

CC is money-capital exchanged for the means of production ('constant capital');

VC is money-capital exchanged for labour-power ('variable capital');
C is productive capital, the means of production and labour-power;
P is the moment of production;
C′ is commodity capital, newly produced commodities;
M′ is expanded money-capital.

The circulation of capital is a simultaneous circulation of use values and value. In Table 4.1 this duality of capitalist circulation is demonstrated in a hypothetical example.[9] Considerable discussion will be devoted to the basis upon which different use values can be aggregated, but at the moment it is simply asserted that aggregation (or measurement) can be in terms of labour time in our two-department (two-commodity) example. In Table 4.1 social production is divided between those use values which are used in production (say, 'steel', measured in tons), and those use values consumed by people ('corn', measured in bushels). On the left side of the table are values (measured in 'labour days'), and on the right side are the corresponding physical quantities.

In the example the capitalists in Department I initiate their production by advancing an amount of money representing 210 labour days, with which they buy 60 tons of steel and hire 100 workers for a day each (shown on the right-hand side). In the second department, where the technical composition of capital is lower (ratio of steel to workers is lower), capitalists advance money equal to 160 labour days, divided in the value-ratio 10:6. For both sectors (or departments) taken together, production involves 100 tons of steel and 200 workers. Part B presents the result of the production process, in which productive capital is transformed into commodity capital. The conditions of production result in 100 tons of steel being produced in the first department and 100 bushels of corn in the second department.

Finally, in Part C of the table there is a summary of the conversion of commodity capital back into money-capital (realisation of commodity capital). The example is one of 'simple reproduction', in which each successive circuit of capital is at the same level of production as the previous one. Thus, the 100 tons of steel produced is sold to each department in the ratio 6:4, duplicating the dis-

9 The example is based on the following parameters. Define one unit of each department's output as what one worker produces in one day. Let X_1 denote the unit values.

$$X_1 = 0.6X_1 + 1;\ X_2 = 0.4X_1 + 1$$

Then, $X_1 = 2.5$ labour days and $X_2 = 2.00$ labour days. Let each worker consume 0.3 units of the consumption commodity per day. The value of labour-power is thus 0.6 labour days, and the surplus value is (1–0.6) labour days per worker. The measurement of value in 'labour days' is discussed in the text.

TABLE 4.1 Hypothetical Example of the Three Moments in the Circuit of Capital

A. Conversion of money-capital to productive capital (M–C)

	Values		Use values	
Dept.	CC	VC	Means of production	Labor power
Dept. I	150	60	60 tons	100 workers
Dept. II	100	60	40 tons	100 workers
Total	250	120		

B. Transformation of productive capital into commodity capital (C ... P ... C′)

	Values				Use values representing:			
Dept.	CC	VC	SV	TV	CC	VC	SV	Total
Dept. I	150	60	40	250	60 tons	24 tons	16 tons	100 tons
Dept. II	100	60	40	200	50 bu.	30 bu.	20 bu.	100 bu.
Total	250	120	80	450				

C. Realization of commodity capital as money-capital (C′–M′)

	Values expenditure by:			Consumption of use values as:		
Dept.	CC	Workers	Capitalists	Means of production	Means of subsistence	"Luxuries"
Dept. I	150	60	40	60 tons	30 bu.	20 bu.
Dept. II	100	60	40	40 tons	30 bu.	20 bu.
Total	250	120	80	100 tons	100 bu.	

See note 9 for derivation of table

tribution in part A of the table. Corn is realised by sales to workers (60 bushels) and to capitalists (40 bushels) for their consumption.

The purpose of the table is to demonstrate the symmetry between the production and distribution of use values (right hand side of the table) and 'value' (left-hand side), the latter being undefined so far, except to equate it with 'labour time'. In Part A of the table (M–C), the capital value advanced (210 in Department I, 160 in Department II) corresponds to a definite amount of use values. Similarly, in Part B the production of value (250 and 200) corresponds to definite amounts of steel and corn. In Department I 60 tons of steel represents output equivalent to the constant capital value advanced, 24 tons to the variable capital advanced, and 16 tons to the surplus value produced. Similarly for the production of corn. With regard to realisation, a definite amount of use values exchanges for the constant capital value advanced for the next period, and the corn production corresponds to the expenditures of workers and capitalists.

Now, in the table there can be no objection to the hypothetical numbers entered on the right-hand side. These numbers reflect the material characteristics of the use values; i.e., steel can be unambiguously measured by its weight, workers by their number, and corn by its volume. However, the left-hand side of the table is more problematical. On what basis can definite amounts of labour time be assigned to quantities of use values? It might appear that this is an easily resolved problem, since corn and steel are both produced by the expenditure of labour time, and we need only sum up the labour time actually carried out in the production processes. The problem is much more complex than this, however, and a moment's reflection shows that merely aggregating actual labour time is unsatisfactory, for it presupposes what we seek to establish.

The first difficulty is that we have two qualitatively different use values. Consider Part B of the table – specifically, the right-hand side. No one would argue that it is legitimate to add steel and corn to get, for example, the 'use value total' of capital advanced. Steel and corn cannot be added. Note that the non-additivity of steel and corn does not arise from an inconsistency in units of measure. It would be perfectly legitimate to measure corn in tons, but this would not make meaningful the addition of corn to steel, now formally possible, except in a very limited way. The aggregation problem is more basic, arising from the physical properties of the two use values. Therefore a common unit of measure does not in and of itself allow for aggregation. This point must be kept in mind when we move to the left-hand side of the table. Here steel and corn are measured in labour time, but that in and of itself no more solves the aggregation problem than measuring steel and corn in tons. The initial difficulty is that the units of measure – labour time – refer to *different types of labouring activity*, just as tons refer to different material objects on the right-hand side.[10]

The production of steel and the production of corn involve qualitatively different labouring activities, what Marx called *concrete labour*. Aggregating these qualitatively different labours is in principle as meaningless as aggregating steel and corn themselves. The fact that these concrete labours can be measured in units of time no more solves the problem of aggregation than the fact that steel and corn can be measured in units of weight. The production of each use

10 This point is elaborated in Weeks 1981.

value involves specific, concrete labour, and for purposes of aggregation what is required is a measurement in units of generalised labour time which abstracts from the particular characteristics of each concrete labouring activity. Marx called such a measure *abstract labour*.

Before developing the concept of abstract labour, we need to note a second difficulty of aggregating on the basis of labour time. Let us consider only one of the departments in Table 4.1; to clearly specify the issue, assume that all the workers in a department perform the same activity, which eliminates aggregation problems due to skill and other differences. Again, a moment's reflection shows that we cannot move from observed or actual labour time expended to aggregation on the basis of that labour time *even in this case of homogeneous labouring activity*. In any actual industry there is a distribution of capitals around some average level of efficiency, so that the product of each production process contains varying amounts of concrete labour time. In Table 4.1, the 'standard' or 'normal' labour time is given in each department on the left-hand side, and this presupposes a process by which a norm is brought about. If one observed the expenditure of labour time in our hypothetical case of homogeneous concrete labour, one would discover that different capitals produced at different levels of labour productivity. The establishment of values is not primarily a problem of the aggregation of labours of different skills. This aggregation, usually called 'the reduction problem', and of great concern to neo-Ricardian writers in particular, is a 'reduction' to homogeneous *concrete* labour. The fundamental transformation in value formation is from concrete to abstract labour. By some means a 'norm' must be established in order to summarise the production characteristics of a department, as we have done in Table 4.1. Marx called this 'norm' *socially necessary labour time*, which involves an abstraction from the differences in efficiency among capitals.

These two abstractions – from concrete labour as such and from the differences in the efficiency of use of concrete labour – are the basis of *abstract socially necessary labour*, or *value*. One method of deriving value is to ignore the two difficulties referred to, and to move *directly* from concrete labour to exchange value. This follows Ricardo's method, and for that reason is correctly designated as *neo-Ricardian*.[11] In essence, this treatment of value directly aggregates use values; for, as we have seen, there is no difference in principle (and practice) between attempting to add steel and corn and attempting to add the labour time involved in producing steel and the labour time involved in

---

11 See Fine and Harris 1979; and Gerstein 1976.

producing corn. This methodological mistake takes many forms; for example, the attempt to calculate 'directly' the value of commodities. Aggregation of use values cannot be done directly, but requires an intermediate form which makes the two abstractions discussed above.[12]

That intermediate form is *value*, and the necessary abstractions are achieved by the interaction of capitals in competition. In Marx's theory, value is not a *physical* property of commodities, but a *social* property. The social nature of value makes it no less real; its reality is a purely social reality, the consequence of particular social relations (namely those of a capitalist society).[13] The abstraction from concrete labour and differences in efficiency among producers is not a *mental* abstraction, but one forced upon producers by the social relations of capitalism. What makes this abstraction appear mental or idealist is that value itself cannot be directly achieved; i.e., it remains hidden, its phenomenal and only observable form being price (what Marx called the 'money form' of value).

Before discussing the process of value formation, it is worthwhile to pursue the sense in which value is 'hidden'. A neo-Ricardian might well agree that value is 'hidden', but would mean something quite different from Marx. In our first presentation of 'value', what is 'hidden' is concrete labour time, since commodities do not come to market marked with hours, minutes, seconds, but with money prices. However, in the neo-Ricardian view, this veil can be lifted for the empirical discovery of value; i.e., concrete labour time expended. In this view, value is 'hidden' in the same way that a coat of paint hides bare boards; selection of a strong enough paint remover will reveal the under lying structure of the wood. In Marx's theory, value is hidden in a completely different sense. It can be 'seen' or discovered only by observing its consequences. Since the value relation is purely social, it is analytically dangerous to seek analogies from the purely physical world, but one might compare value to the force of gravity. Gravity cannot be observed though its regulating force can be inferred from the movement of celestial bodies and their masses. But neither their masses nor their movement *is* gravity. Somewhat similarly, neither concrete labour time nor price *is* value, but value determines the relationship between the two.

Value is established by the interaction of capitals ('competition'), and this interaction presupposes specific social relations; namely, free wage labour and the means of production circulating as commodities. Once these *social rela-*

12 Marx 1970a, p. 56; and Marx 1976b, p. 131.

13 Weeks 2003.

tions exist, organisers of production (capitalists) must necessarily come into contact, as they compete to convert money-capital into productive capital. This conversion is, of course, simultaneously the conversion of commodity capital into money-capital ("realisation") for some capitalists, since the purchase of the means of production (CC–MP) is also the process of the realisation of the means of production. Therefore, the advance of money-capital cannot be separated from the realisation of capital-value, as shown in Table 4.1.

The social relations of capitalist society transform the ingredients of production (labour-power, intermediate materials and machinery) into commodities. As a consequence, each capitalist[14] faces an externally imposed, objective discipline of monetary cost. This monetary cost is the benchmark by which the capitalist discovers if he or she has produced according to the efficiency norm, where the norm itself is established by the interaction of capitals. Thus value arises in production, in that the material carrier of value – commodities – must be produced, and produced with living labour. However, labour has produced use values throughout history, whether or not the use values were exchanged. Unique to capitalist society is the fact that producers are *forced* to interact and this interaction then forces them to operate at normal efficiency or be eliminated.

This interpretation of value reveals value to be not just the hidden regulator of price, but, much more fundamentally, the mechanism by which formally isolated production is rendered social.[15] Basically, the law of value is the law of the social division of labour in capitalist society, one of whose corollaries is the law of price determination.

3 Value and Realisation

My purpose here is not to pursue all the implications of value and the law of value, but to specifically consider the relationship between value formation and realisation. To do this, it is necessary to briefly present the underconsumptionist hypothesis. Simply stated, the hypothesis is that inherent in the circulation of capital is the tendency for more commodities to be produced than can be converted from commodity capital to money-capital. Put purely descriptively, if we assume that workers spend all of their wages, underconsumption

14 It would be more correct to use the word 'capital' here, since each capitalist is merely the personification of a specific socially-created role in capitalist society.

15 Weeks 1981, Chapters 2 and 3; Colletti 1972.

results from the fact that the sum of capitalist personal consumption and the capitalisation of surplus value[16] is less than total surplus value.[17]

For current purposes, the hypothesis need not be explained further; it is simply assumed to be correct and its implications for value theory are explored.[18] Consider again Table 4.1. If all commodities are not converted into money-capital (Part C), this obviously does not affect the fact that they were produced, so that the material production of use values remains at 100 tons of steel and 100 bushels of corn. The consequence of incomplete realisation for the value side of the table depends upon one's theory of the nature of value. If one has the neo-Ricardian, labour embodied view, incomplete realisation does not affect the value calculations either. This should not be surprising, since the left side is treated, in effect, as homogeneous use values, not values. If one thinks that use values can be aggregated directly on the basis of expenditure of concrete labour, then 'value' is determined independently of the interaction of capitals, one aspect of which is realisation. In other words, for neo-Ricardians, value is analysed without considering circulation.

If we follow Marx and make the distinction between concrete and abstract labour (in effect, introducing the concept of *value*), the consequence of systematic and endemic incomplete realisation is quite serious. At this point it is important to note that the two approaches to value theory do not involve semantic, or purely abstract, theoretical differences. In the previous section, it was shown that the construction of the concept *value* requires a resolution of the problems of qualitatively different concrete labours and the differences in efficiency of the use of those concrete labours. These are not primarily theoretical problems, but actual problems of the relationship of production (the qualitative aspect of labour) and exchange (the quantitative aspect of labour). In practice, production and circulation are not only related, but the former *determines* the latter. What is involved is a real transformation of qualitative differences into mere quantitative differences. Value affects this transformation, 'behind the backs of producers'.

In this line of argument, the determining role of value disappears if, in general, there is incomplete realisation of commodity capital. To see this, first consider the case of one commodity, produced under differing conditions of efficiency by various capitals. Assume that the conditions of competition result

16 That is, the conversion of surplus value into money-capital, as opposed to spending it as revenue.

17 This ignores constant capital, of course, which is characteristic of underconsumptionists. For a more detailed algebraic treatment, see appendices to Luxemburg and Bukharin 1968.

18 Weeks 1977b.

in the commodity being realized in such a way that the median capital receives the average rate of profit (where the average rate of profit is determined by the rate of surplus value and the value composition of capital-as-a-whole).[19] Capitals in this industry which produce at below-median efficiency will obviously receive less than the average rate of profit. This reflects the fact that part of the labour time expended in production under the domination of these capitals is unrealisable, or *socially unnecessary*. This redundant labour time does not circulate as commodity capital; i.e., it is not validated by the interaction of capitals as socially useful labour. The competitive nature of capitalist production relations implies that not all working time is transformed into value, even when performed under capitalist social relations. However, there is still a definitive relationship between labour time expended in production and the quantitative relationship between commodities.

This can be explained by referring back to our table. Considering capital-as-a-whole, a value of 370 is advanced as capital, and this results in a production of a value of 450. The quantity of value objectified in the produced commodities is determined by labour time expended if money exchanged against these commodities is equal to a value of 450.[20] If the money exchanged for commodities is less than this, then *in the aggregate* value goes unrealised. Note that we now have two senses in which labour time is not validated in exchange. In one case this is the result of differences in efficiency, and can occur (does occur) when the money exchanged for commodities equals the abstract socially necessary labour time objectified in them through the interaction of production and circulation. In this case the structure of efficiency in each industry and the degree of competition determine total value, which we can take as established, and treat as a benchmark in our analysis.

However, if the realisation of commodities in the aggregate is less than 450, the relationship between the expenditure of labour time and labour time realised as money becomes completely indeterminate. Any proportion of our former benchmark can emerge as realised labour time. In this case, in an abstract, completely capitalist society, production and the interaction of capitals sets the upper limit of realisable abstract labour time, but nothing more. If under-realisation is endemic, and the upper limit is rarely reached, then

19 It is assumed that the average rate of profit has been generalized to all industries *via* the 'transformation process'. See Weeks 1981, Chap. III. Differences between the average and general rates of profit which result from the transformation are ignored.

20 We assume in the Table that all commodities are realized at the same moment. We also abstract from credit and in general from cases where exchange and payment do not coincide. See *Capital*, Vol. I, Chap. I.

it becomes, in effect, merely an ideal, a construction of the mind. Realised abstract labour time in such a case is set by the determinants of the expenditure by workers and capitalists. Production still plays a role, but a very limited one. The differences in efficiency among capitals determine only which survive and which do not. The realized labour time in any branch of industry depends upon how the short-fall in aggregate demand is distributed among those branches.

This can be put another way. In part A of Table 4.1, we begin with certain parameters: the value composition of capital, the rate of surplus value, and the degree and intensity of competition. On the presumption of full realisation, these imply a total value of production. If full realisation is not presumed, these parameters become irrelevant; they give no indication of how much value or how many commodities will be produced and circulated in the subsequent period. The *ex ante* rate of surplus value (exploitation of value in production) no longer determines the profit realized by capital. In summary, labour time expended in production no longer determines either realised abstract labour time nor the profit of capitalists. It is hardly surprising that Baran and Sweezy should abandon the concepts of value and surplus value, and, as a consequence, place no importance on the sphere of production. In an underconsumptionist world, the analysis of production has only 'sociological' relevance.[21]

In the underconsumptionist literature 'foreign' markets are viewed as one method by which unrealised commodities can be transformed into money. Once this possibility is introduced, production determines not even the upper limit of realisable abstract labour time and profit of capitalists. Once an 'external' market is introduced, our table must be 'opened up', and total realisable value is no longer constrained by the labour time expended in production. Obviously, the number of use values produced is not altered, given the technological conditions and the amount of labour employed, but the amount of money which these use values can be exchanged against has in principle no upper limit. In the case of a purely capitalist society the labour time realized is determined by internal aggregate demand on the underconsumptionist hypothesis, and the revenue accruing to workers and capitalists sets an upper limit to this. Production determines maximum realisable labour time and maximum profit, though not the actual levels. With the introduction of external demand, this is no longer the case. If external demand is buoyant, the use values produced can exchange for an amount of money representing labour time far in

21 See Braverman 1974. Though its subject is the labour process, this book refers to surplus value on only seven out of 450 pages.

excess of that expended in production, and the production process determines nothing except the number of use values available for circulation.

Further, it becomes possible for capitalists to realize profit even if the rate of exploitation is zero, since profit can be obtained through exchange with the external market alone. Actually, it is more correct to say that the concept of the rate of exploitation is no longer relevant. As we have seen, if the underconsumptionist hypothesis is correct, we cannot know the abstract labour time each commodity will exchange for prior to knowing the level of aggregate demand (internal plus external). Therefore we cannot know the value of labour-power nor the total abstract labour time which will circulate. In Marx's terminology, we know neither necessary labour time nor surplus labour time prior to realisation. Once realisation occurs, one can calculate the ratio of profits to wages, but this is purely an *ex-post* statistic, determined by demand conditions.

Thus, the underconsumptionists proceed quite logically when they reject the concept of 'surplus value', since for them this is merely another name for profit.[22] The central difference between underconsumptionism and Marxian value theory comes out clearly in our discussion. In underconsumptionist theory, total realisable labour time and total profit are *residual* categories, determined by demand conditions. In Marxian value theory production and the interaction of capitals determine total realisable labour time. Further, the category 'surplus value' is not a residual, but determined just as definitively as the value of variable capital (wages of productive workers).[23] However, these categories are determinant *only* within the context of full realisation of abstract socially necessary labour time. In terms of the circuit of capital, this means that we presume that C′–M′, that commodity capital is converted into money-capital. Clearly, this conversion is not always quantitatively complete. This does not invalidate the labour theory value; on the contrary, it is the labour theory of value, developed within the context of full realisation, which provides an explanation for why realisation at some moments is not achieved in full.

4 Value Theory and Crises

As we have seen, the value of commodities has no meaning in a theoretical model in which the circulation of commodities is continuously restricted by

22 Sherman 1979.

23 That is, the value of labour-power for all workers who produce surplus value. See Fine and Harris 1979, Chapter 3.

incomplete realisation. The analysis based on the labour theory of value presumes full realisation, and then, through an analysis of how values change, reveals the conditions under which full realisation becomes impossible. This is why Marx, in *Capital*, considers the process of realisation prior to elaborating his theory of crisis. At the end of Volume II he presents his famous 'reproduction schemes' (Chapter XX on 'simple reproduction' and Chapter XXI on 'expanded reproduction'). In these reproduction schemes he abstracts from concentration and centralisation, and from all qualitative changes which would make these *accumulation* schemes rather than reproduction schemes.[24] That is to say, he abstracts from changes in the values of commodities. His purpose is two-fold: 1) to demonstrate the abstract possibility of realisation (part of capitalist reproduction) under such conditions, and 2) in doing so, to show that incomplete realisation is the consequence of what he has omitted – changes in values. While doing these things, he has simultaneously justified his previous use of the labour theory of value, which can be methodologically sound only if complete realisation is presumed within the context of a determinant set of values. When he comes to his discussion of the tendency of the rate of profit to fall, he can then argue that changes in values are the disrupting element in capitalist production and circulation. This theoretical argument would have been irrelevant had he not previously demonstrated: 1) that the circuit of capital is not generally disrupted *without* changes in values, and 2) that his central analytical link between concrete labour time expended in production and abstract labour time in circulation is valid.

The process by which productivity change alters values and how value changes generate a tendency for the rate of profit to fall in the accumulation process is beyond the scope of this paper.[25] A few comments can indicate the nature of the process, however. As accumulation proceeds, technical change generates within branches of industry a dispersion of capitals in terms of efficiency around the norm for the consumption of labour-power in the production process, where this norm is socially necessary labour time. As this process continues, the interaction of capitals works to establish new (and lower) values in each branch of industry. This lowering of values implies that some capitals are increasingly unable to realise the labour time expended under their domination. The problem is particularly acute for fixed capital, contracted for in earlier periods when values were higher. The realisation difficulty has nothing to do with underconsumption (inadequate aggregate demand), but occurs in

24 For a discussion of the difference between accumulation and reproduction, see Weeks 1979.

25 Weeks 1981, Chap. 7 and 8; and Weeks 1979; and Fine and Weeks 1980.

the context of full realisation of necessary labour time (i.e., C′–M′); what cannot be realised is that labour time which competition has stamped as socially unnecessary. How this gives rise to a reduction in the rate of accumulation lies beyond this discussion,[26] but when it occurs – 'aggregate demand' (capital advanced) is no longer quantitatively sufficient to realise all socially necessary labour time – the process of value formation undergoes a qualitative change. What had previously proceeded more or less incrementally (the adjustment to lower values) occurs in a dramatic, even catastrophic, adjustment through the forced elimination of socially obsolete means of production – what Marx called 'the moral depreciation of capital'.

We do not pursue this analysis further, for the purpose is not to develop a theory of crisis, but rather the more limited one of demonstrating the incompatibility of underconsumptionist theory and the labour theory of value. Much has been written about whether or not Marx held to some form of the underconsumptionist hypothesis, and quotations from his works are given to support or deny various arguments. There is nothing original in affirming that Marx was not an underconsumptionist.[27] Basically, this is of limited interest, for what is important is not whether one particular person endorses a theory, but whether or not it is a correct explanation of reality. Nor has the purpose of this paper been to refute the underconsumptionist hypothesis directly. Rather, the effort has been to make a methodological point: one cannot simultaneously explain crises in terms of underconsumption *and* employ the labour theory of value as a tool of analysis. In so far as one identifies 'Marxian theory' as a theory based on the labour theory of value, 'Marxian theory' *so defined* excludes the underconsumption hypothesis. The intention in pointing this out is not to preserve a label or to argue over who is or who is not a 'real' Marxist. If underconsumptionists wish to retain the label 'Marxist', then those employing the labour theory of value should seek some other. The particular label used is a trivial matter. But it is not a trivial matter when two methodologically incompatible theories are placed under the same label. Labels should provide clarity, not generate confusion.

26 Ibid.

27 Lenin 1972c.

PART 2

Essays on Development and Underdevelopment

CHAPTER 5

The Law of Value and the Analysis of Underdevelopment

1 Introduction

Karl Marx entitled his first major work on the theory of capitalism an *Introduction to the Critique of Political Economy*,[1] not, it should be stressed, *An Introduction to ... Political Economy*. The inclusion of the crucial 'the critique of' provides the key to Marx's break with classical political economy. As much as he respected the contribution of bourgeois writers, especially Ricardo, he did not consider himself a radical member of the political economy school. That the political economy school's most outstanding members focused upon class relations did not save them from an analysis that, in Marx's judgement, was 'vulgar', in that it focused upon the appearance of phenomena rather than their underlying causes. Political economy focused on relations of exchange, rather than on class relations among human beings. As he wrote famously in an oft-quoted letter,[2] for at least a generation before him bourgeois writers had recognised both class divisions in capitalism and that the basis of profit was exploitation; were these the central elements of his work, his contribution would have been trivial. Marx identified what in his assessment was the central failing of the political economy of Smith, Ricardo, et al:

> Political Economy has indeed analysed, however incompletely, value and its magnitude, and has discovered what lies beneath these forms. But it has never once asked the question why labour is represented by the value of its product and labour-time by the magnitude of that value.[3]

At first reading this passage may seem obscure. It refers to failure of the political economy school to understand that 'markets' are associated with specific social relations in which production, distribution and exchange are organised.

---

1 Indeed, this is the sub-title of volumes II and III of Capital ('A Critique of Political Economy'), though not of the first volume (sub-titled 'A Critical Analysis of Capitalist Production').

2 See Marx and Engels 1965, p. 192.

3 The passage appears in *Capital*, volume I, chapter l, in the famous section, 'The Fetishism of Commodities and the Secret Thereof' (Marx 1906, pp. 81).

 | DOI:10.1163/9789004703193_007

Smith's 'invisible hand' purported to be a social mechanism for all time and all places; what Smith conceived as a guiding principle of self-sufficient individuals, Marx revealed as unique to a society divided between proletarians and capitalists. Marx's formulation of the labour theory of value reveals 1) the laws of reproduction of a capitalist society; 2) that capitalism ('market society') is a historically specific form of class society; 3) that changes in class relations explain the transition from pre-capitalist to capitalist society; and 4) why others explain both the transition and the laws of capitalism in an alternative framework. This four-fold character of the law of value constitutes its methodological break with the political economy school. It is not merely one theory among competitors, but a theory which subsumes its competitors within it by demonstrating that they focus upon the appearance of social phenomena rather than their essence.

Modern political economy ('neoclassical economics') rejected classical political economy's value theory; it shares with the latter its ahistorical methodology. The ahistoricism of both the Classicals and the Neoclassicals is not an oversight that might be remedied by the inclusion of an historical analysis in the chronological sense. Especially Smith, but also other classical political economists, made reference to the historical development of capitalism. Their method was ahistorical. Similarly, neoclassical political economy has produced its own economic historians, but their 'history' is ahistorical insofar as it treats the processes of production, circulation, and distribution of the social product. For the Classicals and Neoclassicals, economic history is the study of relations of exchange. As such, all periods are essentially the same; society has chronology, but no history. Strictly speaking, it is not valid to criticise the Classicals and Neoclassicals for lack of an historical perspective: given their value theory, they should have none.

This paper first develops the core of Marx's theory of value. The main theme is given in the text, with elaboration in footnotes. Value theory is used to reveal the ahistorical character of neoclassical political economy. Then, it is possible to consider the role of value in the passage from pre-capitalism to capitalism. Finally, the insights obtained are employed to develop generalisations about the barriers to accumulation in societies in which capitalism is not fully developed. In order to avoid idolatry, the framework developed will not be called 'Marxist', though Marx was its originator and most influential exponent. Rather, we use the oft-maligned term 'historical materialism' to mean that approach in which the process of social reproduction derives from the social relations in which production is organised.[4] Within this school of thought, the

4 'Marxism' or historical materialism does not argue that social dynamics can be reduced to

analysis of capitalism is that of a particular historical period, in which social reproduction involves the circulation and distribution of the products of labour as commodities. It is within this period and this period only that the law of value prevails.

2 Marx's Theory of Value

In capitalist society, the products of labour appear as 'an immense accumulation of commodities'.[5] That commodities are the product of human labour in itself implies no particular value theory; it is a statement of the obvious. A commodity has a dual nature. For the seller it represents a *quantity* of value, which when realised in generally equivalent form can be used to acquire another commodity through further exchange. This quantity of value is the *exchange value* of the commodity (what it fetches in exchange). For the buyer of the commodity, it represents a *quality* which is sought for a particular purposeful use. This quality constitutes the *use value* of the commodity. The distinction between the quantitative and qualitative aspect of a commodity is obvious and descriptive. It is the pursuit of this obvious and uncontroversial dichotomy that yields the labour theory of value and the laws of capitalist development.

The exchange value and use value of a commodity are not at peace with each other. While the former can vary due to immediate and longer-term influences, the latter retains an intrinsic character; more specifically, improvements in the methods of production can reduce exchange value for a given use value. On the basis of the tension caused by this real dichotomy arises the need for money, which can now be defined as a general equivalent commodity of exchange.[6] At this early juncture in the theoretical discussion, the analytical method should be noted. We did not at the outset presume the existence of money; rather, its role emerged in consequence of considering the nature of commodities.

Out of the 'unpacking' of the commodity arises the need for a further concept. Since commodities do not exchange directly for each other, but through the intermediary form of money, the possibility arises that the exchange value of a commodity can vary as conditions of exchange vary. This raises the ques-

---

economic causes; rather, it argues that social dynamics derive from the social relations in which the collective reproduction of society is organised (Wood 1981).

5 Marx 1906, p. 41.

6 It is beyond the scope of this chapter to explain why value theory implies that the general equivalent is a commodity (i.e. money is produced and has value). See Weeks 1981, chapter 4.

tion of what determines the exchange value of a commodity; i.e. the underlying determinant of exchange value as the money a commodity fetches fluctuates due to stochastic influences. All theories of market prices posit the existence of an underlying determinant of exchange value which is hidden beneath the price form of exchange. In neoclassical political economy the underlying determinant is the 'opportunity cost' of both producers and buyers; for Ricardian political economy it is the technology of production; and for historical materialism it is socially necessary labour, a concept we have yet to unfold. For all the schools, there is a *value* of commodities which lies beneath the surface of exchange. 'Value' has a straightforward and unambiguous meaning: that which determines price, appearing in the form of quantities of money.

Like commodities, money has a contradictory nature. As the general equivalent, it circulates with commodities, but, unlike other commodities, it need not be sold to realise its exchange value (it is exchange value). With this characteristic it can serve as a general store and claim on value. As a claim on value, it can initiate exchange for commodities, commodities which can, in turn, be sold for money again. This process, exchanging money for commodities, then commodities for money, would only be done if the second quantity of money exceeds the initial quantity. It is in this way that money serves as capital, which is defined as self-expanding value; money which through circulation yields more money. To this point an increasingly complex series of phenomenon has been unfolded: from the commodity and its two-fold character, money (implying value), to capital. This unfolding as yet produces no theory of the determination of value; indeed, it can be taken as descriptive of the process of exchange. It allows one to note that exchange can be viewed in terms of two forms of commodity circulation: commodities via money to other commodities, and money via commodities to a greater quantity of money. The former is simpler, selling in order to buy (commodities-money-commodities, C–M–C). This is simple, because it requires little theoretical explanation. It involves disposing through exchange of a commodity whose use value is not desired, in order to obtain money, which can be employed to acquire a desired commodity.[7]

The second, buying in order to sell, is theoretically complex. It demands an explanation of the source of the increased quantity of money. Following Marx, we call the process of buying in order to sell the *circuit of capital*. This increased amount of money that appears through buying in order to sell Marx gave the straightforward name, 'surplus value'. On the surface, surplus value is a simple concept: it is the quantitative difference between the money at the end and

7 Marx called this process 'simple commodity circulation' (Marx 1970a).

beginning of a process of buying in order to sell. The theory of value arises from the need to explain the source of surplus value.[8] Here, again, we must pause and reflect on the implications of what has been, at least superficially, a descriptive discussion. When money does not serve as capital, there is no surplus value[9] to explain, thus no role for a theory of value. Value theory, whatever its logical basis, is historically specific to the circuit of capital, though we have yet to make that historical specification.

We can rule out surplus value deriving in the aggregate from exchange itself.[10] It follows that capital (money) must exchange initially for a commodity whose value increases between buying and selling. A commodity's value increases by entering into a process of production. That value expands in production, would be met with agreement by the neoclassical political economy school,[11] though its view of production would not conform to that of the historical materialist school.[12] Since an increase in value in the aggregate arises from production, it follows that capitalists must pass through production to obtain surplus value. This obvious point implies that the circuit of capital needs expanding to take the form:

M–C ... P ... C′–M′
[Money–Commodities ... Production ... Commodities–Money]

8 In its role as a theory of prices, the theory of value is a theory of prices under capitalism, when prices include surplus value, part of which is capitalist profit. The discussion of the division of surplus value into its phenomenal forms (as it appears in exchange), profit, interest, rent, and unproductive payments (for example, salaries of priests and university professors), lies beyond the scope of this paper (Mattick 1971).

9 'Surplus value' is at this point used in the purely descriptive sense of the difference between the money that initiates the circuit of capital and the money that comes at the end.

10 Consider a two-commodity closed economy. The rise in the exchange-value of one commodity implies a decline for the other. Thus, exchange redistributes rather than creates surplus-value. A neoclassical would not contest this theoretical argument, but would insist that individual and social welfare is increased by exchange. In turn, one following the Marxian method would not contest the neoclassical point, but would judge it to be of little theoretical interest.

11 The neoclassical disagreement would come on two issues: 1) the process by which value is added in production (marginal productivity theory); and 2) what constitutes 'production' (rejecting the distinction between productive and unproductive labour).

12 In neoclassical political economy, market prices oscillate around long run general equilibrium prices. If short run and long run average cost curves have a unique minimum point, and no 'above-normal' profits are earned in any sector (perfect competition), then the general equilibrium set of relative prices is independent of demand. Demand determines the composition of output in general equilibrium, but not relative prices.

The next step in the analytical unfolding is also obvious and non-controversial: the first purchase by the capitalist (M–C), must involve the acquisition of a commodity or commodities which, when used in production, add value. By definition, the elements of production can be divided between workers – the human agency of production – and the material elements of production. We shall call these the labour input and the means of production, where the latter can be subdivided between those that are materially transformed or consumed during production (for example, raw materials, electricity), and those which retain their material form (for example, machines, buildings). Including these elements, the full circuit of capital becomes:

> M–C [L, MP] ... P ... C′–M′
> [Money–Elements of Production ... Production ... Commodities–Money]

To this point the labour theory of value plays no role; it lies latent in the analysis. The fundamental difference between the foregoing analysis and that of neoclassical political economy is that the former has recast the analysis of value as derivative from capital, while the latter treats value as the outcome of the desire by individual human beings for consumption.[13] The point now has come to declare one's value theory. The analysis cannot progress beyond description without an explanation of the origin of the surplus value arising from the circulation of capital.[14] Because of the manner in which materialist analysis describes aggregate reproduction, the neoclassical theory of value cannot be utilised.

Even if one preferred to use the opportunity cost theory of value, our framework, M–C ... P ... C′–M′, precludes it. In the neoclassical theory of value, commodities are not produced in the real-world sense. Stocks of 'primary inputs' ('labour' and 'capital'), when combined with a given technology, generate a flow of new value. In this stock-flow description of the economy an opportunity cost theory of value is consistent, albeit under highly restrictive conditions.[15] The materialist description of aggregate reproduction is not stock-flow, but involves

13 It is this re-casting that eliminates from the materialist analysis the concept of 'utility'.

14 Even as pure description the foregoing is a considerable improvement upon neoclassical analysis, which treats a capitalist society as the exchange between individual agents, or even the Keynesian 'circular flow'. For a critique of the latter, see Weeks 1981, Chapter 1.

15 If production involves more than one output the value theory is consistent only in general equilibrium. See Weeks 1981, chapter 10 and Fine 1980, chapter 3.

the production of commodities by means of commodities, to use Sraffa's term.[16] In this description, the process of reproduction is considered in time periods. In some arbitrarily selected initial time period (in principle one could go back to the Garden of Eden), there is produced a set of commodities which will be the input in the next time period. In the next time period those commodities are transformed into different material objects, during which value is added to them.[17] This view of production formally excludes marginal productivity analysis. It does so not because it allows no substitution between inputs,[18] but because formally there is no difference between material inputs that are consumed during one period of production and those used up over many time periods. Just as electricity is consumed in production and passes on no more value than its own, machinery, buildings, etc., are exhausted of their value over many (though in principle a definite number) time periods, passing on their value but no more.[19] The commodity which can expand value is the labour input. This commodity which capitalists buy is the capacity to work, or *labour-power*. However, this analysis does not as yet provide a theory of value.

The production of commodities by means of commodities framework requires either a labour-based theory of value or the Ricardian technology-based theory. We consider only the former. There is little controversy over whether units of labour time can be employed to *measure* value.[20] Measurement is essentially a trivial exercise for which there are several possibilities. For example, if we consider only material commodities (excluding services), one

16 It would be more correct to write, 'production of products by means of products'. This indicates the generality of the framework; i.e. it is not limited to a system of commodity (capitalist) production. When viewed in this way, production cannot logically be treated in terms of value-added categories alone, but must be analysed in terms of the total social product (value added plus intermediate production). The Keynesian categories of consumption, investment, etc. have their analogues in materialist theory, but are not the relevant categories of analysis. See Weeks 1983.

17 The essence of the production process is the material transformation of objects. The addition of value is a historically specific outcome. For example, a subsistence farmer who plants maize seed does not add value in production; he/she engages in specific and concrete labour which, if successful, results in more maize than was planted as seed.

18 Neoclassical marginal productivity theory is consistent with fixed coefficients of production, as demonstrated decades ago in Dorfman, Samuelson and Solow 1958, chapter 3.

19 At a more concrete level of analysis, the distinction between materials of production (circulating means of production) and tools of production (fixed means of production) is crucial. See Weeks 1981, chapters 7 and 8. Unfolding this argument is beyond the scope of this paper.

20 There is debate over the proper method to the aggregate different quantities of labour. This is discussed below.

could aggregate by weight. However useful this might be for certain purposes, such as planning the transport of commodities, it makes no sense as a theory of value. Similarly, labour time can be used as the unit of measure; the debate is over its significance for understanding aggregate reproduction. Marx's argument proceeds from the tautology that each commodity is the product of human labour. When commodities exchange, they are rendered equal in practice. By definition, the labour that produced them is rendered equal through exchange: the concrete labour expended in production is converted to *abstract labour* in exchange (i.e. into money).

This purely formal conversion of concrete labour into its opposite becomes a real conversion through the process of competition. Competition among producers of a particular commodity establishes a standard input requirement, which Marx called *socially necessary labour*. This is rendered abstract through exchange, becoming abstract socially necessary labour. *The labour theory of value is explanation of the process by which abstract necessary labour is established through a social process* (how the assumption achieves credibility). This breaks with the Ricardian framework, which explicitly or implicitly takes abstract socially necessary labour as given: all labour is treated as homogeneous (or can be rendered so), and all producers of a commodity use the same technology with the same efficiency (or can be treated as doing so). The Ricardian approach does not explain the special historical conditions under which a norm in production is established (i.e., why the functioning of society requires it). Unfolding the nature of commodities has provided the explanation: competition results from the general production of commodities when labour-power is also a commodity; a common norm for the production of each commodity arises from the exchange of inputs and outputs. At each stage in the input-output process capitalists encounter the discipline of exchange.[21] Marx referred to the disciplining effect of exchange when he wrote that 'a commodity is, in the first place, an object outside us'.[22]

We can now summarise the development of the materialist theory of value or *law* of value: commodities are the products of human labour which are produced within the discipline of capitalist exchange, both for the output and the

---

21 Weeks 1990.

22 Marx 1906, p. 41. Pursuing the implications of this quotation takes one through the theory of alienation. A commodity is, among other things, the product of purposeful human activity. Because it must be exchanged, it presents itself to human beings as something external to them, created by a process beyond their control ('the market'). Thus, competition is a process of alienating people from their labour. This is eloquently explained by Marx 1971, chapter 50 ('Illusions Created by Competition').

inputs that are used to create the output. Production is formally private, but essentially social.[23] Every producer participates in social interaction in which his/her commodity is but one part of an organic whole. This system of social reproduction arises from labour-power being a commodity. The commodity status of labour-power results from the separation of producers from the means by which production can be carried out.[24] Producers (workers) are re-united with the means of production through the agency of capital. Having re-united workers and means of production through exchange, capitalists must transform commodities back into money.

3 Theory of Profit

The surplus value arises from the extraction of surplus labour by capitalists in the process of production. This surplus labour is created as a result of the difference between the value of the commodity labour-power and the value which labour-power creates during a production period. We have yet to explain why these two should differ. In as far as labour-power is a commodity, its exchange value is determined by its cost of production. Of all the elements of Marx's theory of value, the analysis of wages is perhaps the subtlest, and only the basic argument is presented here. At a superficial level, it can be treated as a subsistence theory of wages. Without specifying relations of production, society's aggregate labour can be divided between the labour necessary to reproduce the working population, and the labour expended over and above that reproductive minimum. Marx called the former *necessary labour* and the latter *surplus labour*. This division implicitly assumes the division of society into classes, so that there is a dominant group which appropriates the surplus labour.[25]

23 It is essentially social for two reasons. First, within units of production it involves co-operation among human beings, a social process. Second, no commodity is created within one production unit. Every commodity is the result of the production of many commodities, which serve directly and indirectly as inputs to it. Thus, the essence of production is production in the aggregate, with each individual commodity a constituent part.

24 If producers control their means of production and labour-power is not a commodity, then production is essentially isolated, not social. This point is elaborated below. It results in one of the fundamental ironies of a capitalist society: while the production of commodities alienates workers from their labour, by the same process it integrates those workers into a social matrix of production.

25 A society without classes is a society without a surplus; i.e. a surplus product is not basically a technological phenomenon, but emerges from technical possibility to realisation when a class develops to appropriate it from the direct producers.

In a capitalist society this appropriation occurs through the interaction of exchange and production. Capitalists enter into a transaction with workers, in which money (*variable capital*) is exchanged for labour-power. The price at which this exchange occurs (the wage) is determined by the exchange value of the collection of commodities which workers require to reproduce their labour-power. In return, capitalists receive control over the productive potential of workers for a prescribed length of time. Capitalists use the labour-power to produce commodities which they exchange for money. As Kaldor said, workers spend what they get; capitalists get what they spend (plus some, he might have added).[26]

The distinction, between the exchange value of the commodity labour-power and the subsequent exchange value of the commodities workers produce, is not the materialist theory of profit as such. Profit as such results from surplus labour. The existence of surplus labour follows from the analysis of production by means of products: labour is the input to production which can expand value in this framework. The distinction between the exchange value of labour-power and the exchange value of what workers produce provides the analysis of accumulation; i.e. the explanation of how profit can be increased.

Given the exchange value of the commodities required for the reproduction of the labour force (the value of labour-power), surplus labour can be increased in two ways. It can be raised absolutely by the extension of the working day or an increase in the intensity of work. This method of increasing surplus labour has natural limits, but also limits in terms of the norms of 'fairness' in society. Marx called this the raising of surplus value absolutely (or, the production of absolute surplus value); extracting more effort from workers without compensation. He associated this with the early stage of capitalist development, when capitalists faced social relations that limited their ability to introduce technical changes.[27] As the financial system develops, allowing capital to be redistributed towards more efficient producers, and the struggle of the working class

26 There is nothing especially Marxist about the insight that workers are involved in simple commodity circulation and capitalists in the circuit of capital. Indeed, Walt Disney (rather, one of his employees) made the point with succinct clarity in a cartoon strip. Donald Duck (nephew of Scrooge McDuck, the richest duck in the world) receives his paycheque from McDuck Enterprises. He then goes to a McDuck petrol station to fill his car, to a McDuck supermarket to do his shopping, and pays his rent to McDuck Estate Agents. Subsequently, Donald goes to his uncle to ask for an advance on his next week's salary. His rich uncle berates him for lack of thrift and tells him, 'I have no trouble keeping my money'. Had this run in a left-wing periodical, it would have been dismissed as communist propaganda.

27 Weeks 1985.

sets limits to the working day, the raising of surplus value absolutely becomes secondary to the raising of surplus value relatively. Surplus value is raised relatively by the reduction of the necessary labour component in society's aggregate working time.[28]

While individual capitalists can raise surplus value absolutely through their own efforts, it is raised relatively through a social process. Consider a capitalist that produces a commodity that serves as input into a commodity that is part of workers' means of subsistence. A technical change which lowers the cost for one capitalist allows that capitalist to enjoy greater than average profit for that sector of production. This is followed by a process of competition which induces the other capitalists in the sector to adopt the same or similar cost-reducing technology. As all or most capitalists in the sector come to enjoy above average profits, capital migrates from other sectors into the now more-profitable sector. This drives down the exchange value of the commodity, which makes it cheaper for all capitalists that use it as input. In a second competitive round, the commodity using the cheaper input falls in exchange value. Since by assumption this second commodity enters into workers' consumption, the value of labour-power falls. If the standard of living of workers remains the same, then the exchange value of labour (the wage) falls. This process of technical change and competition demonstrates the social character of capitalist production: insofar as any capitalists enjoy a relative rise in surplus value, all do.[29]

It was through his analysis of absolute and relative surplus value that Marx further demonstrated the historically specific character of capitalist production. Surplus labour, appropriated by a dominant class, characterised societies for thousands of years. It was first under capitalism that the increase of surplus labour through the social interaction of producers became a dynamic force of

---

28 Marx used the distinction between absolute and relative surplus value to divide capitalism into two great epochs – the age of manufacture and the age of modern industry (see Weeks 1985b). It may or may not be that Marx believed that extracting surplus value absolutely became of little importance in the second epoch. However, at the end of the twentieth century it is clear that capitalists are constrained in doing so by the strength of the working class, not the logic of accumulation. The neoliberal ideology of 'flexible' labour markets can be seen as a theoretical justification to re-introduce the extraction of absolute surplus value in the advanced capitalist countries.

29 For surplus value to rise relatively, technical change must affect either the inputs into the commodities that workers consume or those commodities themselves. Technical changes that reduce the labour time in commodities not consumed by workers ('luxuries') do not affect the value of labour-power. In neo-Ricardian terminology, non-luxuries make up 'basic' commodities.

accumulation. This dynamism arises from the general production of commodities, in which society's surplus labour takes the form of surplus value (i.e. it must be realised in money form).

4 Value and Social Transformation

Since the elements of production in a commodity society manifest themselves as values in exchange, they are converted in the minds of producers into elements of value.[30] This thrusts upon society a set of exchange categories that define the nature of commodities insofar as they are values: materials costs, wages, profit, interest, rent. These categories are real in that they represent actual payments that capitalists must make. More important, they represent the form by which the social character of production is enforced. An independent producer, such as a farmer who owns her/his own land, finds these categories imposed upon her/his activities. Marx makes this point with concise clarity:

> To himself as wage-worker he pays wages, to himself as capitalist he gives the profit, and to himself as landlord he pays rent. Assuming the capitalist mode of production and the relations corresponding to it to be the general basis of society, this subsumption is correct.[31]

This imputation is the basis for the ahistoricism of neoclassical political economy. As a result of the real subsumption of non-capitalist production to the categories of capital 'the illusion is all the more strengthened that capitalist relations are the natural relations of every mode of production'.[32] Independent producers are not capitalists (they do not hire themselves in a market); they are not landlords (they do not rent their land to themselves); and they are not financial rentiers (they do not lend themselves money). From the imposition of capitalist categories on all social production in a capitalist society, neoclassical political economy moves to the generalisation of the categories to all societ-

30 Excessive quotation from Marx can prove tedious, but on this point it is difficult to improve on his clarity: 'This division of a product into a useful thing and a value becomes practically important only when exchange has acquired such an extension that useful articles are produced for the purpose of being exchanged, and their character as values has therefore to be taken into account, beforehand, during production' (Marx 1906, p. 84).

31 Marx 1971, p. 626.

32 Ibid.

ies in all time periods. Thus, the hunter-gatherer is interpreted as weighing the trade-off between current consumption and the accumulation of capital;[33] the sharecropper's behaviour is analysed in terms of transactions costs. As a result, the social dynamics of all societies are treated as if they occur under the rules of a capitalist order. This gives neoclassical political economy its a – and anti-historical character, rendering it incapable of analysing social change.

In contrast, the materialist theory of value provides both a general (abstract) explanation and concrete analysis. Capitalism is the first form of social production in which class relations are sustained through the general circulation of commodities. Beneath this generalised commodity production lies the separation of labour from the means of production. This separation results in competition among capitals, which is the source of the dynamism of the capitalist mode of production. While in previous societies the products of labour were exchanged against money to varying degrees, this exchange was incidental or at most secondary to the dominance of the appropriating classes over the direct producers. As a result, there was little tendency for exchange value to feedback upon production and create a social norm of efficiency (abstract socially necessary labour). In other words, pre-capitalist production occurs in isolated units, not socially integrated through capitalist markets. In contrast, capitalist production is formally private (based on private property), but socially integrated through commodity circulation.

The prices attached to pre-capitalist products are superficial; they do not regulate the production process. In general, land is not a freely vendible commodity in pre-capitalist societies, so prices do not determine its allocation. Similarly, labour-power is only marginally a commodity, because the direct producers are not separated from the means of production. As a result of the incompleteness of land and labour-power's commodity status, exchange has a limited effect on the social order. To take the most obvious example, it can drive independent producers out of production for exchange, or to the margin of markets, but cannot dispossess them through market processes alone. For this reason Marx made his famous comment that individual private property (petty-bourgeois private property) is everywhere a barrier to the development of the capitalist mode of production.[34] The law of value shows, on the one hand, the source of capitalism's dynamism, the separation of labour from the means of production and the rendering into commodities the natural environment.

33 The hunter-and-gatherer must assess and give priority to his/her use of time (Marx called this 'the economy of time'). However, the tool he/ she might choose to produce in place of immediate consumption is not capital. See Marx 1906.

34 Marx 1971, p. 176.

On the other hand, the law reveals through its absence or limited applicability the historical specificity of its social existence.

In all class societies there are two major sources of conflict: 1) between the appropriating (ruling) class and the producing class over the conditions of exploitation of the latter; and 2) among factions of the appropriating class for control of the state. In pre-capitalist society, the latter conflict manifests itself typically as armed conflict in order to extend control over populations and territories. Under the rule of capital, conflict among factions of the dominant class takes the form of competition among capitals (firms). Over no other issue is the difference between neoclassical and materialist theory more unmistakable than for competition. The former theorists laud it as the mechanism for harmony and social welfare gains; in the analysis of the latter competition is the source of instability and uneven development, which can provoke armed conflict among capitalist states. In materialist theory, warfare is the continuation of market competition by other means.

Conflict in the form of cheapening of commodities does not eliminate armed conflict; quite the contrary.[35] But it is progressive because it results in an unprecedented development of what Marx called humankind's mastery over nature. This development of the productive forces, inherent in competition, is not necessarily a good thing. 'Progressive' is used in a descriptive, not a judgmental sense, to focus on an essential characteristic of the expansion of capital: inherent in it is the progressive development of the power to produce.[36] While technological innovation occurs in other social forms of production, only under capital is it the principal method of struggle within the appropriating class. This makes the dynamics of social change different in pre-capitalist and capitalist societies. Class struggle in capitalist society is driven in great part by the necessity for capitalists to raise surplus value relatively; class struggle in

35 Quite the contrary, the civilised competition in markets produces irresolvable tensions which develop into open warfare. Both World War I and World War II began as conflicts between capitalist countries. The former remained so throughout, while the character of the second became more complicated when Nazi Germany invaded the Soviet Union. The political instability that results from competition in markets was pursued by Marxists within the theory of imperialism, which until after World War II focused primarily on intra-capitalist rivalries. The relationship between advanced capitalist and underdeveloped countries involves the analysis of the interaction of modes of production, discussed below.

36 There is a second, better known, sense in which Marx considered capitalism progressive. Especially in his early writings (see the *Communist Manifesto*) he argued that capitalism is progressive because it creates the proletariat, which will be the historical vehicle for the overthrow of capitalism and exploitation in general. Consideration of this argument lies beyond the scope of this paper.

pre-capitalist society occurs in the context of the appropriating class largely restricted to raising surplus value absolutely.

One can contrast a capitalist society with a pre-capitalist, because all capitalist societies share a common characteristic: human labour-power takes the form of a commodity (for that is what capitalism is). However, other than being divided into classes, pre-capitalist societies share no analogously defining characteristic. That is, they share no universal mode of surplus appropriation which generates a common social dynamic among them. For this reason, a general and abstract discussion of transition from pre-capitalist to capitalist society is by its nature extremely limited in analytical power. Theory tells one the abstract outcome of the transition (the appropriation of a surplus product through free wage labour),[37] but not from where the transition came. It is tempting to construct a false, universal pre-capitalist society which, in effect, is the opposite of an abstract, fully developed capitalism. This treatment of pre-capitalist societies, as what they are *not* rather than what they *are*, de-emphasises to the point of insignificance changes in the social relations of production. The transition to capitalism becomes the growth of exchange relations, rather than a revolution in production and property relations.

The analytical unfolding of value theory reveals the superficiality of using the spread of exchange to explain the transformation of pre-capitalist social relations into capitalist wage labour. Societies maintain their coherence by the effectiveness of the appropriating class in controlling the direct producers. The importance of exchange in a society is derivative from the form that control of the direct producers takes.[38] Exchange, even capitalist exchange, is a surface phenomenon, constructed upon the prevailing relations of production. Marx called the analysis of exchange 'commodity fetishism', meaning that which treats social relations as relations of exchange:[39]

37 The term 'free' wage labour refers to the specific character of social labour under capitalism: 'Free labourers, in the double sense that neither they themselves form part and parcel of the means of production, as in the case of slaves' (Marx 1906).

38 A quite interesting development of this point, with concrete examples, is found in Chapter 20 of volume III of *Capital*, called 'Facts about Merchant's Capital'. For example, '... Of course, commerce will have more or less of a [disintegrating] effect on the communities between which it is carried on. It will subordinate production more and more to exchange-value ... thereby it dissolves the old relationships ... Nevertheless this disintegrating effect depends very much on the nature of the producing community.' Marx 1971, p. 224.

39 He quotes a writer named Fernando Galiani as asserting 'value is a relation between persons', and comments, 'he ought to have added: a relation between persons expressed as a relation between things', Marx 1906, p. 96, footnote.

> [The] money-form [price] of the world of commodities ... actually conceals, instead of disclosing, the social character of private labour, and the social relations between individual producers.[40]

In a capitalist society, exchange plays a role unique unto that society: it conceals the appropriation of surplus labour. All exchanges appear as equal exchanges – the buyer receives the commodity and the seller its exchange value in a formally voluntary transaction. This equality in exchange is then imposed downwards ideologically to production relations, so that each element of the value added, wages, rent, interest and profit, is imputed to a 'factor of production' as reflecting equal exchange. The interpretation of these components as flows of value arising from the contribution of land, labour and capital to newly created value Marx sardonically called the 'Trinity Formula'. These income categories ('revenues' was Marx's term) become relevant only under capitalism. They do not reflect the inherent nature of production, but rather the class divisions in a *capitalist* society. To treat them as relevant to all historical periods is the essence of 'commodity fetishism', ignoring social relations to focus on exchange.

5 Limits to Accumulation in Transitional Societies

Capitalism develops within pre-capitalist society through the conversion of labour-power and land into commodities.[41] This conversion is achieved through a process of coercive social change, such as an armed insurrection or a confiscatory land reform. For a time, perhaps a considerable time, the old social relations persist alongside the emerging relations of capitalist wage-labour. Pre-capitalist relations tend to persist longest in agriculture, because of the difficulty of divorcing the peasantry from the land, and, thus, making land and labour-power commodities. As long as pre-capitalist relations continue in agriculture, this provides a break on the process of accumulation. 'Structuralist' economists have given considerable attention to this problem.[42] In the Latin American structuralist approach, the process of urbanisation generates an increasing demand for food for the growing working class, and the expansion of capitalist production increases the demand for agricultural raw

---

40 Marx 1906, p. 87.

41 The conversion of labour-power and the natural environment into capitalist commodities Marx called 'primitive accumulation'. See Marx 1906, chapter 26, 'The Secret of Primitive Accumulation'.

42 Summarised in Kay 1989, chapter 2.

materials. Backwardness in agriculture results in an inelastic supply of foodstuffs and inputs for industry. As a consequence, relative prices move against the capitalist sector, depressing the profit rate.[43]

While the description is correct, this analysis lacks a clear theoretical foundation. The movement in relative prices is wholly dependent upon an inadequate *supply* of products from the pre-capitalist sector. This inadequate supply results from the specific behaviour attributed to the pre-capitalist landlords, who are assumed not to respond to market signals. The materialist theory of value provides a more analytically general explanation, which is not dependent upon specific institutional arrangements. Consider again the circuit of capital, shown in Table 5.1. Historically, capital emerged first as merchants' capital, which involved buying in order to sell, the form of capital, M–C–M′, without the essential characteristic of capital, wage labour. In this period, prior to the industrial revolution, European merchant houses mediated in the exchange of products arising from pre-capitalist social relations. Profit (M′ > M) arose from the monopoly over trade, buying cheap and selling dear. In this process, the export of commodity capital could reinforce pre-capitalist production relations, since the origin of the products exchanged was of no concern to merchants' capital, as long as their supply was assured. The trade in commodities neither required nor necessarily brought about a transformation in social relations.

By the middle of the nineteenth century, the growth of merchant houses and the emergence of capitalist relations in Western Europe and the United States brought the rise of large financial institutions, whose purpose was the vending of money as such, rather than commodities. In underdeveloped regions, the export of money-capital financed trade, and also provided loans to governments, especially in Latin America, to fund public works such as ports and railroads. As with the trade in commodities, financial houses could pursue their profits without the development of capitalist wage labour.

The export of commodity capital and money-capital had a contradictory tendency in underdeveloped regions, as implied by their position in the circuit of capital. By enhancing the wealth and power of ruling classes in the underdeveloped regions, pre-capitalist social relations could be rendered more tenacious. At the same time, the import of capitalist commodities into underdeveloped regions acted to destroy local artisanal and peasant production. Sim-

43 A similar effect occurs in the famous Lewis model of 'economic development with unlimited supplies of labour'. In that model, the absence of productivity change in the pre-capitalist sector results in a relative, then absolute, decline in food production as 'underemployed' labour is transferred to the capitalist sector.

TABLE 5.1 The life cycle of capital

1. Moment of circulation	**2. Moment of production**	**3. Moment of circulation**
Advance of capital (Money-capital into productive capital)	(Productive capital into commodity capital)	*Realisation of value* (Commodity capital into money-capital)
M–C (MP & LP)	C [LP, MP] … P … C′	C′–M′
[M = C, no change in value]	[C′ > C, value expands]	[C′ = M′, no change in value]
Agency: financial capital	Agency: industrial capital	Agency: merchants' capital
International expansion of capital		
Export of money capital	Export of industrial capital	Export of commodity capital
[capital movement on basis of existing relations of production]	[transformation of the social relations in pre-capitalist societies]	[trade on the basis of existing relations of production]

ultaneously, infrastructure projects financed by the export of money-capital created an emerging class of wage labour. However, even by the early twentieth century internationally traded commodities from underdeveloped countries arose overwhelmingly from systems of forced labour, debt-bondage, and forms of patron-clientage.

Upon this infertile ground of unfree labour, the scope for the export of productive (industrial) capital was extremely limited: the industrialisation of underdeveloped regions required a prior process of the dissolution of pre-capitalist relations. The materialist theory of capitalist development provides few generalisations about the process by which wage labour emerged in each country and region. No general theory of the rise of capitalism is possible, for in each case the failure or success of the relations of capital to take root is dictated by the nature of the pre-capitalist society. However, some general insights are possible. In those underdeveloped regions where the relations of capital took hold, accumulation was limited by its essential incompatibility with pre-capitalist production. From a superficial point of view, pre-capitalist relations appear beneficial, since they could represent a source of cheap labour-power. However, this remains a latent benefit to industrial capital until the pre-capitalist sector unravels and sheds its labour. Even as this occurs, value theory reveals a profound incompatibility that calls the concept of 'cheap labour' into question; i.e. reveals it as an essentially vulgar concept at the level of appearances.

Because pre-capitalist production does not conform completely to the discipline of the law of value, production techniques continue, primarily in agriculture, which would be abandoned by capitalists as unprofitable. Restrictions on the alienability of land and the immobility of unfree labour restrict the ability of capital to transform agrarian relations. However, it is the agricultural sector which provides a large portion of the means of subsistence of the workers that capitalists hire. In an abstract, fully capitalist society, the process of competition reduces the value of commodities, which feeds back through the system to reduce the value of labour-power. Such is not the case for a society in which the means of worker subsistence are produced in pre-capitalist relations.

Other things being equal, a worker with a lower standard of living is 'cheaper' to a capitalist than one with a higher standard of living.[44] However, this refers to increasing surplus value absolutely, and cannot be the mechanism for the progressive cheapening of commodities. No matter how low the standard of living of workers, subsequent cheapening of commodities requires that surplus value be raised relatively in the capitalist sector. As we have seen, surplus value is raised relatively through the reduction of the value of labour-power. In as far as workers consume commodities produced in the capitalist sector, the process of competition, by cheapening these commodities, reduces the value of labour-power. However, the component of workers' subsistence which arises from the pre-capitalist sector is not cheapened by the process of capital accumulation. The fall in the value of commodities produced by capital is not matched by an equal fall in the value of labour-power, resulting in a decline in surplus value per worker, even if the standard of living of workers remains the same. Thus, the interaction of the capitalist and pre-capitalist sectors results in a fall in the rate of profit in the former sector.[45] In simple terms, competition in the capitalist sector results in a transfer of value to the pre-capitalist sector via a movement in relative prices against the capitalist sector.

The fall in the rate of profit does not require that machinery or other means of production are substituted for labour inputs. An autonomous increase in labour productivity[46] is sufficient to bring down the rate of profit. At the ini-

---

44 On the condition, among other things, that the difference in the standard of living is not cancelled by an equal or larger difference in productivity.

45 This process is demonstrated in a formal model in the appendix.

46 'Autonomous' in the sense that more output is achieved from a given input of labour-power and means of production.

tial set of exchange values of outputs and inputs, any autonomous productivity increase appears to the capitalist as cost-decreasing, though it subsequently results in a decline in unit profits. Even if capitalists could foresee the fall in profits due to the productivity increase, they would be forced to adopt by the pressure of competition: if some capitalists did not, others would, in order to reduce their costs and seize a larger market share. The special conditions of underdevelopment force capitalists to adopt productivity-raising techniques that provoke a tendency for the rate of profit to fall.

The process of accumulation in the context of a pre-capitalist sector producing the means of consumption for the workers in the capitalist sector can be summarised as follows. Competition in the capitalist sector results in the introduction of cost-reducing technical changes. By raising the productivity of labour, these technical changes increase the use of materials per unit of labour, and even more if accompanied by an increase in machinery per worker (not considered in this discussion). Were both sectors capitalist, the result of technical change in either sector would be to raise the average rate of profit as exchange values of the means of workers' subsistence fall. Values, then, via competition, prices, would fall. The general cheapening of commodities raises the rate of profit in a purely capitalist society.

When the means of consumption are produced under pre-capitalist relations, the result is dramatically different. As before, competition in the capitalist sector results in the introduction of cost-reducing technical changes. This brings down the price of capitalist commodities. In as far as the capitalist sector uses its own outputs as inputs, the tendency for profit to decline is counteracted. However, this does not affect the distribution of the working day between necessary and surplus labour time. In order that surplus-value rise, it is necessary for the value of labour-power to decline. This will occur if and only if there is a decline in the value of the commodities workers consume, or a decline in the value of the inputs to those commodities. Since the pre-capitalist sector may use capitalist inputs (as in the model), the price of its output may fall, and thus the value of labour-power may fall. But this will be insufficient to keep unit profit from declining in the capitalist sector.[47]

47 Formally, this is equivalent to the oft-demonstrated result that technical change which raises the ratio of means of production to labour-power (what Marx called the technical composition of capital) will result in a decline in the average rate of profit if the value of labour-power remains unchanged. In current discussion, the decline does not result from assuming a constant value of labour-power, but from the relatively lower rate of productivity growth in the pre-capitalist sector.

There are two major tendencies that can counteract the tendency of the average rate of profit to decline in the context of pre-capitalist relations in agriculture. First, in as far as the pre-capitalist sector uses capitalist inputs, technical change in the capitalist sector will lower the value of the means of consumption; i.e. as the pre-capitalist sector comes under the discipline of exchange in its use of inputs. Second, the tendency is counteracted as workers' consumption incorporates commodities produced in the capitalist sector. The specific historical conditions and social relations in each country will determine the strength of these counteracting tendencies. Most fundamentally, removing the limits to accumulation requires a capitalist revolution in agriculture. The inability of the law of value to bring about the progressive reduction of necessary labour relatively to surplus labour reflects the contradictions arising from two systems of social relations which are inconsistent in the long run.

In this context, one can identify a major source of the successful capitalist development of the East and Southeast Asian countries: many of these countries benefited from a fundamental reform of agricultural and tenure prior to their rapid accumulation process. In Latin America, land reforms did not occur at all (for example, Guatemala) or were not complemented by support services necessary for capitalist transformation (Bolivia, Mexico and Peru). The most successful case of capitalist development, Chile, indicates the importance of land reform in laying the basis for accumulation.[48]

6 The Limits to the Progressiveness of Capitalism

An important implication of the theory developed above is that underdevelopment is the incomplete development of capitalism in a society.[49] This would seem to imply that capitalism is the solution to the problem of underdevelopment, a conclusion argued with considerable force by numerous authors who considered themselves Marxists.[50] It is hardly surprising that many on the Left

48 Land reform in Chile was initiated in the early 1960s, then pursued with vigour by the Christian Democratic government (1964–70) and the Socialist/Communist government (1970–3). After the military coup in 1973, the right-wing government continued agrarian modernisation through capitalist farming.

49 This conclusion is in direct contrast to that of dependency theory. The latter concludes that countries are underdeveloped because of capitalist penetration, while materialist theory concludes that underdevelopment reflects the incomplete dominance of capitalist relations over pre-capitalist ones.

50 See Warren 1980.

have drawn back from this conclusion, implying as it does some rather unpalatable political practice. While the logic of the law of value implies capitalism is progressive, it is relevant here to recall Oscar Wilde's aphorism that madness is carrying any argument to its logical conclusion.

The overall progressive nature of the capitalist mode of production is integrally linked to the uneven development which capitalism generates, which is inherent in capitalist competition. From the days of Adam Smith, the political economy schools, both classical and neoclassical, treated competition as a force that produces harmony among capitals ('firms'). This analytical outcome results from presuming that all capitals are identical (the 'typical firm'), entering into the competitive process on equal footing. This assumption presupposes the outcome which the competitive process generates: the tendency for competition to establish a norm of abstract necessary labour in production. By presupposing the outcome, the neoclassical political economy school precludes the possibility of winners and losers in competition. In this framework, competition processes no outcome at all, but rather a harmonious equilibrium among rivals all of whom were identical at the outset and remain so to the end.

This approach, in which capitalist rivals are equals, involves no analysis of competition itself. Indeed, it precludes the very mechanisms by which the competitive struggle is fought. If all 'firms' are 'price-takers', there is no role for price competition, product differentiation, advertising, and the other tactics by which capitalists seek to gain advantage over one another.[51] To understand the uneven development which capitalism generates, it is necessary to reconstruct the analysis of competition on the basis of the law of value. This involves three basic principles: first, that competition be defined as the movement of capital; second, the integration of technical change with the movement of capital; and, third, recognition that within sectors of industry the efficiency of production is unevenly developed. For the analysis of underdevelopment, to these must be added the contradictory impact of the relations of capital on pre-capitalist formations.

As suggested in the discussion of Table 5.1, the impact of the expansion of capital on pre-capitalist relations is determined by the interaction of the form capital takes (commodity, productive, money), and the nature of pre-capitalist social relations. The expansion of capital in commodity and money forms need not generate wage relations which are the basis of capitalism's dynamism. On the contrary, capitalist trade and finance can reinforce the power of pre-capitalist elites, blocking the development of industrial capital,

51 A more detailed critique of neoclassical competition can be found in Weeks 1994b.

both by domestic agents and foreign ones. Further, by expanding international markets for commodities produced in pre-capitalist relations, the expansion of commodity and financial capital can intensify and strengthen systems of unfree labour. In circumstances in which pre-capitalist relations are transformed to wage relations, the process is rarely smooth or harmonious. When labour-power is not completely separated from the land, exchange is a blunt instrument to achieve reallocation. In this circumstance, force may be required, typically executed by the capitalist state, to render pre-capitalist relations vulnerable to capitalist penetration. The 'civilised' warfare of cheapening commodities is constructed upon a violent process of dispossessing peasants and artisans from their means of production.[52]

Even in an abstracted society of purely capitalist relations, the expansion of capital is simultaneously destructive and creative. If, in general, production units within industries vary in unit costs, then it follows that the movement of capital does not reproduce the average production conditions in an industry, but typically seeks to emulate or surpass the most efficient operator. Far from establishing a harmonious equilibrium, capitalist competition disrupts, eliminates the weak and challenges the strong, to force upon industry a new standard of efficiency and cost. The movement of capital to equalise profits across industries is the process of generating uneven development: equilibration in exchange (a single price in a market) hides the generation of uneven development in production. In a capitalist system, regulated but by capital itself, the frontier between the 'civilised' forms of cheapening commodities, on the one side, and banditry, fraud, and violence is easily and frequently crossed.

While capitalist social relations are progressive in the strict sense of laying the basis for a revolutionary development of the productive forces, it does not follow that unregulated capitalism generates this outcome in all circumstances and regions. For example, the current globalisation of commodity and financial markets has been associated with growth 'miracles' in East and Southeast Asia, but has reinforced underdevelopment in Africa south of the Sahara. The latter is as much a part of the dynamism of capitalism as the former. Inherent in the progressiveness of capitalism on a world scale is the simultaneous destructive impact of capitalism in particular regions.

52 Marx termed this process so-called primitive accumulation: 'The so-called primitive accumulation, therefore, is nothing else than the historical process of divorcing the producer form the means of production ... [T]he history of primitive accumulation ... [are] those moments when great masses of men [*sic*! people] are suddenly and forcibly torn from their means of subsistence, and hurled as free and "unattached" proletarians on the labour-market' (Marx 1906, pp. 786, 787).

Further, part of the progressiveness of capitalism arises from the class struggle, out of which restrictions are placed upon the accumulation of capital. The distinction between the absolute and relative extraction of surplus value is at one level of analysis purely formal and definitional. At the more concrete level, it is a critique of unregulated capitalism. In the absence of restrictions on capital, the more primitive absolute extraction is forced upon capitalists by the pressure of competition. Precisely because the raising of surplus value relatively is a social process, it must in part be imposed upon capitalists by limiting their power to raise surplus value absolutely. Historically, limits were imposed through the legal restriction of the length of the working day, regulations on working conditions, and prohibition of child labour. The struggle of workers for workplace rights transforms capitalism from its primitive, repressive stage of absolute extraction, and forces it to realise its more progressive character in which society's surplus labour is increased through the dynamism of technical change.

7 Technical Appendix

In the section, 'Limits to Accumulation in Transitional Societies', it was argued that the persistence of pre-capitalist relations tends to limit the accumulation process. This annex provides a formal proof. At the outset we make a number of simplifying assumptions. Consider a closed economy in which there are two sectors, one capitalist that produces means of production, and one pre-capitalist that produces the means of consumption. The capitalist sector does not use the commodity of the pre-capitalist sector as a direct input to production. The exchange values for each sector can be defined as follows:

$$(p_1 a_1 \beta + p_2 w n_1)(1 + r_1) = p_1 \beta; \quad (1)$$

$$(p_1 a_2 + p_2 w n_2)(1 + r_2) = p_2. \quad (2)$$

where a_i are the units of commodity 1 required to produce one unit of commodity i, $(i = 1, 2)$, (both greater than zero and less than unity); w is the amount of commodity 2 consumed by a worker in a day (greater than zero and less than unity); n_i are the units of labour required to produce one unit of commodity i, $(i = 1, 2)$,(greater than zero); and β is a productivity index (equal to or less than unity). There is no productivity index for the pre-capitalist sector because it is assumed technologically stagnant relatively to the capitalist sector. p_i is the exchange value of commodity i, and r_i the profit rate in the production of commodity i, $(i = 1, 2)$.

While the pre-capitalist sector pays wages, the labour there is not 'free' wage labour, but tied to the dominant rural class through relations of clientage. Land is not a freely vendible commodity, in part because rural labour is tied to the land. As a result, capital cannot move from the capitalist sector to the pre-capitalist, so there is no tendency for the rates of return to equalise. Each commodity's exchange value tends to equal its value. Because of the tendency for exchange values to equal values, the following holds (price in each sector equals the labour time objectified in means of production plus the new or current labour added in production):

$$p_1 a_1 \beta + n_1 = p_1 \beta; \tag{3}$$

$$p_1 a_2 + n_2 = p_2. \tag{4}$$

Therefore

$$p_1 = \frac{n_1}{\beta(1 - a_1)}; \tag{5}$$

$$p_2 = \frac{a_2 n_1}{\beta(1 - a_1)} + n_2. \tag{6}$$

If we substitute (5) and (6) into (1), we obtain (after some manipulation),

$$1 + r_1 = \frac{1}{a_1 + \frac{w n_1 a_2}{\beta} + w n_2 (1 - a_1)} \tag{7}$$

The profit rate in the capitalist sector reduces to a function of several parameters: the input and labour coefficients for each sector, the standard of living (w), and the productivity index of the capitalist sector (β). Inspection shows that a productivity increase (β falling) results in the denominator in equation (7) rising and hence $(1 + r_1)$ falling, and hence r_1 falling.

This occurs even though unit costs in the capitalist sector decline.[53] This decline results from the reduction in the living labour content of capitalist commodities (the reduction in β), in the absence of a tendency for profit rates to equalise across the two sectors. Were both sectors capitalist, the relative

53 Assume that initially β equals unity. Then, cost per unit of output ('cost price' was Marx's term) is $p_1 a_1 + p_2 w n_1$; for $\beta < 1$ unit cost is $p_1 a_1 \beta + p_2 w n_1$ which is lower. The profit rate falls even though unit costs are lower (Marx 1991).

surplus value mechanism explained in the text would ensure that the equalised rate of profit for both sectors would be higher than prior to the productivity increase.[54] In the absence of this equalisation, the exchange value of the means of consumption may fall,[55] but less than would be the case with equalisation, and value is in effect transferred from the capitalist to the pre-capitalist sector.

54 This is the 'Okishio Theorem': any technical change which reduces the cost (cost price) of a commodity at prevailing prices will result in a rise in the system-wide average rate of profit after all prices have adjusted to the new values generated by the new technology matrix. See Okishio 1961.

55 This is because p_1a_2 falls when p_1 declines.

CHAPTER 6

Epochs of Capitalism and the Progressiveness of Capital's Expansion

1 Introduction

That capitalism divides itself into distinct epochs or stages is universally recognised by writers in the Marxian tradition, though there is some variation as to the theoretical explanation for the division. There is considerably less agreement over the characteristics of capitalism in the different epochs. The most important disagreement is over whether capitalism in its advanced stage is 'progressive'. That is, whether it remains the tendency for capitalism throughout its expansion to destroy pre-capitalist social relations and transform those social formations into capitalist formations. This 'progressive' tendency is sometimes narrowly stated as the tendency for capitalism to develop the forces of production. It is argued that insofar as advanced capitalism contains within itself this tendency, it is a progressive force on a world scale; insofar as this tendency has been lost, capitalism is reactionary.

The issue of the progressiveness of advanced capitalism is central to the theory of imperialism, and some have taken the view that capitalism's revolutionary overthrow is justified only if the development of the productive forces has come to an end.[1] Questions concerning the progressiveness of capitalism have appeared prominently in the debate over revolutionary strategy in underdeveloped countries; they are closely linked to the issue of class alliances and whether a 'two stage' revolution is called for. This paper addresses itself to these general issues. In Section II, the periodisation of capitalism is treated and the most important characteristics of capitalism during each epoch arc outlined. In Section III, the question of the progressiveness of capitalism is considered, and it is argued that conclusions on this issue derive from one's theory of capitalist competition. While this analysis has implications for political strategy, these are not pursued in this paper.

1 A famous passage from Marx would seem to support this: 'No social order is ever destroyed before all the productive forces for which it is sufficient have been developed, and new superior relations of production never replace older ones before the material conditions for their existence have matured within the framework of the old society' (Marx 1976a, p. 21).

 | DOI:10.1163/9789004703193_008

When one thinks of the periodisation of capitalism, the most prominent source that comes to mind is Lenin and his famous pamphlet, *Imperialism*. Indeed, it is frequently argued that one of Lenin's most important contributions to Marxian theory was the specification of capitalism's two stages or epochs: the stage of competitive capitalism and the stage of imperialism. We find the first such conceptual division of capitalism in Volume I of *Capital*, with Marx's distinction between the 'stage of manufacture' and the 'stage of modern industry'. It is clear from Lenin's early work that his periodisation of capitalism derives from Marx's division based upon the internal dynamic of the accumulation process.[2] Marx argued that in its first epoch, 'manufacture', the accumulation process is based upon the extraction of absolute surplus value; and in the second, 'modern industry', the production of relative surplus value dominates the accumulation process.

Much of the literature on imperialism has stressed the 'worldwide, strategic character of imperialist penetration'. This literature includes: debate over the strategy of the bourgeoisie in imperialist countries *vis-a-vis* ruling classes in oppressed countries, the possible contribution of the bourgeoisie in oppressed countries to national liberation struggles, and other central issues of revolutionary praxis. What follows does not address itself directly to these crucial questions, though it is integrally related to them. Rather, an effort is made to identify the historical tendency of capital's development. The most important issue at this high level of abstraction is the question of capital's tendency to transform pre-capitalist social formations into capitalist formations. If this is the major tendency, then capitalism is said to be 'progressive'. This does not imply that *capitalists* in advanced or backward countries are progressive. That question lies at a more concrete level of analysis. While the nature of capital's development and the strategy of the imperialist bourgeoisie are related, the two are not mechanically linked by abstract logic. Rather, their relationship is mediated by the concrete history of each country.

But while the abstraction to capital as a whole moves one far from the analysis of conjunctural circumstances, it provides a number of fundamental insights which allow for a rigorous consideration of the concrete. The most general and basic conclusion is that the fundamental nature of capitalism does not change as capitalism matures, but rather that those aspects which were latent in immature capitalism come to dominate. In particular, this analysis rejects the 'monopoly capital' school of thought which argues that developed capitalism is characterised by different laws of operation than those operative in the

2 Lenin 1972c.

previous stage.[3] The most important of these is the competitive contradiction, which the 'monopoly capital' school sees as disappearing in modern capitalism. While the implications of the 'monopoly capital' view are not pursued, they are seen as the implicit basis for much of the theorising about the causes of underdevelopment in the imperialist epoch.

2 Epochs of Capitalism

2.1 *Stage of Manufacture*

Capitalist production is based on the separation of producers from the means of production. This separation involves as its most important aspect the forceable expulsion of labour from the land. Once this separation occurs ('primitive accumulation' Marx called it), the necessary conditions for capital's birth are present. In the 'freeing' of labour from the land, capital is set free by allowing money to be a claim on wealth in general. Once labour is no longer in possession of the means of production, it can only be united with those means of production through the initiative of capital. This point is shown by reference to the circuit of capital, given below.

$M\text{–}C^{MP}_{LP} \ldots P \ldots C'\text{–}M'$

M — money-capital
C — productive capital: means of production (MP) and labour power (LP)
P — moment of production
C′ — commodity capital
M′ — expanded money-capital

The capitalist epoch dates from the domination of the work process by capital. Prior to this domination of production, capital existed in extremely restricted form as merchant's capital. Merchant's capital had the basic form of capital, buying in order to sell (M–C–M′), but it did not exert its control over the production process. It is the control of the production process by capital which not only characterised a new historical epoch, but made capitalist society dynamic and progressive compared to previous epochs. Marx characterised this initial control of production as the 'formal subsumption of labour to capital'. The division of labour within the production process in the period of manufacture reflected the social relations and technology which evolved within artisanal production. The dynamism which capital generated was the result of the new social relations of wage labour.

3 Baran and Sweezy 1966.

In this first stage of capital's development, the sources of expanded accumulation were the concentration of capital and the raising of surplus value absolutely. Because of the artisanal nature of the production process, the possibilities for raising productivity were extremely limited. Machinery was largely a product of craft workshops, expensive and limited in supply. In part due to this technological limitation, individual capitals expanded by concentrating more workers into workplaces, rather than by transforming the production process. In such conditions, surplus value was raised primarily by lengthening the working day and increasing the intensity of work. Marx called this the production of absolute surplus value.

Capital's reliance on the production of absolute surplus value was dictated by the primitive state of capitalist social relations even more than by technological constraints. In the period of manufacture, the progressive tendencies of capitalism manifested themselves not primarily in the development of productive forces, but in the destruction of anachronistic social relations. Particularly important was the credit system, underdeveloped and oriented to the needs of merchant's capital. Achieving dominance over the credit system was perhaps the single most important task for industrial capital in order to make the transition to 'modern industry'.

The accumulation of capital is achieved by the conversion of surplus value into new capital, additional means of production and labour power. For capital as a whole, the rate of accumulation depends upon, and its upper limit is set by, the mass of surplus value which is realized as profit. In the period of manufacture, individual capitals tended to be similarly limited, with their expansion based upon the surplus value produced in the individual production processes. This reflected the underdevelopment of the credit system. In effect, the institutional framework of capitalism was too primitive to allow for the redistribution of surplus value among capitals, which is the function of banking or financial capital.[4] Limited to their own profits, individual capitals could not undertake the large investments which the revolutionising of the means of production required.

These limitations on the accumulation process gave the period of manufacture its particular character. Competition was restricted to struggles within branches of industry by relatively large numbers of producers. First, with the credit system underdeveloped, more efficient capitals were constrained in the rate at which they could expand and eliminate weak competitors. Second, this same credit constraint made it difficult for capital in one branch of industry to

4 Weeks 1981, Chapter v.

invade other branches. To use Marx's term, this was the period of the concentration of capital (growth of individual capitals), with little scope for the centralisation of capital (redistribution of existing capital among fewer capitals). This implies that in the period of manufacture 'capital as function' (capital's productive aspect) dominated over 'capital as ownership' (capital's distributive aspect).

It is this early and primitive stage of capitalist society that bourgeois economists eulogise as the golden age of competition. This view is both romantic and ahistorical. What appears as 'free competition' was *constrained* competition, competition in embryonic and primitive form. The bourgeois theory of 'perfect competition' is merely an ahistorical abstraction from a brief and fleeting moment of capitalism's youth. To treat this primitive period of capitalism as the theoretical basis of commodity producing society is to invert reality, for the major tendencies within accumulation remain latent in this stage.[5]

At this point it is useful to elaborate what is meant by 'latent', since this concept plays an important role in the analysis. Obviously capitalism has changed over time, and its appearance in the twentieth century is quite different from its appearance in the late eighteenth century. One can account for this in two ways. One way would be to treat capitalist society as affected by forces related to but separable from capitalist social relations themselves, such as technical change, and to argue that capitalism adapts itself to a new environment or is transformed by that environment. The approach here is different. It is argued that capital in its incipient form contained within itself contradictory elements, and the progressive resolution of these contradictions gave rise to the subsequent concrete manifestations of capital's reproduction. To be specific, the rapid process of centralisation of capital and the union of financial and industrial capital which occurred at the end of the nineteenth century was not an alteration in the nature of capitalist accumulation, but the realization of contradictions which had been present in capital's reproduction one hundred years before. At some risk, we can venture an analogy with an acorn: the growth of a great oak tree represents not adaptation or change in response to the environment, but a process latent in the acorn itself (though obviously the environment has a quantitative effect on its growth).

The early stage of capital's development should now be considered; in this manufacturing stage capitalism is clearly progressive within its own domain.

5 I refer to the process of the centralisation of capital, production of relative surplus value, and the two tendencies that arise from these: the tendency of the rate of profit to fall and the counteracting tendencies *w* the falling rate of profit.

The progressiveness of capitalism is the consequence of capital seizing control of the production process (moment C … P … C′ in the circuit of capital) and through accumulation bringing more and more people into wage labour. In the stage of manufacture, the progressiveness manifests itself at different levels of abstraction. First, the growth of capitalist production is the growth of the proletariat, which lays the basis for the struggle between the two great classes of modern society. Second, capitalist social relations have a liberating effect on the development of the productive forces, heralding a new epoch in man's mastery over nature. Third, what Marx called the 'necessary illusion' of equal exchange between capital and labour transforms the ideological context in which the exploitation of labour occurs. The ideology of capitalism is based on the formal equality of capital and labour in exchange, and in the political sphere this manifests itself in the bourgeois concept of individual freedoms. These freedoms functioned in the early stage of capitalist development to liberate capital from feudal constraints. One necessary aspect of this liberation of capital was the separation of labour from the means of production, a process that freed workers from extra-economic coercion in order that they might be made available for capital.

On a world scale manufacturing capitalism was limited by the same underdevelopment that restricted accumulation to the production of absolute surplus value. Because of the rudimentary character of the credit system, the export of both money-capital and productive capital could not be easily achieved. The term 'export of money-capital' is used to designate lending by financial institutions, usually in the form of state or private bonds, to other countries, developed or underdeveloped. 'Export of productive capital' refers to the setting up of productive enterprises in other countries (plantations, factories, railroads, mines) under the direct operating authority of foreign capital.

The existence of pre-capitalist social relations left little scope for such export to Africa, Asia, Latin America, and Eastern Europe in the nineteenth century. Pre-capitalist societies are not predominantly commodity-producing, though they may be drawn into capitalist exchange. As long as labour power is not a commodity, or is available only to a limited extent, capital lacks the basis for its unique system of exploitation. That is why the first export of productive capital was for mining and plantations, which were outside the pre-capitalist economy and produced for the overseas capitalist market.

One needs no special theory to account for the predominance of the export of commodity capital in the stage of manufacture, and certainly no underconsumptionist argument. Capitalist production recognises no national boundaries, and the export of commodity capital is the consequence of commodity production itself. To a certain extent, the export of commodity capital was stimulated by the need for raw materials required from pre-capitalist formations. But the theoretical issue is not why commodity capital was exported in the stage of manufacture, but why money-capital and productive capital were not. The explanation lies in the nature of capitalist society on the one hand, and of pre-capitalist formations on the other.

2.2 *Stage of Modern Industry*

The process of accumulation in the stage of manufacture concentrates the working class into larger productive units, laying the basis for the development of working class power. This power asserted itself in a struggle over the conditions of work and control of the labour process. The most decisive aspect of this struggle was the conflict over limiting the working day, or, more precisely, the struggle over who would determine the length of the working day, capital or labour. The victory of the working class in establishing limits to the degree to which capital could dictate the length of working day ushered in the stage of modern industry.[6]

Once the working day was no longer unilaterally set by capital, the scope for raising surplus value absolutely reached its limit. While this form of increasing the surplus was not eliminated, it ceased to be the major element in the competitive struggle among capitals, giving way to what Marx calls 'relative surplus value'. This requires that in a given working day the 'necessary labour time' be reduced relative to the 'surplus labour time'. The primary method for achieving this result is the introduction of technological improvements into the production process. The emergence of relative surplus value as the dominant basis for accumulation did not end oppressive methods of intensifying labour on the shop floor; i.e., capitalism did not mellow its exploitative character in the stage of modern industry. To the extent that work became less oppressive, this resulted (and results) from the continuous struggle of the working class over hours, conditions, and intensity of labour, not as a result of rising productivity itself. The development of the credit system provided the additional money-capital necessary for the expansion of the scale of production which greater use of machinery required. The need to marshal large amounts of money-capital led to the growth of financial capital, with profound consequences for the nature of the capitalist system. In Marx's words, it represented the ascendancy of capital-as-ownership over capital-as-function; or as Lenin put it, the domination of industrial capital by finance capital. Lenin's emphasis on finance capital has been commonly interpreted to imply the decline of competition in the stage

6 For an excellent discussion, see Fine and Harris 1979. See also Harris 1983.

of imperialism. In recent years, a growing school of theorists rejects this interpretation of Lenin's writings and the argument that competition declines.[7]

Rather, the truth is that the development of the credit system and finance capital intensifies the competitive struggle. In the stage of manufacture competition tended to be restricted to what bourgeois economists call the 'product market', price competition among existing capitals. With modern industry capitalist competition develops to a higher level, manifesting itself in the flow of capital between branches of industry, and eventually between countries. Like so many aspects of capitalism, the tendency for competition to intensify is obscured. The movement of capital can at times result in capitals monopolising markets. This tendency increases as capitalism develops, but it is a manifestation of capital's competitive contradiction, not the elimination of competition.[8]

While all production is social, production in the stage of modern industry becomes socialized to a qualitatively advanced degree. Capitalist production appears to be atomised, isolated production, the sum of the production of many capitals. In the stage of manufacture, this appearance somewhat corresponds to reality, since exploitation is to a great extent achieved by the domination of individual capitals over their workers – the extraction of absolute surplus value. In the stage of modern industry, exploitation is socialised; the relationship is between capital as a whole and the working class. Raising the rate of exploitation depends upon the rate at which the integrated system of production can raise productivity generally and thereby reduce necessary labour time (the value of labour power). In such an advanced phase of capitalist development, one capitalist increases exploitation of labour insofar as all do.[9] Marx called this the development of 'social capital'.

The age of modern industry facilitates the export of money-capital and later productive capital. Again, no special theory of capital export is required, for the tendency to export money and productive capital arises from developments internal to the capitalist mode of production. Once financial capital achieves maturity, it seeks out profitable fields, including those in pre-capitalist formations. This interpretation implies that while it is not erroneous to periodise

7 See footnote 24, and Weeks 1984, Chapter 1.

8 Marx put this well in *The Poverty of Philosophy*: 'In practical life we find not only competition, monopoly, and the antagonism between them, but also the synthesis of the two, which is not a formula, but a movement. Monopoly produces competition, competition produces monopoly ... The synthesis is such that monopoly ca n only maintain itself by continually entering into the struggle of competition' (Marx 1976b, p. 197).

9 This follows from the manner in which surplus value is raised *relatively*. See Marx 1906, Chapter 12; and Weeks 1981a.

capitalism in terms of the forms that the export of capital takes, it is imprecise analytically to do so. Periodisation based on the form in which capital is exported can be misleading in two ways: 1) it stresses the differences between the epochs of capitalism rather than their basic continuity; and 2) it suggests that the stage of modern industry should be divided into a period in which the export of money-capital is primary and a further one in which the export of productive capital is primary. The second point we develop below.

Finally, to periodise capitalism by the forms of capital export is to accept a criterion based on the sphere of circulation. Basing arguments on circulation is not a *prima facie* sin of analysis. However, most Marxian theorists would agree that phenomena of circulation are derivative from the sphere of production.[10]

3 The Export of Capital and Its Effects

3.1 *Export of Commodity Capital*

As already noted, capitalism from its birth engaged in the export of commodity capital (C′–M′). Observation of this fact gave rise to an early critique of capitalism based on an underconsumptionist theory and denying the progressiveness of capitalism. Early writers to take up this position were Sismondi and Proudhon, who argued that the development of wage-labour relations, by destroying the peasantry and artisanal classes, reduced the 'home market' for commodities. The analytical shortcoming of this school of thought is that it fails to recognise the circulation of commodities as the circulation of capital, as Lenin cogently argued.[11]

The expansion of commodity production in the capitalist homeland transforms society through the ruination of the independent petit-bourgeois producer – a ruination that appears to take place through the 'civilised' form of price competition. In the periphery direct force is applied to non-capitalist formations by the bourgeois state (what Marx referred to as 'so-called primitive accumulation').[12] It has been often pointed out that commodity capital export

10 Marx wrote: 'the structure of distribution is completely determined by the structure of production', and 'the immensity of exchange, its extent and nature, are determined by the development and structure of production' (Marx 1973, pp. 28).

11 Lenin wrote: 'Do we deny that capitalism needs a foreign market? Of course not. But the question of a foreign market has *absolutely nothing to do with the question of realisation and* the attempt to link them into one whole expresses … the romantic inability to think logically'. Lenin 1972a, p. 162, emphasis in original. I have dealt with this issue in Weeks 1983.

12 'Direct force. outside of economic conditions, is of course still used [in nineteenth-century

frequently had the effect of destroying pre-capitalist production in underdeveloped areas, particularly artisanal production. Some writers state that this generated capitalist transformation or created the conditions for such a transformation.[13] Whatever validity such conclusions might have, it is essential to note the central place of force in early capitalist development and the role of the bourgeois state in the violent process of 'primitive accumulation'. Historical evidence suggests that exchange alone is insufficient to generate capitalist relations; it does so only when active steps are taken to generate bourgeois social relations out of the destruction created by exchange and competition.[14]

For the most part the pre-capitalist countries and territories invaded by commodity capital lacked a bourgeoisie. Moreover, the export of commodity capital was not controlled by the industrial bourgeoisie, but by merchant capital. Merchants of the capitalist centre generally traded with pre-capitalist ruling classes in the underdeveloped areas, and as a consequence, the production of commodities in the latter region maintained its pre-capitalist character. As trade expanded, there often was a tendency for the pre-capitalist relations to be strengthened, not weakened. The pre-capitalist ruling classes simply extracted a larger surplus product through the intensification of existing forms of exploitation.[15]

The rapid growth of world trade in the stage of manufacture reflected the progressive development of wage-labour relations in the capitalist countries, but in the underdeveloped world it strengthened the rule of pre-capitalist exploiting classes. The emergence of a bourgeoisie in the underdeveloped areas was thus retarded by an alliance between foreign merchant capital and local pre-capitalist exploiting classes, the latter controlling the state.[16] The dynamic growth of capitalism in a small part of the world engendered its opposite in the rest of the world.

Britain], but only exceptionally ... It is otherwise during the historical genesis of the capitalist production. The bourgeoisie, at its rise, wants and uses the power of the state to "regulate" wages. i.e., to force them within limits suitable for surplus value making, to lengthen the working day and to keep the labourer himself in the normal degree of dependence. This is an essential element of the so-called primitive accumulation'. Marx 1906, p. 809.

13 For example, Taylor 1981.

14 'The particular functions or money ... point, according to the extent and relative preponderance of the one function or the other, to very different stages in the process of social production. Yet we know by experience that a circulation of commodities relatively primitive, suffices for the production of all or these forms [of money]. Otherwise with capital. The historical conditions of its existence are by no means given with the mere circulation of money and commodities' (Marx 1906, p. 189).

15 This is developed in more detail in Dore and Weeks 1978, pp. 81–4.

16 See Brenner 1977.

3.2 *The Competitive Contradiction*

With the transition of capitalism to the stage of modern industry, international economic relations assumed a new character. Within capitalist formations the socialising tendency of commodity production reached full expression, and internationally capital assumed its imperialist character.[17] In the stage of modern industry not only does the export of money and productive capital become possible, but the character of the export of commodity capital is transformed. Merchant capital, an anachronistic survivor of the mercantile period, becomes subservient to the interests of financial capital, which itself is based upon industrial capital. At this point capital begins to be internationalised in all of its forms, and the capitalist transformation of pre-capitalist formations becomes an immanent tendency.

Before considering the contradictory nature of this tendency, it must be stressed that the export of money-capital and productive capital (and the continuing export of commodity capital) should not be conceived as only involving capitalist countries and pre-capitalist formations. Put another way, imperialism is not simply a relationship between the developed and underdeveloped worlds.[18] A primary aspect of capitalism's international relations in the stage of modern industry has been the export of capital to advanced capitalist countries and the resulting competitive contradictions between the ruling classes of those countries.[19] The relationship between advanced capitalist countries and underdeveloped countries in the age or modern industry is thus a component part of the internationalisation of capital, not its definitive aspect.

17 Marx comments: 'With the development of social production the means of production cease to be means or private production and products of private production and can thereafter be only means of production in the hands or associated producers. ... However, this expropriation appears within the capitalist system in a contradictory form, as appropriation of social property by a few' (Marx 1971, p. 317). In the same vein Lenin writes: 'Capitalism in its imperialist stage leads directly to the most comprehensive socialisation of production; it, so to speak, drags the capitalists, against their will and consciousness, into some sort of new social order, a transitional one from complete free competition to complete socialisation' (Lenin 1981, p. 205).

18 Lenin criticised Kautsky for defining imperialism as the relationship between developed and underdeveloped areas. He wrote of Kautsky's definition: 'This definition is of no use at all because it is one-sided, i.e., arbitrarily singles out only the national question ... The characteristic feature of imperialism is precisely that it strives to annex *not only* agrarian territories, but even most highly developed regions ... [A]n essential feature of imperialism is the rivalry between several great powers' (Lenin 1964, pp. 268–9).

19 The overwhelming majority of productive capital export is to advanced capitalist countries. For example, in the late 1970s, 75 percent of the overseas assets of North American corporations were in advanced capitalist countries; in the late 1950s, the percentage had been less than sixty percent. See Weeks 1984, Chapter 2.

The theory of imperialism has three interrelated aspects: 1) inter-capitalist rivalry, 2) the impact of capital export on social formations in underdeveloped areas, and 3) the 'national question'. It is the second aspect, sometimes called 'the articulation of modes of production', that involves the issue of the progressiveness of capitalism in the modern epoch. The decisive question is: does the internationalisation of capital tend to break down pre-capitalist relations and engender capitalist relations of production?

Since the end of World War II, the most widely accepted answer to this question by writers on the left has been that provided by what is called 'dependency theory'. Writers in this school differ in their analytical premises, but they generally agree that the export of capital has blocked, and continues to block, capitalist development in underdeveloped countries. At the same time, however, they argue that most underdeveloped countries are predominantly capitalist.[20] This apparently inconsistent argument rests on the concept of 'dependent' or 'distorted' capitalist development, in which accumulation possibilities exist but are extremely limited.

While dependency theorists use an eclectic range of arguments to support the concept of 'dependent capitalist development', the key element in the theory is that the world economy is characterised by monopoly, not competition among capitals.[21]

Indeed, this is a consistent argument. If modern capitalism has lost its competitive contradiction, in effect evolving into what Kautsky called 'a single world trust', then further development of capitalism anywhere is blocked. If competition has been eliminated, then the pressure to revolutionise the productive forces is absent, and the world economy tends toward stagnation (rather than cyclical crisis), as Baran and Sweezy argued in the 1960s, specifically for the North American economy.[22] One's view concerning the progressiveness of capitalism in the modern epoch derives from one's conclusion about competition.

Earlier in this paper it was argued that competition intensifies as capitalism develops. It follows from this analysis that the 'monopoly capital' view of the world economy confuses the *form* in which competition manifests itself and the *underlying cause* of competition. While competition must necessarily manifest itself in the form of many capitals in conflict, the cause of competition resides in capital as a whole. The monopoly capital school, in common with bourgeois theory, treats competition only in its most concrete form, in the

20 For a typical presentation, see Laclau 1971.

21 See Weeks 1984, ch. 1.

22 Baran and Sweezy 1966.

interaction of individual capitals. Marx, by contrast, dealt with competition at this level hardly at all.[23] He argued that competition is part of the inner nature of capital as a social relation, and its manifestation in the interaction of many capitals derives from the internal dynamics of capital as a whole. At issue is not whether individual capitals compete; this is an empirical matter, and concerns only the form of competition. The basic question is whether capitalist society subsumes within itself a competitive contradiction.

Feudal society by its nature stifles competition. When labour is united with the land, the vast majority of products cannot circulate as commodities. As capitalism comes into being, the process of primitive accumulation dispossesses labour, frees it for exploitation by capital, and transforms the concrete labour of individuals into alienated labour. The competitive contradiction arises from the fact that labour power is a commodity, and its commodity status requires that the products of labour circulate as commodities. This competition manifests itself on many levels: 1) most profoundly, in the competition between capital and labour over the conditions of exploitation; 2) in the competition among capitalists for labour power; 3) in the movement of capital among branches of industry to equalize the rate of profit; and 4) in the immediate conflict of capitals within a branch of industry.

In the stage of manufacture, the last of these is most important, due to the relative immobility of capital. As capitalism develops, however, it is the third, the movement of capital (centralisation) which defines the competitive struggle among capitals. This movement of capital involves the competition among capitals for labour power, which itself is possible only because labour has been dispossessed (implying the struggle between capital as a whole and the working class as a whole).[24] In the stage of modern industry, the free movement of capital results in periods of violent competitive conflict, such as in the consumer electronics industry today, and periods of subdued struggle, in which capitalists achieve an unstable cooperation among themselves. In the first two decades after the Second World War international competitiveness was relatively dormant due to the overwhelming hegemony of US capital, a hegemony now on the wane. It is no accident that the monopoly capital school and dependency theory flourished during this period of US economic hegemony. However, the period of subdued competition was the calm before the outbreak of a competitive process marked by the centralisation of capital on a world scale.

---

23 For a discussion, see Fine 1991.

24 Weeks 1981, Chapter 6, where this argument is elaborated. Sec also Clifton 1977; and Shaikh 1980.

3.3 *Export of Money-Capital*

If one considers capitalism to be characterized by competition, then the expansion of capital follows logically and no further explanation of the movement of capital is required for the concrete case of international capital movements. The dynamism of capitalism in the stage of manufacture generated the export of commodity capital. In the case of underdeveloped areas, this resulted in the blocking of capitalist development through an alliance between merchant capital and local pre-capitalist ruling classes. The transition to modern industry swept away the mediating role of merchant's capital in trade and also created the possibility for the export of money-capital and productive capital.

In order to understand the consequences of capital export in these two latter forms, let us first consider the movement of money-capital in the abstract. Banks lend money on the condition that it be repaid with interest. Whether or not the money is used as capital by the borrower does not alter the fact that to the banker it is self-expanding value, money-capital. For example, in a developed country, a bank may lend to a worker, who uses the money to have his house painted, pay medical bills, etc. No productive labour may result, nor even a use value be produced, yet the money is capital for the lender. The same conclusion applies when banks lend money to the capitalist state, which may use the money to pay military salaries or unemployment benefits. Thus the movement of capital need not stimulate capitalist activities even in a purely capitalist society, though most lending is from capitalist to capitalist in bourgeois economies. In this way financial capital is formally symmetrical with merchant capital. Both have the appearance of self-expanding value (M–M′ and M–C–M′, respectively), and neither requires capitalist production in order to expand its value, at least formally.

There is a major difference between merchant capital and financial capital, however. Merchant capital predated industrial capital, so its independence of bourgeois production has not only a formal but a real basis. Indeed, as merchant capital increasingly traded the products of industrial capital, its importance declined. Financial capital, on the other hand, developed as a consequence of industrial capital, and its independence of bourgeois production is merely formal. It exists everywhere as a partner (perhaps senior partner) with industrial capital.

It is now possible to summarise how capital export operates in the stage of modern industry (imperialism). The export of money-capital to underdeveloped countries, beginning in the second half of the nineteenth century on a large scale, was not for capitalist production for the most part. On the contrary, much of it was to governments which represented pre-capitalist states. Therefore, the export of capital tended to strengthen pre-capitalist ruling classes, as the export of commodity capital had done. Lenin's comment on the reactionary nature of imperialism was an astute assessment of this relationship of financial capital to pre-capitalist classes. However, just as the export of money-capital grew qualitatively more important than the export of commodity capital in the mid-nineteenth century, so the export of productive capital assumed precedence over the export of money-capital in the mid-twentieth century. Once the export of productive capital to underdeveloped countries reached major proportions, the capitalist transformation of the underdeveloped world was (and is) a necessary consequence. In other words, the major tendency of capitalism in the period of the export of productive capital is the progressive elimination of pre-capitalist formations and the emergence of the industrial proletariat as an economic and political force.

It is this phenomenon which Lenin treated in detail in *Imperialism*, for this form of capital export characterised capital's expansion from the 1860s to the First World War. In the nineteenth century money-capital moved chiefly among advanced capitalist countries and served as capital in the hands of the borrowers. During the second half of the century, for example, large amounts of money-capital flowed from Britain to North America, financing railroads and manufacturing enterprises. On the other hand, most of the money-capital export to underdeveloped areas was to governments representing pre-capitalist states or to mercantile interests engaged in overseas trade.[25]

The effect of the export of money-capital to underdeveloped areas was contradictory, reflecting the fact that financial capital is formally independent of industrial capital, on the one hand, but is engendered by it historically, on the other. By lending to pre-capitalist states, financial capital strengthened the rule of pre-capitalist classes in their struggle against the emergence of local bourgeoisies. The alliances forged between financial capital and the landed oligarchy in Latin America were extremely long lived, persisting to this day in the more backward countries of the region.[26]

While in the political sphere the export of money-capital strengthened pre-capitalist rule, in the economic sphere it was the leading wedge of capitalist penetration and transformation of pre-capitalist social relations. It is this aspect of finance capital which Lenin stressed.[27] Money-capital exported to underdeveloped areas was a potential source of financing capitalist enterprises; whether this happened depended upon the extent to which the previous

25 See Lenin 1981, and Hilferding 1981.

26 For a brief discussion, see Taylor 1983.

27 Lenin 1981, p. 243, where Lenin writes, 'The export of capital influences and greatly accelerates the development of capitalism in those countries to which it is exported'.

export of commodity capital had generated a dispossessed labour force. In extremely backward areas, such as the interior of Peru, the construction of railroads, financed from abroad, occurred with forced labour. At the same time, capitalist enterprise was restricted to 'enclaves' – mining and plantation agriculture – because pre-capitalist Latin America provided extremely restricted markets for commodities. Moreover, in m any cases the mining and plantation enclaves strengthened pre-capitalist relations. In Peru, the sugar plantations were first based upon virtual slave labour (Chinese immigrants) and later on the debt-servitude of peasants from the highlands. Mining activity had a history of forced labour from colonial times, and the new mining enterprises of the late nineteenth century were only nominally capitalist in their social relations.[28]

Thus, the effect of the export of money-capital was not a simple matter of reinforcing pre-capitalist states on the one hand while undermining pre-capitalist production on the other. For latent within the export of money-capital there was the progressive thrust of productive capital. But since the lingering effect of the export of money-capital was to block the development of wage labour, a considerable passage of time was required to link the revolutionizing power of productive capital to the export of money-capital. It is an indication of Lenin's deep understanding of capitalism's dynamics that he could see that the export of money-capital would necessarily revolutionise social relations in underdeveloped areas. But this insight was in advance of events, and some supporters of Lenin's position were too optimistic about the speed at which pre-capitalist societies would be transformed.[29]

3.4 *The Export of Productive Capital*

No Marxist would take issue with defining capitalism as progressive if its expansion tends to break down pre-capitalist formations and in the process generates wage labour relations. Such a judgment is not an endorsement of the capitalist system of exploitation, but reflects the conclusion that the working class is the agent of the overthrow of capitalism and all forms of exploitation. Judging the expansion of capitalist labour relations as progressive is what distinguishes utopian from scientific socialism.[30] Therefore, the expansion of productive

28 See Dore 1981.

29 For example, the Indian Marxist Roy judged India to be predominantly capitalist before the Second World War. Roy 1922.

30 Stedman-Jones puts it well: 'What was designated "utopian", according to this approach [Engels' *Socialism: Utopian and Scientific*] was the imagination of the possibility of total social transformation involving the elimination of individualism, competition and the

capital in underdeveloped countries is necessarily progressive, since it means the growth of the proletariat.

This does not imply that the *export* of productive capital is necessarily progressive. The export of productive capital is a retarding force if it has the effect of not expanding capitalist relations in underdeveloped countries. A necessary but not sufficient condition for this would be that the export of productive capital did not result in the growth of the working class. The growth of the working class necessarily implies the development of capitalism, since it draws labour out of pre-capitalist relations and expands the market for commodities. Capitalism can, of course, break down pre-capitalist relations without a growth of wage labour. This occurs when capitalism eliminates artisanal or peasant production but throws the displaced workers into the reserve army of the unemployed. This may well have occurred during the stage of manufacture in Europe, when the dispossession of the peasantry and the ruination of the artisanal class proceeded much more rapidly than the growth of the capitalist employment of labour. A similar decline is occurring in many underdeveloped countries today. But the relevant criterion for judging the development of capitalism is the growth of the proletariat (employed and unemployed), not the condition of the peasantry and artisans, which capitalism necessarily undermines. The destruction of the local capitalist class by foreign capital, sometimes called the 'denationalisation of ownership', is itself largely irrelevant to the issue of the progressiveness of capitalism. What generates a new era in the class struggle is the growth of the proletariat, irrespective of who has ownership of the capital which dominates labour. The issue then is under what circumstances is productive capital exported to underdeveloped countries, and why does it not accumulate once it is in place in those countries?

Dependency theorists argue that this occurs because foreign capital in the age of imperialism is monopolistic. Foreign monopolies presumably enter underdeveloped countries, destroy local capital, and then protect their markets. In the absence of competition, there is no pressure for accumulation and further capitalist development is blocked.[31] This argument is contradicted by empirical evidence. Throughout the underdeveloped world the proletariat is larger than it was a decade ago, particularly in Latin America. Further, the monopoly view of international capital cannot be sustained theoretically if

---

sway of private property, without a recognition of the necessity of class struggle and the revolutionary role of the proletariat in accomplishing the transition' (Stedman-Jones 1991).

31 This argument is quite old, going back to the nineteenth-century utopian critics of capitalism (See Lenin, *Collected Works*, Vol. 1). After the Second World War, it was revived by Baran and more recently offered again by Dietz. Baran 1957; and Dietz 1979, p. 23.

monopoly is understood to mean the absence of competition. The monopoly argument and its stress on the blocking of the development of national capital has much in common with Sismondi's critique of capitalism made 150 years ago. Just as Sismondi stressed the ruination of the peasantry and saw the expansion of capital and wage labour as impoverishing and weakening society, so dependency theorists stress the ruination of national capital and deny the general expansion of capital.

After the Second World War, the disintegration of pre-capitalist formations, particularly in Latin America, was sufficiently advanced to elicit the export of productive capital on a large scale. With this development, the revolutionising impulse of capitalist relations, an impulse which had largely exhausted itself in the advanced countries, became the dominant tendency in the underdeveloped world. In the last three decades Lenin's far-sighted prediction of the rapid development of capitalism throughout the world has been realized.

4 Conclusion

The theory of periodisation developed here is based on the internal dynamics of the accumulation process. The major foundations of capital's history are the production of absolute surplus value and relative surplus value. Other writers who use the same theoretical basis propose a third stage. Fine and Harris call this stage 'state monopoly capitalism', and Mandel uses the term 'late capitalism'.[32] While these writers provide important insights into the changing character of capitalist institutions, it has not been established that they have defined a separate *stage* of development.

Because capital can be exported in three forms, it is tempting to draw the conclusion that capitalism passes through three stages. The different forms of capital export certainly represent three ways (or even stages) in which capitalism penetrates pre-capitalist formations, but these are stages in the disintegration of those formations, not necessarily stages in the development of the capitalist system as a whole. Many changes have occurred within capitalism in the last one hundred years which are profound, but they do not therefore signal a new stage of capitalism's development.

The theory of periodisation presented here shows that the export of capital to underdeveloped areas first strengthens pre-capitalist rule (export of commodity capital), later continues to do so in a contradictory way (export of

32 Fine and Harris 1979; and Mandel 1975.

money-capital), and finally acts to destroy pre-capitalist social relations and construct capitalist ones in their place (export of productive capital). Using the term 'progressive' in its strict Marxist sense, the conclusion follows that capitalism is progressive in the stage of modern industry (imperialism), though more than one-half century passed before the progressive tendency clearly emerged.

The fact that the export of capital tends to develop capitalism in the underdeveloped world does not imply that accumulation in those countries will be continuous or that they will eventually enter the ranks of the advanced capitalist countries. The manner in which capitalism develops in the underdeveloped countries, and in particular the limits to accumulation in the context of underdevelopment, though an issue of major importance, is not considered here. But its consideration must be based on the recognition of the progressive expansion of capital in underdeveloped countries, not on a 'monopoly' analysis that denies that expansion.

CHAPTER 7

Equilibrium, Uneven Development and the Tendency of the Rate of Profit to Fall

Since the publication of Volume III of Capital, *debate has raged over Marx's theory of the tendency of the rate of profit to fall in advanced capitalist society. Unfortunately, the debate often takes an extremely rarefied form, so rarefied that its implications for theory, much less for practice, are at best obscure. This is indeed unfortunate, since the debate, abstract as it may seem at times, is fundamental to political practice. What is at stake is whether capitalism is by its nature stable and capable of sustained dynamism or whether the accumulation of capital is self-limiting. It must be stressed that the issue is not whether 'Marx was right' or whether his theory can be defended, but rather what is the actual nature of capitalist accumulation and the correct way to analyse it.*

The link between theoretical analysis and the political outlook and practice of particular individuals cannot be made mechanistically. However, the debate over the tendency of the rate of profit to fall does correspond to the debate over revolutionary strategy. If, as argued below, the process of capitalist accumulation is inherently unstable (the tendency of the rate of profit to fall being the fullest expression of that instability), then it follows that a system of commodity production cannot be altered in such a way as to eliminate that instability. Rather, commodity production must be abolished.

If, on the other hand, the accumulation of capital finds its limits in aggregate demand ('underconsumption') or in wage pressures ('profit squeeze'), then a managed, rationalised system of commodity production becomes a political possibility, at least as a transitional social formation on the road to a fully proletarian state. Obviously involved here is the debate over the possibility of a 'peaceful' road for socialist transformation. The purpose of these comments is not to label underconsumptionists and profit-squeeze theorists as 'reformists' and to bless others as 'revolutionaries'. Such labels close out debate among comrades rather than facilitating it. Our point is that the debate over the tendency for the rate of profit to fall relates directly to key questions of political strategy – the role of the wage struggle and 'economistic' demands, possible divisions within the capitalist class and their significance, and class alliances for the overthrow of capitalism and the construction of socialism.

 | DOI:10.1163/9789004703193_009

1 Introduction

The hearts of untold thousands of Marxists must have sunk to read the obituary of Marx's theory of the tendency of the rate of profit to fall. We are not told where the funeral was held, but one can presume that the theoretical remains were laid to rest in Highgate Cemetery alongside the great revolutionary himself, marked by a tombstone financed by subscriptions from 'orthodox' Marxists. Despite this grave passing, while the ground is still fresh, so to speak, it is worth considering whether we have here a case similar to Samuel Clemens reading his obituary in a newspaper and commenting, 'the reports of my death are greatly exaggerated'.

The apparently deadly blow to the law of the tendency of the rate of profit to fall (LTRPF) occurs in an article by Nobuo Okishio. That article was published almost twenty years ago, but his arguments have continued to be developed by others.[1] In what follows we consider Okishio-type arguments, particularly their analytical method and their treatment of competition, money, and fixed capital. The Okishio argument is disarmingly simple: if one considers two static equilibria, holding the standard of living of the working class constant, technical changes which lower the unit costs of commodities must raise the equilibrium rate of profit. For some, this buries the LTRPF forever, since it appears to contradict Marx's central argument that it is the progressive development of productive forces which gives rise to the LTRPF, which undermines accumulation.[2] For Marx this is 'the single most important law of political economy'. In what follows, we evaluate the Okishio argument and how it has been elaborated by others, to see if, like in the famous story by Poe, we have a premature burial.

2 The Argument Elaborated

In the introduction, I briefly summarised the Okishio argument, and now I present that hypothesis in more detail so that it be clear what is under criticism. There are similarities between the Okishio method and the general Sraffian approach, so much so that the former can be interpreted as part of the lat-

1 What we refer to as 'Okishio models' can be found in Okishio 1961; Roemer 1977; Roemer 1979; and Van Parijs 1980. One should also mention two articles which present the mathematics of the argument clearly and, at the same time, are more modest in their conclusions: Alberro and Persky 1979; and Himmelweit 1974.

2 The theory appears in Part III of *Capital*, Chs. XIII–XV (Marx 1971).

ter world view. However, it is not the purpose of this article to undertake a critique of Sraffian theory. The purpose is the much more limited one of critiquing the recent literature on the tendency of the rate of profit to fall, which bases itself on what is called the 'Okishio theorem'. Within this limited context, fundamental issues of scientific method arise, such as the proper method of abstraction. All theoretical disagreements can be carried back to differences in method of abstraction, but the present critique will not locate itself at such a fundamental level. As important as such debates are, to enter into them here would obscure and push to the background the specific issue at hand; namely the importance and implications of the Okishio critique of the law of the tendency of the rate of profit to fall. The fundamental questions of method have been debated elsewhere,[3] and those familiar with the debates will recognise their implicit presence as our argument unfolds.

The Okishio theorem is quite straightforward and can be summarised without reference to esoteric mathematics, though those mathematics provide a rigour of proof with which we take no exception. Let a closed production system be uniquely defined by a prevailing technology in each department (sector) of production and a unique standard of living for the working class, where the latter is some unique collection of commodities. In this production system, a positive rate of profit for the system as a whole is implied, assuming that the prevailing techniques allow a level of productivity for which the net product of the system exceeds the production necessary to satisfy the standard of living for all employed workers. In the terms Marx used, this means necessary labour time is less than total current labour time; though it is unnecessary to use Marx's terminology to explain the Okishio theorem, and probably misleading to do so.

The heart of the Okishio critique of the theory of the tendency of the rate of profit to fall is the analysis of the consequence of the availability of a new technology in one or more sectors of the production system (while holding the standard of living of workers constant).[4] The first crucial step in the analysis is the specification of the decision rule upon which capitalists act when considering the adoption of a new technology. The decision rule reflects common sense; capitalists will adopt a new technology if and only if the new technology is anticipated to lower unit costs of production. The unit cost calculation

3 For example, see Fine and Harris 1979; Rowthorn 1974; Himmelweit and Mohun 1978; and Fine 1980.

4 Here and throughout this article, we consider only 'basic' sectors; i.e., those which produce products which workers consume or inputs for those products; or inputs for inputs, etc. See Suskewicz 1979.

is assumed to be on the basis of prevailing prices, both of the inputs and the output(s), though obviously technological change will in general alter relative prices over time. However, the calculation of costs on the basis of current prices is a strength of the Okishio theorem, for it does not apparently require capitalists to predict the consequences of the technical change beyond the parochial impact on their immediate production costs. It is then possible to demonstrate that all technological changes which conform to this rule, when adopted by all capitalists in a sector, will have the effect of raising the implicit rate of profit for the closed production system as a whole. And if we postulate some process by which the rate of profit equalises across sectors, this equalised rate of profit – the rate of profit realized by capitalists in each sector – will also be higher than the rate of profit that prevailed before the new technique(s) were generally adopted. The reason for this result is that the technical change(s) introduced under the decision rule must necessarily reduce the total labour time, current and past, necessary to produce the products within the production system. The theorem can be summarised as follows: given the standard of living of the working class, technical changes which rational capitalists will introduce, when generally adopted, will raise the overall rate of profit. Or even briefer, *ceteris paribus*, technical change raises the rate of profit.

Anyone familiar with Marx's theory of the tendency of the rate of profit to fall will immediately see the apparently devastating implication of the Okishio theorem. Whether or not one thinks that Marx had a 'profit squeeze' theory of the tendency of the rate of profit to fall,[5] it is universally agreed that he sought also (or instead) to formulate a theory of the tendency of the rate of profit to fall for a given standard of living of the working class. And in this theory, the tendency of the rate of profit to fall is the consequence of technological change; or more explicitly, of increases in the productivity of labour, defined as more output per worker per unit of time. The Okishio theorem apparently refutes this: Marx said that productivity changes cause a tendency for the rate of profit to fall; Okishio showed that productivity increases cause a tendency for the rate of profit to rise. Marx apparently stands refuted.

I will argue that the law of the tendency of the rate of profit to fall is not refuted by the Okishio theorem; indeed, that the theorem is largely irrelevant to the tendency of the rate of profit to fall, unless one interprets the law a particular way. It should be noted that my purpose is not primarily to defend Marx,

5 We have argued that he did not, but this is irrelevant to the current discussion. See Weeks 1979.

even less to compare the Okishio critique to Marx's writings. Rather, my purpose is to demonstrate that there is a tendency for the rate of profit to fall in capitalist society, and that the Okishio theorem has not refuted the existence of this tendency.

To initiate my critique, I point out several characteristics of the Okishio analysis, each of which demands attention. First, in terms of formal mathematics, all sectors of the production system are treated as if each could be aggregated into a single production unit, or single capital. This notwithstanding, the analysis of technical change is at the level of individual capitals. Implicitly involved here is the familiar assumption of the 'representative firm'. The only way that one can both treat a sector as an aggregate and consider the behaviour of one capital within it as typical is by assuming all the capitals within the sector to be the same. The point is a logical one, and its implications will be pursued below. At this point, I am not making a criticism, but only identifying the characteristics of the model.

Second, and related to the first, the Okishio theorem compares two states of static equilibrium in order to draw its conclusion. This is stated explicitly by Van Parijs, who writes that 'it is impossible for a fall in the equilibrium rate of profit (due to a rise in the organic composition) to generate crises'. Throughout the Okishio analysis we are dealing with equilibrium profit rates, equilibrium prices, and equilibrium values. Further, the equilibria are presumed to be stable, for otherwise a dynamic analysis would be required and none is offered.

Third, in the Okishio analysis there is no exchange as such, for in equilibrium we always view the production system after all markets have been cleared, and cleared at equilibrium prices. As a consequence, money as such plays no part in the analysis. This point in and of itself is not a criticism or an original observation about static equilibrium models. It becomes important, however, in the context of a dynamic analysis of the tendency of the rate of profit to fall.

Fourth, the critique is formulated within a model in which there is strict division between variables and parameters, which is characteristic of static equilibrium analysis. On the one hand, the model treats technology and the standard of living of the working class (and implicitly, the value of money) as exogenously determined. These two central elements are not analysed, but are taken as given. Within the model, the manner in which they can change is not specified, except for the indirect constraint on technical change set by the cost-price decision rule. On the other hand, wages, prices, and profits are variables, determined in effect by the parameters. This dichotomising of the elements of the theory has two consequences. First, the variables are explained by elements which themselves go unexplained. The indeterminacy of one set of elements is solved by assuming but not explaining another set of elements. Further, the structure excludes an analysis of how the variables might exert causality upon the parameters. To be explicit, the dichotomy between variables and parameters rules out the possibility of one of the parameters, namely technology, undergoing change out of equilibrium. Of course, it would not be impossible for the elabourators of Okishio's critique to formulate a model in which technology and the standard of living are endogenous. But they have not done so, and this omission is not accidental. We shall argue that if they did so, their results would be quite different.

Overall, the approach is one of comparing static equilibria, which is ill-designed by its nature to analyse the dynamic passage from one equilibrium to the next. In comparing static states, the question of stability of the equilibria is not treated, but rather subsumed under the rubric of competition. This use of equilibrium analysis has the consequence of excluding time from the model, except in a purely formalistic way. The treatment of time is formalistic in that the past, present and future in the theory are perfectly interchangeable. The 'time' sequence of the different equilibria can be altered merely by changing the subscripts on the equations. We are not dealing here with chronological time, but logical steps from one equilibrium to another – Robinson's famous islands characterised by different technologies, and the islands can be visited in any order. This implication of the Okishio critique becomes extremely limiting analytically when an attempt is made to treat fixed capital, as we see below.

As a final note before a counter-critique, I should stress that my characterization of the Okishio model has not been made to accuse it of lack of 'realism', though it is not realistic, if by 'realism' one means corresponding to the concrete. Rather, the purpose has been to show the limited phenomena which the model can treat, whether realistically or unrealistically. My argument will be that the tendency of the rate of profit to fall is a law of capitalist accumulation, a law of uneven development. Firmly located in equilibrium theory, the Okishio model cannot incorporate this law in any way, so it has not so much refuted it as excluded it logically. I do not exclude the possibility that the defenders of the model could render their analysis dynamic. It is, however, for them to demonstrate that their analysis is relevant to the dynamic processes of capitalist accumulation. Such an attempt would be welcomed, not in small part because it would probably support the argument which follows.[6]

6 See Persky and Alberro 1978, cited in Van Parijs 1980.

3 The Okishio Model and the Harmony of Competition

Central to the Okishian model is a particular and ahistorical view of competition. In the model competition renders all things the same, generalising the adoption of the most advanced techniques, which is necessary for their stable equilibria. This view of competition is essentially neoclassical and counter-intuitive in its treatment of the interaction of capitals. In neoclassical economics competition is a mechanism which renders capitals identical. Competition here creates equilibrium, a situation of harmonious co-existence of many capitals within each sector of social production. This homogenising effect of competition is absolutely essential for the analysis, for without it no static equilibrium is possible. Consider a sector of the economy in which there are capitals of varying efficiencies, enjoying different rates of profit by virtue of selling at different cost-prices. Such a circumstance is by definition inconsistent with equilibrium, since the conditions are present for the expansion of some capitals relative to others. As a consequence, price, market shares, total production, and the average conditions of production are not uniquely determined. The disequilibrium nature of such a situation is easily demonstrated. If, within a sector, different capitals use different production techniques, then the average conditions of production are not independent of the distribution of output within the sector. Further, it is not justified to assume that the distribution of output by capitals is given, since the heterogeneity of techniques implies a heterogeneity of cost-prices, and capitals with lower cost-prices will tend to expand compared to those with higher cost-prices. Thus, for a stable equilibrium, competition must be defined as a homogenising force; or if there is uneven development, it must be assumed to operate *between* sectors (equalising the rate of profit), but not *within* sectors where it would change the distribution of output by capital ('firm') and invalidate the assumption of a unique and exogenously given technology in each sector.

We can compare the neoclassical view of competition to the analysis of a tennis match. The average tennis fan would analyse a field of, say, sixteen contestants, by predicting that the competition among the players would be resolved, in general, by one player emerging victorious over the others. This prediction would be based on an assessment of the relative abilities of the contestants. The Okishio model, on the other hand, would argue that in the process of play, the weaker players would improve to the level of the stronger, and that the tournament would reach a state of equilibrium in which all matches were continually at 'deuce' point. Such an equilibrium is as unlikely in the competition among capitals as at Wimbledon. Yet this is the 'competitive' relationship required in the analysis of the Okishio model.

As pointed out before, we are not arguing that the Okishio model cannot incorporate uneven development. However, were it to do so, the static equilibrium framework would have to be discarded, and it is for the defenders of the model to show that their critique can be generalised when general equilibrium does not hold.

Central to the model is this view of competition, and missing from the treatment is competition as the *struggle and conflict among capitals*. This omission derives from treating competition ahistorically and divorced from dynamics. Competition as an equilibrating force is ahistorical in that it is divorced from the circuit of capital, a circuit which develops and changes qualitatively over time. In the early stages of capitalist development (Britain in the first half of the nineteenth century, for example), the extent and intensity of competition were quite limited. The underdevelopment of competition reflected both the characteristics of production and circulation in this early period.[7] With regard to production, both the class struggle and the development of the productive forces (obviously inter-related) had not created the basis for raising surplus value relatively.[8] The basis of raising profits was the production of absolute surplus value (e.g., lengthening the working day) or increasing the mass of profit by the concentration of capital.[9] In this rude state of technology, which Marx called 'manufacture', the technical conditions for large-scale expulsion of living labour were not present. Along with this, the social relations facilitating the centralisation of capital were not well developed. The credit system was unsophisticated, making it difficult for capitalists to obtain large amounts of money-capital.

Under such circumstances, the expansion of individual capitals was through the capitalisation of realized surplus value, a method which severely limits the qualitative changes in the work process which could be achieved, as well as limiting expansion quantitatively. To the extent that the Okishio view of competition has any historical referent, it most closely coincides to this early period of the struggle among capitals, when the circumstances of class struggle, technical development, and relations of circulation greatly limited the extent to which one capital could attack others. The relatively slow pace of technical change (because machinery was not mass produced) limited the degree to which individual capitals would gain cost-price advantages over other capitals. Credit relations restricted increases in the scale of production, circumscribing

7 For a discussion of the historical development of competition, see Clifton 1977.

8 For an elaboration of this, see Fine and Harris 1979 and Weeks 1981, Chap. 3.

9 Where *concentration* refers to the growth of individual capitals, and *centralisation* involves the redistribution of capital among many capitals.

the stratification of capitals by size. The bourgeois view of competition is, in effect, an idealised extension of this period of capitalism, with emphasis upon the most historically primitive aspect of it.

With overall development of the productive forces and the working class victory to limit the working day, capitalism entered into the epoch of the production of *relative* surplus value, the reduction of necessary labour time relative to surplus labour time by the reduction of the values of commodities. The Okishian analysis addresses itself to this epoch in its treatment of technical change, but retains an idealized theory of competition based upon the earlier epoch of the production of absolute surplus value. The law of the tendency of the rate of profit to fall is a law which manifests itself when the production of relative surplus value becomes dominant in the process of accumulation. The competition which Okishio models invoke to refute the law is an anachronistic, as well as idealised, concept.

In order that one can move conceptually from one static equilibrium state to another, competition must play the role of rendering all capitals identical within a sector of industry. Thus, the analysis of static equilibrium requires not only the assumption of competition, but the assumption that all new capitals enter a sector with a technique of production identical to that of the most efficient capital; and further that all resident capitals also adopt this most efficient technique or cease production. Now, under what conditions would competition generate this result? It must be noted that it is not justified here to assume that the most efficient technique is generally known and established, as Roemer does in his critique of Persky and Alberro,[10] for this is to assume what remains to be proved. What must be shown, if the static equilibrium analysis is to be accepted, is that competition leads to even development – identical capitals. To say that techniques are known to capitalists and their development predictable, as Roemer does, is merely to make the assumption of even development in other words. What is at issue is whether competition itself engenders revolutions in the productive forces.

One can only argue for a harmonising competition if one has previously assumed that alternative production processes are given to capitalists independently of competition. Then, homogenisation of capital follows as a logical conclusion, since a capitalist would have to be stupid to choose a less efficient technique. Under what circumstances would techniques be generally known and predictable in their emergence? This would occur when technical change was occurring slowly. And this corresponds to the period of the production of absolute surplus value, in the early stage of the development of capitalism.

10 Roemer 1979, p. 388.

Once the means of production are mass-produced and the credit system develops, the competition among capitals assumes greater intensity and becomes the mechanism of uneven development. Once the development of the productive forces becomes continuous, competition itself is motivated by the discovery of new techniques. Capitals enter into sectors of industry armed with new techniques, implying lower cost-prices. Across sectors, this tends to equalise the rate of profit; but within sectors it generates uneven development, the stratification of capitals by levels of efficiency. The equalising tendency of competition across sectors is continuously contradicted by the effect of competition within sectors. What appears in the static Okishian analysis as an equilibrating force is actually a process of cumulative uneven development. Roemer criticises this portrayal of competition generating uneven development on the grounds that it presumes that capitalists cannot correctly anticipate the pace of technical change. But such an argument presupposes the general equilibrium which competition itself is required to bring about. What must be 'anticipated' is not merely technical developments themselves, but the profit and cost flows in the future from these developments. These can only be 'anticipated' if the static equilibrium upon which the price calculations are made will actually occur.

The internal circularity of Okishio-type arguments is quite clear when their treatment of competition is scrutinised. The analysis bases its critique upon comparison of static equilibrium states in which each sector of the economy can be treated as a single capital. This, in turn, requires some mechanism to render all capitals in a sector identical. The mechanism is labelled 'competition'. In order that the assumption of 'competition' not be the same as merely assuming all capitals to be identical, the argument must specify how the competitive struggle would lead to similarity among capitals. This is achieved by granting capitalists perfect foresight and this requires knowledge of future static equilibrium prices and costs. But such knowledge is irrelevant unless the static equilibrium will actually come to prevail. And it will come to prevail only if competition generates even development. Having followed this line of argument, we see that 'competition' in this theory is nothing more than the assumption of static equilibrium itself.

In summary, we see that the movement of capital among industries to equalise the rate of profit is also the process of uneven development; the struggle among capitals has the contradictory effect of tending to equalize returns among sectors and to generate unequal returns among sectors. It is a mistake to conceive of the struggle among capitals as an equilibrating mechanism, for it does not establish a stable, sustainable, relationship among capitals. The tendency of the rate of profit to equalize hides a fierce competitive struggle within industries.[11] By ignoring the struggle among capitals, Okishio, like neoclassicists, treats the interaction of capitals as an equilibrating force, though in fact it is the source of uneven development. Consideration of competition among capitals, as opposed to competition in the abstract divorced from social relations of production, renders static equilibrium comparisons irrelevant.

A further point needs to be made. The model, in its treatment of competition, equates the tendency for profit rates to equalise with the equalisation itself, and therefore interprets Marx as an equilibrium theorist because he postulated an equalising tendency. Whether Marx was or was not is of limited interest, for in terms of logic there is no reason why a tendency need result in an equilibrium, for a tendency can set in motion forces which contradict it. Because of the nature of capitalist social relations, capital is mobile and forced by competition to move in response to differences in profit rates across industries. This movement is not just a movement of money-capital, but also involves the reorganisation and reallocation of the elements of production, one aspect of which is technical change. Even if the movement of capital results in a momentary equalisation of profit rates across industries, there is no logical basis for presuming that the conditions of competition within each sector (uneven development) are such as to maintain this momentary situation.

4 Money Briefly Considered

The capitalist mode of production is the first in which the reproduction of class relations and class rule involves the general circulation of the products of labour as commodities. As commodities, these use values must be exchanged against money in order that capital may realize value in a general social form, a form in which that value can again be employed as capital. Marx symbolised this unending circulation with the symbols M–C … P … C′–M′ (money-capital is exchanged against the means of production and labour power; this productive capital is consumed in the labour process to create commodity capital; and the commodity capital is reconverted into money-capital). No consideration of capitalist production is possible without a treatment of money. This point is not novel, but the Okishio model does not appreciate its importance.

A moment's reflection shows that comparative statics in effect define money out of existence. To understand this, we need briefly to treat the functions

11 '… (in competition) all determinants appear in a position which is the *inverse* of their position in general. There price determined by labour, here labour determined by price, etc., etc' (Marx 1973, p. 580).

of money in capitalistic society. The most obvious role of money in capitalist circulation is as means of circulation. In this role, money is the agent of the movement of commodities, circulating commodities which fall out of circulation to be consumed in the production process or directly by workers and capitalists. This function necessarily implies other functions. A capitalist must exchange his commodities against money or the surplus value latent in those commodities goes unrealized and cannot be converted into capital. However, once commodities are realized as money, the possibility of an interruption in circulation is created. Since money is the generalised expression of social labour, it can be held as a claim on all other commodities (as a store of value); i.e., money need not be *realized*, since it is by definition and practice realized value, generalised wealth in the abstract.[12]

In and among states of equilibrium this function of money as store of value has no significance. By definition, in equilibrium all exchanges have already occurred smoothly or are occurring smoothly without interruption. In equilibrium there is no 'motivation' by capitalists to hold money idle, unless one presumes hoarded 'cash balances', which must also be in equilibrium consistent with the stability conditions of the static state. As a consequence, the assumption of static equilibrium assumes away the fundamental contradictions of a money economy, the division between *money as means of circulation* and *money as means of payment*. These, in turn are closely related to money as a store of value and the possibility of an interruption in the circulation of capital.

In the process of accumulation, exchanges between capitalists for the means of production occur on the basis of credit, so that a pyramid of indebtedness builds up as accumulation proceeds. Here, credit is serving as a *means of circulation*. At some later point, these debts must be paid off, at which time money acts as a *means of payment*. In its role as *means of payment*, money does not circulate commodities, but cancels debts contracted by the circulation of commodities during a previous period. If the analysis restricts itself to states of equilibrium, the distinction between means of circulation and means of payment is trivial. In equilibrium, by definition any incongruity between circulation of commodities and payment for commodities has been eliminated. However, if we allow for the cumulative uneven development generated by the competition among capitals, then the possibility of credit crises presents itself.[13] These crises can result from changes in the values of commodities or

12 See Marx 1906, Chap. III; and Weeks 1981.

13 'In so far as actual payments have to be made, money does not serve as a circulating

from changes in the value of money itself. If either or both occur, capitalists may be unable to cancel the debts they previously incurred.[14]

All this is ruled out by considering equilibrium states, for in equilibrium all markets are cleared, including financial markets. By restricting itself to equilibrium states, the model first rules out any disruptions in accumulation arising from the process of value formation,[15] and, second, rules out any contradictions in the circulation or non-circulation of money which results from the process of value formation. In such an analysis one searches in vain for a crisis theory; it has ruled out the forms crises necessarily take in capitalist society. In effect, we are offered a model of capitalist society without money. The importance of this is demonstrated in the next section.

5 Fixed Capital and Circulation

The omission of any meaningful consideration of money by Okishio becomes particularly glaring when others 'generalise' the critique of the tendency of the rate of profit to fall to include 'fixed capital'. The latter term must be placed in inverted commas, since their analysis fails to distinguish fixed capital from circulating constant capital in a meaningful way. In the context of static equilibrium, fixed capital for the Okishio model is constant capital which lasts longer than one production period. As Marx pointed out, this is merely the *basis* of the distinction, not the distinction itself.[16] It fails analytically because it does not recognise the two-fold nature of fixed means of production; like all commodities they are *both values and use values*.

medium, but as the individual incarnation of social labour, as the independent form of existence of exchange value, as the universal commodity. This contradiction comes to a head in those phases of individual and commercial crises which are known as credit crises' (Marx 1906, p. 155).

14 '[S]ince the circulation process of capital is not completed in one day but extends over a fairly long period until the capital returns to its original form, since this coincides with the period within which market-prices equalize with [prices of production], and great upheavals and changes take place in the productivity of labour and therefore also in the *real value* of commodities …' (Marx 1968, p. 495).

15 By this we mean uneven development, which results in a spectrum of techniques in use. This implies a momentary indeterminacy in normal conditions of production, which must be resolved by competition. See Section III.

16 'This difference in the behaviour of the elements of productive capital in the labour-process forms however only the point of departure of the difference between fixed and non-fixed capital, not this difference itself' (Marx 1956, p. 118).

When considering the production of value (and surplus value), the relevant distinction is between constant and variable capital. Constant capital is exchanged against the means of production whose value is passed on unchanged in production. Variable capital is exchanged against labour power, which when consumed by capital, expands value. However, when one analyses the circulation of capital, the relevant distinction is between fixed and circulating capital, for the production of value is presupposed. Fixed capital has two characteristics important for the circulation process. First, the use value of fixed means of production does not circulate, only its value does. Unlike other means of production, fixed means of production undergo no change of material form in the production process. Part of their usefulness is exhausted through 'wear and tear'. What is transferred to commodities in the labour process by consumption of fixed capital is *value*, and value alone. Second, and related to the first point, fixed means of production impart their value to commodities piecemeal, over several production and circulation cycles. As a result, a portion of the value of fixed capital *does not circulate*, but remains 'fixated' in material objects.

This second characteristic lends a special character to the circulation of fixed capital. Since fixed means of production have been purchased with money (they are capital), they must be replaced by a subsequent money exchange when their usefulness is exhausted. Their value is transferred, passed on to the commodities continuously, but they are replaced discretely.[17] This reflects the two-fold nature of fixed means of production. As values, they shrink with their material wearing out, and this value is accumulated continuously as money for their replacement. As use values, they are replaced all-at-once. By reference to concepts previously employed, we can summarise by saying that the transformation of fixed means of production from productive capital to money-capital occurs continuously with the realization of new commodities in money form (money-capital). However, the transformation of money-capital back into pro-

17 'In the performance of its function that part of the value of an instrument of labour which exists in its bodily form constantly decreases, while that which is transformed into money constantly increases until the instrument of labour is at last exhausted and its entire value, detached from the corpse, is converted into money. Here the particularity in the turnover of this element of productive capital becomes apparent. The transformation of its value into money keeps pace with the pupation into money of the commodity which is the carrier of its value. But its conversion from the money-form into a use value proceeds separately from the reconversion of the commodities into other elements of their production and is determined by its own period of reproduction, that is, by the time during which the instrument or labour wears out ...' (*Capital*, III, p. 166).

ductive capital for these fixed means of production is a separate, discontinuous process. Realization of value and replacement of use value are separate processes.

It should now be clear why fixed capital is defined by how it circulates. In all societies labour processes have included means of production with a life span longer than a single production period. This is only the basis of the difference between fixed and circulating capital. The difference itself is the manner in which value is transmitted and use values replaced in each case. For circulating capital, value is transmitted completely and the use values replaced upon resumption of the circuit of capital. For fixed capital, value is transmitted incrementally and replacement of use values necessarily deferred.

We can now see that the attempt to 'generalise' to fixed capital within the Okishio framework is no generalisation at all, but merely a mathematical treatment of fixed capital as if it were circulating capital. By considering states of equilibrium, the difference between how fixed capital transmits its value and how fixed capital is realized is eliminated from the analysis. What we observe in an equilibrium state is a moment after both transmission of value and realization of value have occurred. What has been done in essence is to define the turnover period between equilibrium states to be equal to the time period necessary to realize all the value objectified in fixed means of production. In short, fixed capital is 'incorporated' into the Okishio analysis by treating it as circulating capital. In effect, fixed capital is treated as a commodity which circulates (a 'joint product').

Out of equilibrium, the difference between the transmission and realization of the value of fixed capital assumes a contradictory character. The possibility exists that conditions may change such that the transmission of value cannot quantitatively correspond to the *realization* of that value. The struggle among capitals turns this possibility into an actuality. As technical change proceeds, the value of commodities falls. Older means of production progressively become less efficient compared to new ones. As values fall, part of the value in old means of production becomes unrealizable. In effect, part of the value of old means of production becomes socially unnecessary, and must be absorbed by individual capitals by monetary losses.[18]

It should be clear that this contradiction between value transmission and value realization is closely entwined with the division between money as means of circulation and money as means of payment, considered in the previous section. There we pointed out that changes in values can create a situ-

18 See Marx 1956; Marx 1973.

ation in which the money realized upon sale of commodities is not sufficient to act as means of payment for means of production previously contracted for with credit money. Competition stimulates technical change, which devalues existing fixed capital, so that the total value it transmits to commodities is less than its initial value. The money-capital which returns after realization of commodities will be less than the money-capital advanced for fixed means of production. Such difficulties are inherent in capitalist circulation due to the devaluation of fixed capital by technical change.

This process of devaluation is lost by treating static states. In equilibria, all capitals are assumed identical, so uneven development is ruled out by definition. All exchanges have occurred under equilibrating assumptions, so there is no difference between sale and payment for commodities (money as means of circulation and means of payment). The transmission, realization and replacement of fixed capital are simultaneous and instantaneous, so no devaluation of fixed capital can occur. It is hardly surprising that Okishio models get no tendency for the rate of profit to fall or crises in their system.

6 Accumulation and Dynamics

Throughout history, humanity's struggle to control nature and produce the products which society requires has been characterised by uneven development of the productive process. In feudal Europe, for example, productivity varied among manors, due to the natural condition of the soil, if for no other reason. In capitalist society, this uneven development of the productive forces takes on fundamental importance, for in capitalist society the productive forces are mobile. This creates a contradiction within capitalist society, between the uneven development itself and the competitive nature of capital as a social relation. These two contradictory elements were elaborated by Marx in two laws, the law of the tendency of the rate of profit to fall and the law of the counteracting tendencies to the law of the tendency of the rate of profit to fall. The first, 'the law as such', is a law of the development of the productive forces. The second is a law of the interaction of capitals. In effect, the Okishio model considers only the 'law as such', and divorces the development of the productive forces from the social relations within which that development occurs.

In order to develop these two laws we must first consider the nature of technical change, which in the first instance impacts upon the labour process itself. Therefore, it needs to be treated as the relationship between use values before its impact on values, prices, wages, and profits can be considered.

Increases in the productivity of labour involve, by definition, workers producing more products per unit of time. This is achieved through the division of labour within the labour process. The division of labour comes about by use of more machinery, so that each production task is reduced to a simple operation carried out mechanically. Marx called this 'the expelling of living labour from the production process' (the general law of capitalist accumulation). The result of technical change, therefore, is in general to increase the technical composition of capital, or the relationship between the mass of the means of production and the labour power required to operate and process those means of production.

The new technology implies a new set of values for the economy and a new set of relative exchange values. However, at the moment the new technology is introduced, the new values and new exchange relationships are only latent in the new technology, and must await the interaction of capitals (competition) to realize them. This point does not refer to merely a logical progression, but to the actual process of accumulation. Technical change first alters conditions in the sphere of production, and subsequently conditions in the sphere of circulation. Okishio models treat the two as occurring simultaneously.

A rise in the technical composition of capital has the immediate impact of raising the ratio of constant to variable capital at the prevailing values. Since the prevailing values also determine the rate of surplus value, a rise in the technical composition of capital has occurred but the rate of surplus value has not changed. This process is 'the law as such'. The technical composition of capital measured in the values prevailing when the new technology was introduced was called by Marx the 'organic' composition of capital.

At this point the development of the productive forces is inconsistent with prevailing values, and a dynamic process of adjustment is necessary. This process of adjustment is the operation of the law of the counteracting tendencies to the tendency of the rate of profit to fall. The interaction of capitals leads to the reduction of values, which cheapens the commodities which go to make up constant and variable capital. The technical composition of capital undergoes revaluation as values change. The valorised composition of capital consistent with the new technology Marx called the 'value' composition of capital. These two concepts, the organic and value compositions, enable us to analyse two distinct but interrelated phenomena within the process of accumulation: the development of the productive forces and the adjustment in circulation to that development. The adjustment to that development (the process of value formation) counteracts the tendency of the rate of profit to fall in two ways. First, the commodities which make up constant capital may fall in value more than the commodities that make up the normal consumption of the working class. This would counteract the rise in the *organic* composition of capital. Much more important is the rise in the rate of surplus value due to the cheapening of commodities.

What the Okishio model does in effect is to eliminate completely the process of value formation. It takes the technical changes as given, interprets them narrowly as nothing more than changes in technical coefficients in an input-output table, then calculates the exchange relationships they would imply were they to prevail in each sector. This equilibrium calculation abstracts from the social relations of capitalist reproduction – competition, money, and the capitalist nature of fixed means of production. These are precisely the elements which create instability within a capitalist economy.

With this in mind, we can see the insight provided by the Okishio critique. Abstracting as it does from the social relations of capitalist society, the critique demonstrates that it is not the development of the productive forces as such which limits the accumulation process. On the contrary, if the productive forces could develop smoothly and evenly, capitalist society would not be inherently unstable. Capitalist society is beset by crises because the productive forces develop in the context of specific social relations (see Sections III and IV) which make that development uneven, and that even development calls for resolution in the form of economic crises.

We therefore owe Okishio a debt, for he has rigorously demonstrated the primary role of social relations in capitalist society.

CHAPTER 8

The Expansion of Capital and Uneven Development on a World Scale

This paper explains the divergence among countries in level of development in terms of primary and secondary uneven development, both resulting from the process of accumulation. Primary uneven development arises because of the more dynamic expansion of capitalist countries relatively to countries in which capitalism is incipient. This difference is inherent in the social relations of capital. Secondary uneven development occurs within the group of predominantly capitalist countries, due to competition and adoption of technical innovations within the social relations of capital. The former generates divergence; the latter exhibits a cyclical pattern of convergence and divergence, with convergence the long-term tendency.

1 Introduction

That the development of capital is *uneven* is a fundamental conclusion of the Marxian analysis of accumulation, which distinguishes it from the equilibrium approach of the neoclassicals. In the neoclassical approach, competition and the movement of capital are equilibrating forces which narrow differences among firms, regions, and countries. Indeed, an apparent anomaly in neoclassical analysis is its prediction of a convergence of development among these, and persistent inequality among agents, with the latter arising because the 'initial' distribution of productive assets is taken as given. Recent work, especially by UNCTAD (1997) and Pritchett (1997c), has demonstrated that over the last one hundred years there is no evidence of a levelling convergence of growth rates, and, therefore, levels of per capita income.

This paper provides further evidence of the uneven development of capitalism on a world scale, and offers a theoretical explanation for the phenomenon. We explain divergence in terms of *primary* and *secondary* uneven development. *Primary uneven development* arises because of the more dynamic expansion of capitalist countries relative to countries in which capitalism is incipient. This difference is inherent in the social relations of capital. *Secondary uneven development* occurs within the group of predominantly capitalist countries, due to competition and adoption of technical innovations within the social relations of capital. The former generates divergence; the latter exhibits a cyclical pattern of convergence and divergence, with convergence the long-term tendency.

The issue of divergence is introduced by an elaboration of the orthodox or neoclassical argument that trade, and trade combined with capital mobility, should result in the convergence of levels of development world-wide. As for so much of orthodox theory, this analysis is instructive by demonstrating the highly restrictive conditions under which its conclusions follow logically. The discussion then turns to the Marxian framework. At a superficial level, Marxian theory could also be interpreted as producing convergence, that non-capitalist social relations are swept away in favour of capitalist relations. However, this interpretation reads Marx's contribution from a neoclassical perspective. After developing an analysis of divergence or uneven development, empirical evidence is presented, in order to inspect the particular form divergence has taken over the last four decades.

2 Convergence in Neoclassical and Marxian Theory

The task of a theory of growth and development has been succinctly summarised by Pritchett:

> Any theory that seeks to unify the world's experience with economic growth and development must address at least four distinct questions: [1] What accounts for continued per capita growth and technological progress of [the developed capitalist countries] ...? [2] What accounts for the few countries that are able to initiate and sustain periods of rapid growth in which they gain significantly on the leaders? [3] What accounts for why some countries fade and lose the momentum of rapid growth? [4] What accounts for why some countries remain in low growth for very long periods?[1]

While a theory of capitalist development must address Pritchett's four questions, he poses them without a specification of the nature of capitalist accumulation. Analytically prior to his four questions is, why does uneven development characterise the world? This implies a second, historical, question: how does one account for the relative concentration of capitalist development in Western Europe and the settler colonies of Western Europe?[2]

1 Pritchett 1997c, p. 15, numbers added.

2 The only developed country not in these two categories is Japan. Singapore qualifies on per

According to neoclassical economic theory, the distribution of levels of development on a world scale should be a simple phenomenon, derivative from internal characteristics of each country, and trade and capital flows. Since economic phenomena are governed by universal laws of the behaviour of individual agents, there is no theoretical basis to expect some countries to develop faster than others.[3] External factors, also universal in character, would tend to eliminate all but minor differences in levels of development. Consider first the convergence process implied by the neoclassical static trade model. Exchange between countries, even in the absence of any movement of capital or labour between countries, should result in a tendency for wage rates and profit rates to equalise (so-called factor price equalisation). Thus conclusion is based upon a number of specific assumptions: 1) all countries have access to the same technology of production (implying that every country can potentially produce the same range of commodities);[4] 2) output results from capital and labour, which can be substituted for each other in the production process;[5] 3) the domestic structure of demand in each country is the same; 4) if one measures the 'factor-intensity' of a product by the ratio of capital to labour, and ranks all products by this ratio, the ordering is not affected by changes in wage rates or profit rates, and 5) markets internal to each country are perfectly competitive.[6]

Under these assumptions, let a country shift from a closed economy ('autarky') to so-called free trade. Each country will export the commodities that use intensively the factor of production that is abundant, and import commodities that are intensive in the factor which is scarce in the country. As a result of the shift in resource use, the demand for the abundant factor will rise (increasing its price), and the demand for the scarce factor will fall (decreasing its price). When all adjustments are complete, wage rates and profit rates will

capita income, but for analytical purposes should be viewed not as a country but a city-state (e.g., it has no agricultural sector).

3 See Jones 1997, where he argues that all countries would tend to have similar rates of investment.

4 In a neoclassical world, every product is generated from a 'production function' that allows for substitution among inputs.

5 The theory can be generalised to include labour of different skills and capital equipment of different types, as long as these are available to all countries. The factor price equalisation conclusion does not follow if there are production inputs that are specific to countries.

6 This eliminates so-called 're-switching', in which case changes in the ratio of profits to wages can result in what was previously a 'labour-intensive' technique becoming relatively 'capital-intensive'. See Weeks 1989, Chapter 10.

be the same in all free-trading countries. Even in its own terms, the conclusion is absurd. It implies, for example, that average wages should have fallen more or less continuously in the advanced capitalist countries over the last one hundred years (including the wages of the skilled), not merely to have risen slower than in the underdeveloped countries.[7] However, the absurdity of the theory is instructive. In a world in which all countries apply the same technology there would be no basis for major differences in levels of development. The concrete equivalent of the abstract assumption of perfect competition is that product and input markets operate effectively to allocate resources. For this to occur, it would be necessary for production to be organised within capitalist social relations. If all countries were fully capitalist, utilising the same technology, then, indeed, 'factor prices' would tend to equalise, though the process would be uneven. Therefore, neoclassical trade theory reaches an absurd theoretical conclusion, which is refuted by empirical evidence, because it excludes from its analysis the causes of uneven development.

If one extends the neoclassical analysis to allow for capital flows, then the static convergence conclusion becomes dynamic: the combination of specialisation according to comparative advantage and the movement of capital from labour scarce (developed) to labour abundant (underdeveloped) countries should combine for a powerful levelling effect. In neoclassical analysis the convergence conclusion is unassailable theoretically, and refuted empirically. There is no apparent exit from this contradiction within the neoclassical paradigm. The standard, off-the-shelf neoclassical explanation for disappointing growth rates is 'bad policies' by governments (the Policy Hypothesis). This is hardly a credible argument when low growth has persisted for at least one hundred years for many countries.[8] Even were this persistence not the case, state policy as an explanation for different growth rates in the long run offers no explanation for our second (historical) question: how the presently developed countries initially achieved their status (i.e., why policy wisdom was so geographically concentrated for one hundred years).

While not neoclassical, Gerschenkron's analysis of the 'advantages of the late-comer' (Gerschenkron, 1962) has been employed in the mainstream literature to make sanguine predictions that differences in level of development will tend to narrow over time. The essence of his argument was that 'backward' countries have the advantage of drawing on a stock of technology that was

7 Wages in developed countries, as well as not declining in the long run, have risen relatively to wages in most underdeveloped countries.

8 Pritchett, 1997a, p. 199. One would expect that neoclassically rational policymakers would, after a few decades, learn the 'correct' policies for growth.

developed by the advanced countries.[9] Therefore, producers in backward countries can pass over less efficient technologies and move to the most developed ones. This, combined with appropriate institutional arrangements,[10] can produce growth rates for 'late-comers' considerably higher than those of advanced countries during their underdeveloped period. There is clearly some insight in this analysis, but if taken as a general prediction, it collapses empirically. Most underdeveloped countries have not closed the development gap with advanced countries; very few have done so. The analysis may establish the possibility of faster growth rates for 'late-comers', but does not explain why it occurs so infrequently.

On a mechanistic reading of Marx, his theory of capitalism can be interpreted as predicting convergence of levels of development. If the spread of capitalist social relations is inexorable, then it would be only a matter of time until capitalist transformation of the entire world occurs. If capital moves seeking the highest rate of profit, and if profits are higher in underdeveloped countries, due to lower wages, then there would be net capital flow from developed to underdeveloped countries. As in the neoclassical case this would, through time, result in a narrowing of levels of development. An argument quite close to this is found in the work of Warren.[11]

This interpretation of capitalist development implies that capitalism is everywhere an engine for development; and a country is underdeveloped because its social relations are incompletely capitalist. The Dependency Hypothesis is the best-known attempt to escape from this politically unpalatable and empirically questionable conclusion. The Dependency Hypothesis maintains that the development of the advanced countries has been at the expense of the underdeveloped countries. Dependency writers proposed various mechanisms by which this would occur, all of which reduce to underdeveloped countries suffering 'surplus' extraction by developed countries. Like the Policy Hypo-

9 A contemporary example of the application of the Gerșchenkron thesis is found in Jones 1997. 'Output per worker grows in the long run because of the creation of ideas', 'Ideas diffuse across countries … eventually', and, thus, 'All countries eventually grow at the average rate of growth of world knowledge' (Jones 1997, p. 25). It would be difficult to find a better example of a syllogism. Among other things, this spurious logic ignores the possibility that the diffusion of 'ideas' (undefined) has a cost, and that 'knowledge' (also not defined) might be controlled by the 'creators' of that knowledge.

10 Gerschenkron placed great emphasis upon actions by the state to facilitate capital accumulation. This aspect of his analysis is rarely stressed in the current literature. For a discussion, see Griffin 1989b, pp. 100–1.

11 E.g., Warren 1973.

thesis, the Dependency Hypothesis fails to address the historical question: how did one set of countries emerge as the extractors of surplus, and another as the losers of surplus.[12]

Even if the historical question were solved, the Dependency Hypothesis proves fatally flawed by its inability to produce a logically consistent and empirically verifiable mechanism for surplus extraction. The 'profit remittance' mechanism fails on both counts. It is a logical contradiction to argue, on the one hand, that capital flows to underdeveloped countries because of high rates of return, and, on the other, to maintain that profits are remitted rather than re-invested. Therefore, it should not surprise one that empirical evidence indicates that the magnitude of profit remittances between underdeveloped and developed countries is far below what would be necessary to have a substantial growth impact, at least, before the debt crisis of the 1980s.[13]

Dependency writers proposed 'unequal exchange' as an alternative mechanism for surplus extraction. The most common form of this is the 'declining terms of trade' argument, whose more mainstream manifestation is the Prebisch-Singer thesis. This is essentially an empirically-based argument: in international trade relative prices tend to move against underdeveloped countries due to the internal characteristics of developed and underdeveloped countries.[14] While this may be the case for some primary products, such as tropical beverages, empirical studies have not demonstrated that it systematically operates between the two sets of countries. An alternative, somewhat immune to empirical refutation, is the argument that differences in wage rates among countries result in systematic transfers of surplus.[15] The logic is deceptively simple: if all countries use the same technology, then profit rates will be higher in countries with lower wages. The movement of capital to equate profit rates will lower prices in low-wage countries and raise them in high-wage countries. While international prices will appear as equal exchange, they mask a transfer of surplus.

---

12 Weeks 1982b, pp. 119–20.

13 Weeks 1984, Chapter 2.

14 In the Dependency interpretation, unequal exchange arises from the difference in power relations between 'centre' and 'periphery' countries. In the Singer-Prebisch argument, it is the nature of markets. In the peripheral countries, producers are competitive, and productivity increases are passed on as price reductions in traded goods. In the centre countries, product markets are non-competitive, and productivity increases manifest themselves in part in higher prices in trade. Thus, the world prices of exports from peripheral countries tend to stagnate or fall, while the prices of exports from centre countries tend to rise. The Singer-Prebisch argument was a product of the 1950s and 1960s, when economic rivalry among developed countries was latent, due to the dominant position of US capital.

15 Amin 1976 and Emmanuel 1972.

This version of the unequal exchange argument is logically inconsistent.[16] If the commodities in question are internationally traded, it is not possible for them to sell at different prices in different countries without *ad hoc* institutional assumptions. Profit rates cannot equalise, because prices must do so, except for non-traded commodities.[17] Even were there a tendency for profits to equalise, despite the contradiction of a common price in international trade, the analysis would imply a net movement of capital to underdeveloped countries to equalise profit rates. If this occurred, underdeveloped countries would grow faster than the developed, resulting in convergence, not the divergence that the hypothesis seeks to predict.

Finally, there is an underlying flaw in most versions of the Dependency Hypothesis: it does not attribute uneven development to capitalism. The initial division of the world between developed and underdeveloped countries is taken as given (the historical question is begged), and the surplus transfer mechanisms could apply to any historical period.[18] The task is to produce an analytical framework which accounts for divergence during the capitalist epoch, when differences in national and regional levels of development increased far beyond any that previously occurred.

3 Competition and Uneven Development

The explanation of divergence in levels of development has two parts: the character of capitalist accumulation and the nature of underdevelopment. In the Marxian literature these are 1) the process of accumulation, and 2) the articulation or interaction of modes of production. The historical emergence of capitalist social relations, wage labour within commodity production, produced the primary manifestation of uneven development, which is the division of the world into developed and underdeveloped countries. The interaction of technical change and competition within the developed capitalist countries generates a secondary uneven development, across industries and regions of

16 Dore and Weeks 1978.

17 For logical consistency, a given product must sell at a common price in international trade, regardless of its country of origin (ignoring transport costs). Then, profits cannot equalise across countries because wage rates differ and the technology of production is the same (Krugman 1987).

18 This is not true of the Emmanuel-Amin version of unequal exchange. Their approach implicitly presumes the full development of capitalist social relations, or otherwise capital would not flow freely among countries.

the capitalist countries. To explain these assertions, one must consider the process of capitalist development and accumulation.

A capitalist society reproduces itself through the production and circulation of commodities. The general production of commodities that characterises capitalism derives from the exploitation of direct producers through wage labour. The development of wage labour resulted, and continues to result, from the separation of workers from their means of production. The most obvious form of this separation is the dispossession of agricultural producers from the land, but it also applies to artisanal production. Having been dispossessed, producers are reunited with the means of production via the agency of capital. They become, in effect, the instruments of capitalist production. This change in social relations is the basis for the dynamism of the capitalist mode of production. With labour 'free' from the means of production, capital in the form of money can marshal resources flexibly. Capitalist countries and the capitalist epoch are characterised by the movement of capital, as it shifts labour and other resources among industries and regions. While labour remains in possession of its means of production, capital is constrained in its movement. The division of the world during the late eighteenth and nineteenth centuries into advanced and backward countries, into colonial powers and colonies, arose from the dynamism of capitalist relations. This division represents the primary aspect of uneven development on a world scale: the United Kingdom, the United States, France, Germany, etc., on the one hand; and the myriad of colonies (e.g., India) and semi- colonies (Latin American countries), on the other.

In developing his analysis, Marx made methodological innovations that distinguished him from other critics of capitalism. Others, for example Proudhon and Sismondi, criticised capitalism for excesses caused by monopoly power. These allegedly produced an unequal exchange in which capitalists appropriated value from petty commodity producers and workers. In contrast, Marx argued that what appears as excesses of capitalism are the systematic outcomes of the process of competition. Competition, not the lack of it, is the source of instability, crises, and uneven development. This analysis of competition is the antithesis of the neoclassical approach, in which competition is the source of equilibrium and *even* development. Neoclassical theory treats competition in terms of the 'representative' firm, and competition creates a harmony in exchange.[19] In general, radical critics of capitalism have accepted this approach. If one attributes the ills of capitalism to monopoly, one implicitly accepts that competitive capitalism would produce a more benign outcome.

19 The orthodox theory of competition is treated in Weeks 1994a.

Much of dependency analysis implicitly or explicitly relies upon a concept of monopoly to explain underdevelopment.[20]

The nature of capitalist competition is revealed by beginning with the neoclassical analysis. In a neoclassical world, markets in the short run can be afflicted with 'firms' earning excess profits. The entry of new firms eliminates these so-called rents, by driving down prices, until profits have been equalised across all markets. The resultant prices are socially optimal, in that they reflect the social cost and benefit of each product. In this schema, competition not only generates market clearing and equilibrium; in the long term, it also produces a socially desirable outcome. Non-Marxist critiques of this line of argument have tended to focus upon the absence of competition in actual markets, due to various sources of market power. This 'market failure' approach accepts the fundamental orthodox argument: that competition is the mechanism that brings forth the benign aspects of capitalism. Neoclassical economists and most of their critics reach this conclusion because competition is treated independently of its capitalist nature, and because production is ignored.

In a capitalist society, technical change creates the potential for variations in unit costs within sectors. At any moment in time, capitalist enterprises operate with machinery and plant whose total value (capital value) has not been recaptured through production and sales. If capitalists scrapped existing techniques and replaced them with more efficient ones when the latter first appear, most capitals would incur losses. The capitalists in an industry will, if possible, delay introducing new equipment, to achieve the optimal trade-off between current operating costs and losses on capital value. The problem need not be that lack knowledge of superior techniques, nor that capitals lack the finance to acquire them, though for some capitals, one or both may be true. The problem is more fundamental, involving a contradiction between the forces and relations of production. On the one hand, technical change offers more efficient methods of producing commodities. But, techniques are ruled by capitalist rationality, and their use or non-use is motivated by the drive for profit. Until the social relations of capital are satisfied, the law of private profitability delays innovations.

The delay in introducing innovations by some capitalists results in an uneven development of productive forces within an industry. At the level of

20 Dore and Weeks 1978. Consider for example, the contradictory dependency view that profit rates are higher in underdeveloped countries, but profits are remitted to the developed countries, thus reducing the investible surplus. This contradiction can be superficially resolved by assuming that foreign capital establishes monopoly positions in underdeveloped countries (Amin 1974).

appearances, competition fosters harmony and equilibrium, a tendency for a common price among producers of a similar product. Beneath this appearance uneven development rules, with enterprises earning different profit rates due to different production techniques. If there is a systemic crisis of capitalism, which takes the form of a drop in industry demand, higher cost producers will become non-viable. A systemic crisis can provoke a wave of bankruptcies across industries, and is the vehicle by which uneven development is reduced. In the absence of a systemic crisis of aggregate demand, an industry can be disrupted through invasion by a new producer, who comes armed with more advanced techniques and without obsolete capital whose value needs recovering. The entry of new capital into an industry involves not the process of equilibration, but is the vehicle to punish high cost producers for delaying technical change.

The movement of capital among industries has a contradictory effect: at the level of appearances it brings a tendency for profit rates to equalise; beneath this distributional form, it creates instability and crisis for resident enterprises. Therefore, it is the putatively benign aspects of capitalism, competition and innovation, which generate uneven development and crises.[21] This interaction between the forces of production (technical change) and the relations (competition) both undermines and rejuvenates the process of accumulation. This contradiction gives rise to the secondary aspect of uneven development, the decline and rise of industries and regions within societies that are dominated by capitalist relations. Certain industries, regions within countries, and even countries may decline, suffering from slow growth and unemployment. Such declines create the basis for their reversal, since they are associated with falling wage and non-wage costs. The ebb and flow of capital within predominantly capitalist societies creates at any moment relatively backward regions, but these change over time.

This analysis predicts that primary uneven development, between capitalist and non-capitalist countries, will be enduring and difficult to overcome, while secondary uneven development will change with the movement of capital within and among the predominantly capitalist countries. It predicts a long-term tendency for convergence among predominantly capitalist countries, and a long-term divergence between these countries and other countries, whose social relations are predominantly non-capitalist relations.

21 See Weeks 1981, Chapters 7 and 8.

4 Divergence Observed

The concepts of primary and secondary uneven development provide the analytical basis for our review of the empirical evidence over the last four decades, 1961–97. By chance major changes in the world economy occurred that roughly coincided with decades. In 1971, the United States government de-linked the dollar from gold, ending the post-war system of fixed exchange rates. Thus, the 1960s represented the last years of the post-war, Bretton Woods system of international economic management. To exchange rates instability were added two waves of oil price increases, in 1973–4 and 1978–9, which made the 1970s a decade of economic profound economic disorder. The debt crisis dominated the subsequent decade, during which average growth rates of almost all countries fell below their trend values. At the end of the decade, the Soviet Union collapsed, profoundly altering the international system. Thus, the period covers the last decade of what some have called the 'Golden Age' of twentieth-century capitalism, its breakdown, and the subsequent international disorder.[22]

From the perspective of the OECD countries, the 1960s were, indeed, a Golden Age, when growth rates across countries averaged more than five percent (see Table 8.1). This was also the period of fastest growth for the North African and Middle Eastern countries, and, at the least, 'silver' for the countries of the sub-Sahara and Latin America. For the Asian groups of countries, growth rates were higher subsequently, in the 1970s for the East and Southeast Asia group, and in the 1980s for South Asia. GDP growth rates are not the most accurate indicator of development, because of differences in population increase across country groups. Table 8.2 shows the ratio of per capita income for each group of underdeveloped countries to the OECD average. The ratio for the was lower in 1996–7 than in 1961–1965 in every case but East and Southeast Asia group. For example, the average for the sub-Saharan countries fell from 3.4 percent to 1.5 percent, and Latin America from fifteen to eleven percent.

Primary and secondary uneven development are indicated in Figure 8.1, which presents the standard deviation of annual growth rates (in natural logarithms) across countries, within each regional grouping of the underdeveloped countries and the OECD countries. For the thirty-seven years, in only four is the variation among OECD countries equal to or greater than for any group of underdeveloped countries. Further, for no group of countries is there a trend. The variation across countries tends to be low among the developed capitalist countries, and high among the underdeveloped countries. Further,

22 Marglin and Schor 1988.

TABLE 8.1 GDP growth rates by country groups, 1961–1997

Group Period	OECD	SSA	LA	ESEA	SoAsia	NAME
1961–1971	5.2	4.2	4.9	6.7	4.3	8.5
1971–1980	3.5	3.8	4.2	7.2	3.4	6.8
1981–1989	2.9	2.5	1.1	5.7	5.1	3.3
1990–1997	2.4	2.0	3.9	5.6	4.5	3.5
average	3.6	3.1	3.5	6.4	4.4	5.6
World Bank Predictions, 1997–2006	2.8	4.1	4.2	6.0*	5.9	3.6

*The World Bank predicts a GDP growth rate for East and South East Asia of 7.6 percent per annum, and per capita as 6.6. This has been reduced to 6.0 for GDP and 4.5 for GDP per capita for two reasons: 1) the collapse of ESEA growth rates in 1997 and 1998 makes 7.6 an impossible target; and 2) the implied rate of population increase (one per cent per annum) is certainly too low. North Africa and Middle East group covers 1993–1997. China excluded from Asia groups.

OECD (Organisation of Economic Cooperation and Development, developed countries) – Australia, Austria, Belgium, Canada, Denmark, Finland, France, Germany, Ireland, Italy, Japan, Netherlands, New Zealand, Norway, Portugal, Spain, Sweden, Switzerland, United Kingdom, United States of America.

SSA (Africa south of the Sahara) – All continental countries south of the Sahara except Eritrea, Djibouti, Namibia, South Africa, Somalia

LA (Latin America) – All Spanish-speaking countries (except Cuba) and Brazil.

ESE Asia (East & Southeast Asia) – Hong Kong, Indonesia, South Korea, Malaysia, the Philippines, Singapore, Thailand.

SoAsia (South Asia) – Bangladesh, Nepal, India, Sri Lanka, Pakistan.

NAME (North Africa & the Middle East) – Algeria, Egypt, Israel, Morocco, Oman, Syria, Saudi Arabia, Tunisia

SOURCE: WORLD DEVELOPMENT INDICATORS, CD-ROM (1961–1995), UNITED NATIONS (1998), & WORLD BANK (1997)

there is a strong cyclical element for the developed capitalist countries. Growth rates among these countries tended to diverge when the cross-country average growth rate were low, and to converge when average growth was high.[23]

23 Over the twenty-seven years, 1961–97, the correlation between the average rate of growth for seventeen countries and the standard deviation of the growth rate (across countries by year) was 0.68.

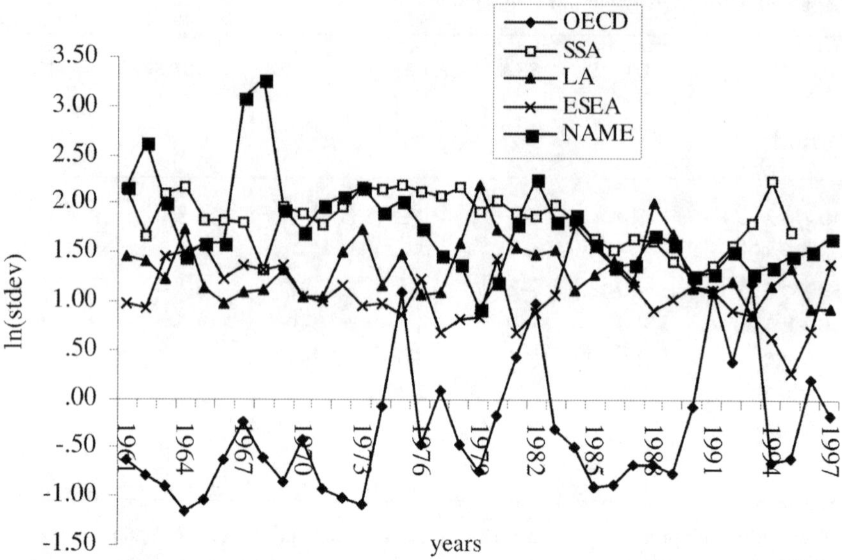

FIGURE 8.1 Standard Deviation of Growth Rates (natural log) by Region, 1961–1997 (secondary uneven development)

This implies that during periods of rapid accumulation, the levels of development among the capitalist countries tended to narrow. For none of the groups of underdeveloped countries is there a significant correlation between growth rates and their standard deviation. These statistics suggest that when the average rate of growth across all countries of the world was high, the developed capitalist countries tended to converge, while the underdeveloped countries did not, either among themselves, or relatively to the developed countries.

The extent to which underdeveloped countries have diverged from the developed capitalist countries over the last forty years is shown in Figures 8.2 and 8.3. These charts show the annual difference between the growth rates of each region and that of the OECD countries. Inspection of Figure 8.2 indicates that for the sub-Saharan countries, divergence has been the rule. For Latin America, only during a brief period, 1971–6, did per capita income rise relatively to the OECD countries. For the North African and Middle Eastern countries, growth was above the OECD average in the 1960s, but continuously below in subsequent years. The South Asian countries (Figure 8.3) grew at a rate slightly above that for the OECD countries from the late 1970s, allowing for a minuscule increase in relative per capita incomes, from 1.6 to 1.8 percent of the OECD level. At this rate of increase, it would take just over five hundred years for South Asian per capita income to converge to that of the OECD countries. The

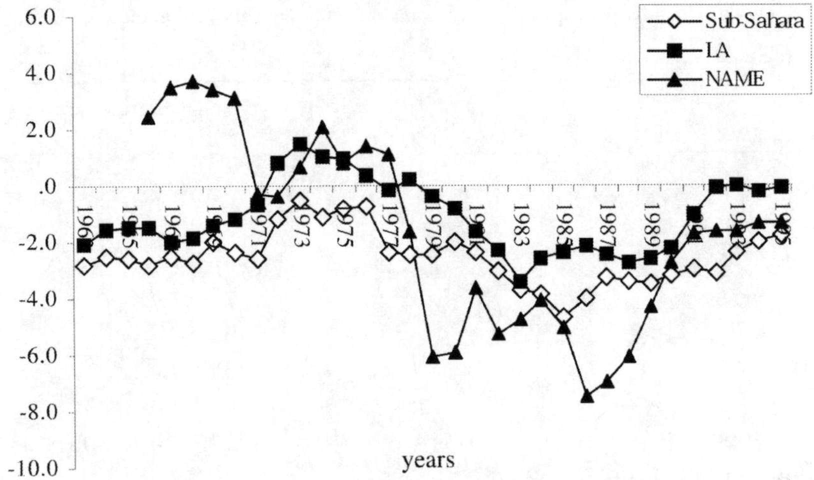

FIGURE 8.2 Differences in Per Capita Growth, the Sub-Sahara, Latin America & NAME, and the OECD Countries, 1961–1997 (five year moving average)

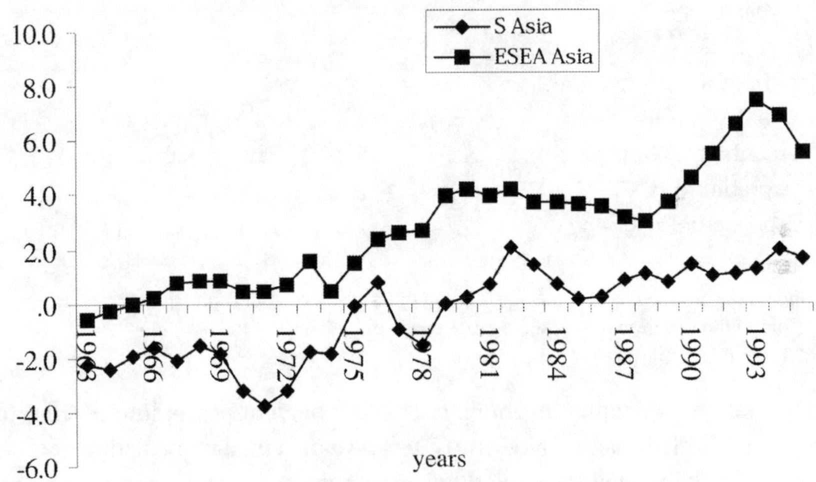

FIGURE 8.3 Differences in Per Capita Growth, ESEA and South Asia, and OECD Countries, 1961–1997 (five year moving average)

only strong convergence is for the East and Southeast Asian countries, which may well have been reversed for the foreseeable future by the regional financial crisis of the late 1990s.

Returning to Table 8.2, we can calculate the growth rates for country groups that would be necessary to return each group to its percentage level of the early 1960s. We assume that the OECD countries continue to grow at their long-

TABLE 8.2 Relative per capita incomes by region, 1961–1997 (absolute numbers in US$ of 1990)

	OECD	SSA	LA	ESEA	SoAsia	NAME
PCY 1961–65	9015	306	1391	155	185	1232
% of OECD						
1961–65		3.4	15.4	1.7	2.0	13.7
1971–75		2.7	13.7	*1.8*	1.6	*15.7*
1981–85		2.2	13.6	*2.4*	1.6	13.6
1991–95		1.6	11.3	*3.8*	*1.7*	8.8
1996–97		1.5	11.2	*4.6*	*1.8*	8.5
PCY 1996–97	21,540	326	2405	982	395	1826
Rate of increase of PCY, 37 years*	2.7	0.2	1.7	*5.7*	2.3	1.2
Rate required to regain 1961–65 ratio to OECD in 37 years		5.3	3.8	Not app	3.1	4.3
(Speculation) World Bank Predictions, 1997–2006	2.3	1.2	2.7	4.5**	4.1	1.1
(actual 1994–97)	(2.7)	(0.3)	(2.0)	(4.1)	(2.6)	(1.2)
Percentage of OECD, 2006, WB predictions		1.4	11.6	5.6	2.2	7.2
(2006, actual 1994–97)		(1.2)	(10.4)	(5.2)	(1.8)	(7.3)

Note: A rise in a region's percentage is noted by italics. PCY – per capita income.
* Compound rate, average of 1961–65 to average of 1996–97.
** See note to Table 8.1.

term rate of per capita income increase (2.7 percent per annum).[24] To return to their relative position after thirty-seven years (equal to the period, 1961–97), the sub-Saharan countries would need to grow at over five percent per capita per annum. This is a full five percentage points above the average rate for these countries over the previous thirty-seven years. For Latin America, a four percent rate would be required, well above the region average in any decade since 1960. More credible, but still unlikely, is the three percent rate for South Asia.

24 Pritchett points out that the growth of per capita income in the advanced countries has been remarkably stable. He shows that, if in 1961 one had estimated the per capita income of these countries for the early 1990s on the basis of previous long-term growth rates, the resulting estimate is within ten percent of the actual value (Pritchett 1997a).

TABLE 8.3 GDP Growth correlations: OECD and country groups, 1961–1997

Country group	Elasticity	R^2	F-stat
SSA*	0.643	0.345	.01
Latin America	0.789	0.294	.01
ESEA	0.637	0.252	.01
South Asia	-0.257	0.042	ns
NAME	0.884	0.138	.05

* On OECD growth lagged one year. The elasticity using current periods is .518, with an R-squared of .222.

For what they are worth, World Bank estimates of regional growth rates for 1997–2006 confirm the probability that divergence will continue (bottom of Table 8.2). The World Bank projects that of the five underdeveloped regions, growth of per capita income in two will be below the OECD average (the sub-Sahara and North Africa and the Middle East). For Latin America and South Asia, the World Bank projects rates above the OECD countries', and well above historical performance. Only for the East and Southeast Asian countries is the projection consistent with the past. The 1997–8 financial crisis of these countries casts doubt upon their ability to match past performance. Alternatively, we can take growth rates during 1994–7 as indicating the future trend, when every country group's per capita income growth was *above* its long-term trend (with the exception of East and Southeast Asia). Were these high rates maintained to 2006, the relative position of all groups except the East and Southeast Asia would deteriorate.

Table 8.3 provides a crude measure of whether divergence can be explained by the degree to which a country group is linked to OECD growth. It suggests that lack of integration into the world economy cannot explain the long-term deterioration of relative per capita income for most underdeveloped countries. The table reports the simple correlation between annual growth rates of the OECD countries and each underdeveloped region. Of the five regions, the correlation is highest for the sub-Saharan countries. Growth for the sub-Saharan countries has tended to rise and fall with OECD growth, such that a one percent rise in the latter is associated with a .64 percent rise in the latter. However, over the long term, OECD growth has been considerably higher. For all groups but the South Asian, there is significant correlation with OECD growth, but this has been associated with divergence, not convergence, in levels of development.

We interpret this divergence to be the result of primary uneven development: the tendency for growth to be more rapid within predominantly capitalist social relations.

From a neoclassical perspective, part of the explanation for divergence can be explained by the absence of substantial redistribution of capital from advanced to underdeveloped countries. Table 8.4 shows net direct foreign investment by the major industrial economies, with the United States, United Kingdom, Germany, and Japan listed separately. In contradiction to the prediction of orthodox theory, the largest capitalist country, the United States, was a net *recipient* of foreign investment in all years. For all countries, there was a net flow to underdeveloped countries in the second half of the 1980s and 1990s, but relatively small. Even for the 1990s, foreign investment into the United States (seventeen billion US dollars) approached the total for all underdeveloped countries (twenty-one billion). For the most part capitalist enterprises in advanced countries invest in their 'own' or other advanced countries.

Figure 8.4 shows the relatively low level of foreign direct investment from advanced to underdeveloped countries. Except for China, foreign investment played a relatively small role in gross domestic investment. In Latin America, foreign investment was consistently below ten percent of total investment for the entire twenty-six year period, with no trend if one accounts for the cycle of depression and recovery; i.e., foreign investment accounted for about the same percentage in the mid-1990s as in the early 1970s. For the major Asian countries, foreign investment in no year reached as much as four percent of total investment. Contrary to what one might expect, foreign investment has been of greater relative importance in the sub-Saharan region than in Asia (the former greater than the latter in all but three years),[25] though considerably more volatile. The only major country in which foreign investment has played a substantially increasing role in total investment has been China. If China is excluded, the relative quantitative importance of foreign direct investment in underdeveloped countries was no greater in the 1990s than in the 1970s.

In this context, we can note that the evidence that most foreign direct investment is among developed capitalist countries, not from these countries to underdeveloped regions, is consistent with our concept of primary uneven development. One would expect that capital would flow to countries and regions characterised by capitalist social relations, for the persistence of non-capitalist relations is associated with institutional barriers to such flows.

25 Most of the investment in the sub-Saharan region was in the mining sector, and had limited impact on affecting social relations in the countries.

TABLE 8.4 Net direct foreign investment flows into major industrial countries, 1980–1996 (billions of current US dollars)

	USA	UK	Germany	Japan	Other	Total
1980	9.5	-2.5	-2.7	-2.1	-2.2	0.0
1981	26.2	-5.3	-2.7	-4.7	-9.1	4.4
1982	19.9	-0.8	-1.8	-4.1	-0.2	13.0
1983	18.6	-1.5	-1.4	-3.2	-1.4	11.1
1984	28.3	-5.2	-2.5	-6.0	-4.1	10.5
1985	21.3	-4.3	-3.3	-5.8	-10.5	-2.6
1986	26.4	-3.7	-7.5	-14.3	-9.7	-8.8
1987	47.3	-9.0	-7.8	-18.4	-10.0	2.1
1988	52.1	-5.3	-10.1	-34.7	-6.9	-4.9
1989	51.5	3.7	-7.4	-45.2	-15.9	-13.3
1990	53.0	24.5	-17.1	-46.3	-15.8	-1.7
1991	27.1	9.7	-17.5	-30.2	-12.9	-23.8
1992	4.6	5.5	-16.1	-14.6	-0.8	-21.4
1993	5.0	-1.4	-12.6	-13.7	0.1	-22.6
1994	24.2	-3.3	-9.7	-17.2	-13.5	-19.5
1995	5.9	-5.8	-23.9	-22.6	17.8	-28.6
1996	35.4	6.7	-27.1	-21.7	-4.0	-10.7
annual average						
1980–85	20.6	-3.3	-2.4	-4.3	-4.6	6.1
1986–90	46.1	2.0	-10.0	-31.8	-11.7	-5.3
1991–96	17.0	1.9	-17.8	-20.0	-2.2	-21.1

SOURCE: UNITED NATIONS (1986, 1991, 1998)

Overall, the evidence is clear: during the three decades international capital did not dramatically accelerate its expansion into the underdeveloped world. On the contrary, the dramatic expansion was within the advanced capitalist countries. One would not expect capitalism to foster an equitable distribution of income and wealth on a national level. Nor did it foster a general convergence of capitalist development around the globe. Within capitalist relations, accumulation fosters convergence; while growth among countries at quite different levels of capitalist development produces divergence.

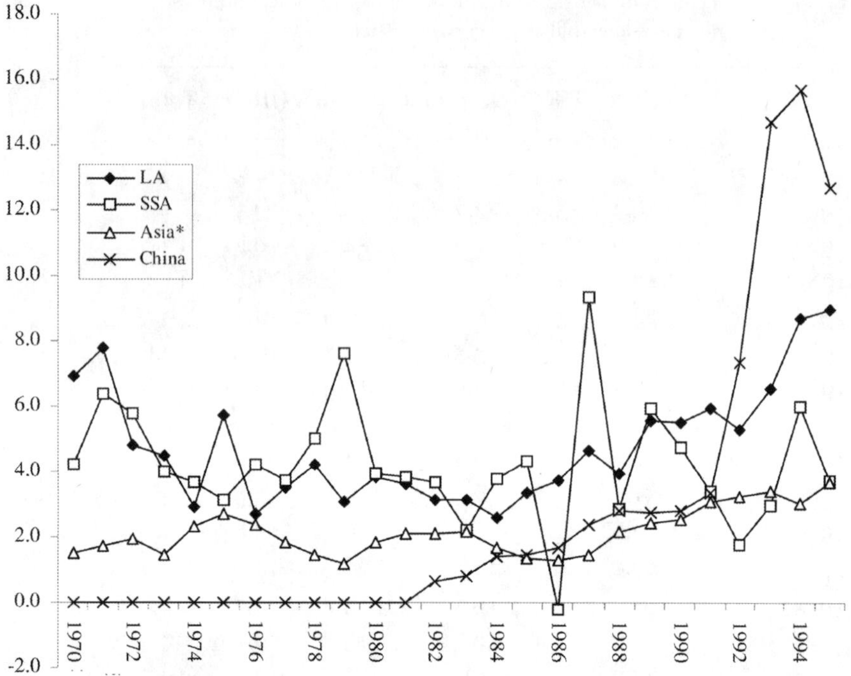

FIGURE 8.4 Foreign Direct Investment as a Percentage of Gross Domestic Investment, by Region and China, 1970–1995

5 Convergence and Divergence

Our general conclusion, that capitalist countries converge among themselves,[26] and diverge from countries in which capitalist relations remain underdeveloped, does not explain the historical division of countries into the two groups. The historical explanation is straightforward: the transition from slow to rapid economic growth is achieved through the development of capitalist social relations. This is essentially a process internal to each social formation, influenced, but not determined, by external factors. The extent to which trade and investment flows foster capitalist development within a social formation is primarily determined by the nature of the non-capitalist relations themselves. Since non-capitalist relations can take many forms, no general theory of transition to capitalism is possible.

26 This is a central conclusion of the empirical work of Pritchett 1997b.

Through a process taking several centuries, capitalism developed in Western Europe,[27] establishing itself as the dominant mode of exploiting labour during the second half of the eighteenth century. During the nineteenth century, capitalism spread through the countries of this region. Because of the close integration of these countries in trade and finance, the development of capitalism in this region should be viewed as a single historical process; i.e., it should not be analysed as a number of separate transitions. The next 'wave' of capitalist development, in the late nineteenth and early twentieth centuries, involved only two *transitions*, Italy and Japan. In these countries, feudal and semi-feudal social relations were replaced by the social relations of capital. The other countries that emerged as capitalist during this period were settler states: the United States, Canada, Australia, New Zealand, and, unsuccessfully, Argentina and Uruguay. If the history of global capitalist teaches any lesson, it is that the transition is a protracted process, dominated by uneven development, in which divergence is the rule and convergence the exception.'

27 That is, the United Kingdom, Ireland, France, Germany, the Low Countries, and Scandinavia.

CHAPTER 9

International Exchange and the Causes of Backwardness

1 Introduction

The unequal development of the productive forces was shown by Marx to be a fundamental law of capitalist accumulation; and, in general, it is this law which produces uneven development on a world scale and inequality among countries. While all Marxists agree that the explanation of inequality in levels of development between countries lies in the laws of uneven development,[1] there is less agreement upon the mechanism by which this uneven development is produced and reproduced on a world scale. One can distinguish two broad approaches, (a) those which explain inequality in levels of development among countries primarily in the sphere of circulation, emphasising the appropriation of the surplus of one country by another country,[2] and (b) those which place the cause of inequality in the sphere of production, and, thus, as a relationship between classes reproduced on a world scale. The purpose of this paper is to critique the former position and to develop further the latter.[3]

Briefly summarising our position and the themes we develop: (a) exploitation is a relationship between classes, not between countries, and international transfers of value are understood from this standpoint; (b) inequality among

1 An apparent exception to this generalisation is Samir Amin. In the writings of Marx, Lenin, and Stalin, even Trotsky, 'uneven development' refers to the development of the productive forces. As we see below, Amin, who identifies himself as a Marxist, explicitly argues that the productive forces are equally developed throughout the world (Amin 1973, pp. 1–2, 9).

2 This is the more common position of the two we consider and is set out clearly in Baran (1957) and Frank, (1969). A special and narrow branch of the school that sees inequality arising in the sphere of circulation is the work of the neo-Ricardian A. Emmanuel. Below we consider this approach. By "neo-Ricardian" we mean those theorists who do not treat capitalism as a historically unique mode of appropriation, who treat production as a technical process, and as a result do not consider the concept of mode of production. The work of Samir Amin is treated as part of the "unequal exchange" school.

3 This second position is presented in Bettelheim (1972) and Brenner (1977). Our paper was first circulated for comments in 1976, then again in a second draft in January, 1977. Subsequently, the Brenner article appeared, which takes the same general position as our paper, though his is much more historical in its theoretical discussion.

 | DOI:10.1163/9789004703193_011

countries is the consequence of class exploitation in backward countries and the reproduction of this class exploitation through imperialism; (c) the initial development of capitalism in Western Europe and subsequent accumulation there and elsewhere (in North America and Japan) was not based upon the extraction of riches from backward countries; and (d) to the extent that trade has a detrimental effect on backward countries, it is the result of trade, not primarily the consequence of the terms, by which it occurs. While stressing that exploitation is a relationship between classes, it must also be stressed that the spread of capitalism on a world scale, particularly in the imperialist epoch, leads to oppression of countries and nations, as well as national minorities within countries. This oppression is inherent in imperialism and falls upon all classes in the oppressed nation or country. The objective function of such oppression is to facilitate class exploitation, which is a relation in production.

2 'Surplus Extraction' as the Source of Backwardness

2.1 *The Work of Baran and Frank*

By far the most prevalent explanation of the inequality in level of development among countries – leaving bourgeois apologists aside – is that 'surplus' is extracted from backward countries and is appropriated and subsequently used in the advanced countries. To analyse this view, emphasis here will be first on the work of Baran and Frank, because of their clarity of exposition and consistent (one might even say obsessive) use of this explanatory thesis. It may be argued that these writers are 'out-of-date', or that their analytical errors have been 'laid to rest'. We disagree. The mistakes of Baran and Frank reappear in the works of many other authors, whose influence is still quite strong. Some of these, particularly Amin, we consider below.

The appropriation of surplus product has a twofold consequence in the work of Baran and Frank: it impoverishes the backward country and enriches the advanced country. Frank writes:

> … [T]he metropolis [advanced capitalist country] expropriates economic surplus from its satellites [backward countries] and appropriates it for its own development. The satellites remain underdeveloped for the lack of access to their own surplus and as a consequence of the same polarization and exploitation contradictions which the metropolis introduces and maintains in the satellite's domestic economic structure … One and the same historical process of the expansion and development of capital-

> ism throughout the world has simultaneously generated – and continues to generate – both economic development and structural underdevelopment.[4]

Similarly, Baran, after stressing the role of surplus extraction as the cause of underdevelopment,[5] adds:

> … [W]hatever may have been the fractional increase of Western Europe's national income derived from its overseas operations, they multiplied the economic surplus at its disposal. What is more: the increment of the economic surplus appeared immediately in a concentrated form and came largely into the hands of capitalists who could use it for investment purposes. The intensity of the boost to Western Europe's development resulting from the 'exogenous' contribution to its capital accumulation can hardly be exaggerated.[6]

This emphasis placed on the extraction and appropriation of surplus product as the cause of backwardness, and as crucial to accumulation in the advanced countries,[7] demonstrates a misunderstanding of (a) the nature of exploitation (and, thus, of surplus appropriation), (b) the origins of capitalism, and, therefore (c) the nature of capital itself as a social relation. What in essence is being suggested is that capitalism does not develop primarily on the basis of exploit-

4 Frank 1969b, p. 9, emphasis added.

5 It is not being suggested that Baran stresses this to the exclusion of all other causes. Indeed, his discussion of the classes which imperialism supports in backward countries is integral to his analysis, and is referred to below.

6 Baran 1957, pp. 142–3. While Baran may have thought that there was no danger of exaggeration, Marx clearly warned against such emphasis. Referring specifically to the imports of gold and silver from the New World (as Baran is doing in the quotation cited). Marx wrote:

> The capitalist mode of production – its basis being wage labour … can assume greater dimensions and achieve greater perfection only where there is available in the country a quantity of money sufficient for circulation and the formation of a hoard … promoted by it. This is a historical premise, although it is not to *be taken* to mean *that* first a sufficient *hoard* is formed and then capitalist production begins (Marx 1956, p. 209, emphasis added).

Of course, an isolated quotation from Marx contradicting Baran does not make the latter wrong prima facie. Below we analyse why Marx reached this conclusion.

7 The same view is expressed in the following: 'It is characteristic of capitalism that the development of some countries takes place at the cost of suffering and disaster for the peoples of other countries … The colonization [of backward areas] made possible the rapid development of capitalism in the West' (Kuusinen n.d.: pp. 247–8).

ation of the proletariat, but upon the basis of the exploitation of countries, a basic revision of Marx's method.[8]

Inherent in the 'surplus extraction' argument are two theses: (a) that exploitation can be seen as a relationship between countries, and (b) that the capitalist mode of production is an incomplete mode of production; i.e., it cannot generate its own reproduction. We shall seek to demonstrate that the concept of surplus appropriation, and thus the concept of exploitation, has been robbed of its scientific content by these two theses. First and foremost, surplus product arises in the process of production. Whether it is exchanged and/or eventually moves across a geographical border, in no way alters the fact that it must first be produced. How it is produced is both a technical and a social process. Its production involves classes and its appropriation is by a dominant and non-producing class from direct producers at the point of production. The surplus product is not a magical or mysterious thing; it is a material phenomenon, in that the surplus labour of the direct producers must at some point assume a material (use value) form such as labour services or material products of the labour process. Exploitation is the appropriation of this surplus labour in natural (use value) or money from by a class of nonproducers. To analyse appropriation in the context of countries is to ignore the process of production and to obscure the class nature of societies.

Obfuscation of the class question is shown clearly in the quotation from Frank, where he says 'their own surplus', referring to countries by the possessive pronoun. This use of pronouns is not merely semantic. By separating appropriation from production and classes, the necessity for exploitation at any level becomes lost in the analysis and the surplus product becomes a mysterious thing. In other words, if exploitation is treated as a relationship between countries, it becomes a characteristic of capitalism, but not a necessary condition for that mode of production.[9] Further, it becomes a characteristic which is not unique to capitalism, but of all modes of production (except socialism). We are not here chiding Frank for not being faithful to Marx, though he is not, of

8 Bettelheim 1972a makes this point forcefully. It is not accidental that Marx devoted only one chapter of Volume I of *Capital* to a discussion of colonies. We should stress that we are not faulting Baran and Frank for disagreeing with Marx per se, but in abandoning his method, which we argue is a scientifically correct method (see Brenner 1977, pp. 31–3, 51–3).

9 Here we deal primarily with Baran on this point, but it also applies to Frank, who argues that Latin American countries were able to develop fastest when the external link to the advanced capitalist countries was weakened or broken. At the very least, this is suggestive that he does not see the exploitation of backward areas as a necessity for capitalist countries, particularly in light of the fact that one of these periods of weakening was during a period when capitalism was in greatest need of aid – the Great Depression.

course. The important issue is not that he is obscuring Marx's analysis (though he is), but that he is obscuring reality. A surplus product arises in production and appears in circulation (if exchanged). By dealing with countries only, one considers the appearance of reality, not reality itself. What is missing here is the concept of mode of production.

A mode of production is characterised by the specific social relations which determine how the surplus product is produced, the method whereby the surplus product is appropriated, and the superstructural forms which are implied by these social relations of production and appropriation. All societies in which there is class differentiation are characterised by exploitation, and the particular class structure of a society is not accidental, but determined by the specific method of appropriation. The plunder of one geographic area for the enrichment of a class (or classes) of expropriators in another geographic area has been a characteristic of virtually all historical epochs. If such plunder and appropriation is used to explain the inequality in the level of development among countries, there is no need to introduce capitalism into the analysis – capitalism becomes an unnecessary 'fifth wheel' in the discussion of only polemical significance. Put another way, plunder and appropriation of surplus product by one country at the expense of another derives from domination, and while it continues under imperialism (the monopoly stage of capitalism), it is no more characteristic of capitalism in its imperialist stage than it was characteristic of competitive capitalism or of ancient Rome. What is unique to capitalism is the appropriation of the surplus product of labour through the exploitation of labour in the social form of labour power (free wage labour).[10] The particular mechanisms which reproduce the inequality in levels of development among countries in the capitalist epoch derive from this historically unique character of the capitalist mode of production; or, if not, then a discussion of capitalism is irrelevant to the question of the inequality among countries. Thus, it must be shown that the inequality is produced and reproduced under capitalism because of the exploitation of labour as a commodity.

Failure to recognise that capitalism is a unique mode of production, based on the buying and selling of labour power, leads either to self-contradiction or reformism in the explanation of backwardness. This comes out strikingly in the work of Baran. While seeming to argue that exploitation between countries is inherent in imperialism, he discusses the possibility of an exploitation-free international capitalism:

10 For an excellent discussion of this, see Takahashi 1967, p. 31.

> [I]f the most advanced countries' contact with the backward world had been different from what it was, if it had consisted of genuine cooperation and assistance rather than of oppression and exploitation, then the progressive development of the now underdeveloped countries would have proceeded with incomparably less delay, less human sacrifice and suffering. A peaceful transplantation of Western culture, science, and technology to the less advanced countries would have served everywhere as a powerful catalyst of economic progress.[11]

What is being suggested is the possibility within capitalist relations of production of a 'peaceful', non-exploitative expansion of capitalism. Here, Baran is not, apparently, speaking hypothetically. He goes on to assert that such an expansion actually occurred:

> A comparison of the role played by British technology in the development of the United States with the role played by British opium in the development of China fully epitomizes this difference.[12]

This extraordinary argument is the logical reductio absurdum of the surplus extraction thesis. What is being asserted is that the inequality among countries is not the result of capitalism itself, but of a 'country' losing 'its' surplus. If capitalism is characterised by general laws, then these must be manifest in all cases, in the United States or China – though not with the same concrete results. They cannot be intrinsically benevolent in one case and malevolent in another. In the above quotation we have a total denial of these laws and of the class nature of societies, ascribing surplus product to national states rather than appropriating classes.[13] This personification of countries implies that even under capitalist relations of production the economic surplus, if it remained in the backward country, would be used for the general benefit of the population; in other words, that the local capitalist class is not primarily a class of exploiters, but part of a commonweal of national interests.[14] Like Proudhon, the advocates

11 Baran 1957, p. 162.

12 Baran 1957, p. 162.

13 This is an error made repeatedly by Frank. For example: 'Thus the metropolis expropriates economic surplus from its satellites and appropriates it for its own development. The satellites remain underdeveloped for lack of access to their own surplus …' (Frank 1969b, p. 9, emphasis added).

14 Again, Baran 1957 is clear. 'It would have been … an entirely different India … had she been allowed … to realize her destiny in her own way, to employ her resources for *her* own benefit, and to harness *her* energies and abilities for the advancement of her own people' (Baran 1957, p. 150, emphasis added).

of the surplus extraction thesis are arguing that inequality lies not in commodity production, but in the unfairness of the trading (or plundering) relationship, i.e., in commodity circulation.

Again, the fundamental error of the surplus extraction thesis is that its proponents lack any concept of the mode of production. While they may refer to classes in backward countries (particularly Baran), they never find it necessary to consider that '"whatever the social form of production, labourers and means of production always remain factors of it … [but], the specific manner in which this union is accomplished" distinguishes the different economic epochs of the structure of society from one another'.[15] 'The specific manner in which the union is accomplished' determines, within certain limits affected by historical circumstances, the class structure, the nature of the state, the system of laws, and other superstructural forms.

Without considering the mode of production, "the specific manner" in which the means of production and labour are unified, the analysis of relations between geographic areas becomes subjective and idealistic, easily slipping into romanticism and utopian speculation, as Baran does in the last quotation. By ignoring the mode of production, production itself is ignored. Once the analysis loses touch with the process of production, the fundamental social axiom that all societies, save the most primitive and the most advanced (socialist and communist), are based upon the exploitation of direct producers disappears from view. And without the mode of appropriation (and thus exploitation) at the heart of an analysis of societies, a discussion of classes has no scientific content, and subjective and idealistic conclusions cannot be avoided. This idealism is obvious in Baran's work, where he suggests the possibility of a benign encounter of the third kind between expanding capitalism and pre-capitalism. The impossibility of such an encounter follows from a materialist analysis. Frank is similarly idealistic, but in an 'ultra-revolutionary' form. Because he sees the wealth of capitalism to be the result of surplus extraction, he does not analyse capital itself, but fetishises it as a relation between countries rather than as a relation between classes. He rejects implicitly Baran's benign alternative and asserts the impossibility of the development of the forces of production in backward countries.[16] He dismisses the national bourgeoisie as a potential

15 Marx 1956, pp. 22.

16 It is important to note similarities between Frank's position – and the position of 'dependency' writers in general, and that of Sismondi (and later the Narodniks in Russia). The argument that capitalist development is impossible except for those countries that got there first is almost as old as capitalism itself (Lenin 1972a).

momentary ally in an anti-imperialist struggle, leaving only a leap to socialism as an alternative to 'underdevelopment'.

Errors of theory in the analysis of backwardness are inseparable from errors of political practice. These errors can only be avoided by an analysis of the mode of production. Thus, before we can understand the impact of the spread of capitalism upon backward countries, we must understand capitalism itself, as a historically specific mode of production. As Lenin wrote, '... if production relations remain unexplained (for example, if the process of the production of the aggregate social capital is not understood), all arguments about consumption and distribution turn into banalities, or innocent, romantic wishes'.[17]

3 Surplus Extraction Submerged in Underconsumptionism: The Work of Marini

Before going into what we consider the correct approach to the question of unequal development,[18] we turn to other presentations of the surplus extraction thesis. In essence, Marini, Cardoso, and Amin, who have attempted to further develop dependency analysis, are no different from the presentation by Frank. The essential similarity of all dependency writers is not readily apparent because this school has a strong eclectic tendency, which comes out clearest in Cardoso and Amin. As a result of this eclecticism, the primary and secondary aspects of the theories are frequently presented on equal footings, and arguments which are inherently contradictory are presented as complementary, as if they merely refer to different aspects of a complex phenomenon. In consequence, by drawing out the implicit core of dependency theory, whatever its variations, one appears to "distort" the work of each particular author.

In order to analyse the surplus extraction thesis as presented in the form of an underconsumptionist argument, we treat the work of Marini. This form of the argument is quite common, found also in the work of Cardoso,[19] for example, who is better known than Marini, at least in the English-speaking world. However, Cardoso's extreme eclecticism makes a concise critique of his

17 Lenin 1972, pp. 202–5.

18 We use this vague term instead of 'uneven development' because to us the latter implies the further phrase '... of the productive forces'; and it remains for us to demonstrate that the 'uneven development of the productive forces' is the cause of backwardness. Thus, we use the term at this point precisely because of its theoretical ambiguity and confusion (i.e., 'unequal development' of what?).

19 See Cardoso 1972, and Cardoso and Faletto 1972.

work extremely difficult. Marini takes an important step forward compared to Frank and Baran by pointing out that the analysis of capitalism must be based in the sphere of production.[20] However, he argues, this applies to capitalism 'at the centre', and since 'peripheral' or 'dependent' capitalism is conditioned primarily by circulation, it is to phenomena in circulation that we must look in order to understand 'dependent' capitalism. Unfortunately, this formulation of the issue is not very helpful; it assumes what it seeks to establish analytically. If it is the case that the sphere of circulation is primary in Third World countries, then it is certainly correct to centre one's argument there – in exchange and distribution. But the mere fact that a world market exists and that foreign capital plays a dominating role in 'peripheral' or 'dependent' economies does not establish the primacy of circulation. It merely establishes that the analysis must at some point incorporate world-market relations and the export of capital; it does not establish that these are best analysed by preceding from circulation rather than production.

After setting his framework, Marini contrasts the function of 'distribution' in developed and underdeveloped countries, treating 'distribution' in the very limited neo-Ricardian sense of the distribution between wages and profit.[21] He argues that in the underdeveloped capitalist countries, the role of the working class is that of producers, and the product of its labour is exported. Since the product is exported, there is no need for this working class to serve as consumers, and its wages can be forced down without limit, this, of course, follows as a tautology: if it is the case that the central role of wages is in the realization of value produced and if the commodities produced are exported, then wages have no further function and can be depressed without limit. Clearly, the exported commodities from 'dependent' capitalist countries must be realized somewhere – they cannot be dumped into the sea. The commodities are realized, in Marini's schema, by the consumption of the working class in the developed capitalist countries, and this necessity for realization requires that wages be high there. Here arises a wage theory which is developed in more sohpisticated form in the work of Amin – the wage-profit distribution in the developed capitalist country is determined independently of the sphere of production, determined purely by the need to realize the value produced at 'home' and 'abroad'. Marini points out that his analysis implies that the opposition

20 The following is based on Marini 1972.

21 That is, he treats distribution of society's production from the value side only, ignoring the material side, which ignores the two-fold nature of commodities. This is at the heart of his underconsumptionist analysis. See Marx on Adam Smith's similar error (Marx 1956, p. 226ff.).

between labour and capital in the developed country is overcome in the sphere of circulation since both classes share a common interest in having wages high.[22] Thus workers are superexploited in the 'dependent' country, and there is no mechanism for their wages to rise since they are not needed for realization. Since wages do not rise, the internal market does not expand, and accumulation in the dependent country ('acumulación dependentista') is retarded or 'deformed'.

On the face of it, this theory seems to have little in common with Frank's or Baran's, whether it is correct or not. However, hidden beneath the underconsumptionist analysis is the surplus extraction thesis. In essence, Marini is arguing that surplus value is produced in the 'periphery' and appropriated at the 'centre'; underconsumptionism merely provides the mechanism by which this appropriation occurs. While Frank and Baran are vague on the actual mechanism, seeming to give emphasis to appropriation through profit remittance, Marini sees the appropriation occuring through the consumption by workers and capitalists in the advanced country of consumer commodities produced in the 'dependent' economies. The high living standards in developed countries, particularly for workers, is achieved by consuming in material form the surplus value produced in the Third World. 'Development' is implicitly defined in terms of living standards rather than in terms the development of the productive forces. In this theory, the living standards of the working class are, in fact, determined independently of the development of the productive forces.

Wage levels, which are equated to living standards, confusing the use value and exchange value which the wage represents,[23] are determined purely by the 'need' for realization, both in the backward and the advanced capitalist countries.

In fact, Marini has gone beyond Baran and Frank in his stress of surplus extraction. Baran, at least to an extent, sees the appropriated 'surplus' being used productively, as a source of accumulation, in the advanced capitalist countries. Marini treats the appropriated surplus purely as a consumption fund for the advanced capitalist society as a whole. Without the 'dependent' economies, the standard of living in the developed capitalist economies would fall drastically and the rate of profit would collapse, since the commodities exported from the periphery are both the source of higher consumption (in their material form) and embody the surplus value for the capitalist class in the advanced

22 Marini 1972.

23 Dore and Weeks 1977, pp. 1–18.

country (in their value form). Now, there are serious problems with this formulation of the 'surplus extraction' argument, not the least of which is, how is it possible for workers to be paid sufficiently to realize surplus value, yet not eliminate profit? This problem is not resolved, but only confused, by introducing two countries into the analysis. That is, if workers consume the material form of surplus value, they must also have previously been paid its value equivalent. If they have not been paid its value equivalent, then they cannot buy it.

The underconsumptionist argument to explain barriers to the expansion of capital is not original with Marini; he simply applies it to backward countries. The argument, in its most sophisticated and developed form, originates with Luxemburg (1968). Nor are the criticisms of the argument new. Perhaps the clearest is that of Bukharin who points out that there is, in fact, no 'realization problem' (problem in converting surplus value into profit) since the major portion of the realization of value occurs not through workers' (or even capitalists') consumption of the means of subsistence (the products of Department II in Marx's schema), but through the productive consumption of the means of production (the products of Department I).[24]

In summary, Marini's argument is basically the surplus extraction thesis. As such it liquidates the role of production entirely, and on this basis draws erroneous conclusions regarding the role of classes.

4 Surplus Extraction in the Form of 'Unequal Exchange'

In recent years the most influential form assumed by the surplus extraction thesis is that put forward by A. Emmanuel in his book *Unequal Exchange* (1972). While the work is quite long and filled with a great number of numerical examples to demonstrate various aspects of his theory, the central idea is quite simple. Much of the length is the consequence of Emmanuel's attempt to justify treating 'the wage as an independent variable', and 'factor claims' in general as logically prior to values or prices; that is, to establish the validity of treating exchange value as the sum of costs, rather than exchange value being determined by the socially necessary labour time embodied in commodities. He is particularly determined to show that this approach is consistent with Marx's analysis. Since Marx explicitly criticised this method, attacking Adam Smith for it, Emmanuel has a difficult task in establishing his position.[25]

24 Bukharin 1968.

25 Marx wrote, '… and here Adam Smith's ridiculous blunder reaches the climax. After start-

The purpose of Emmanuel's work is to determine the conditions establishing the exchange ratios of commodities in international trade. It should be noted that this is not the same as determining the operation of the law of value on the international level, since the law of value is not merely a law of pricing; i.e., it is not the Marxian version of 'supply and demand'. We are not criticising Emmanuel for this, but merely making clear the scope of the problem he has set for himself. In his analysis, all capitalists in all countries are treated as having available to them the same technical production possibilities, regardless of the level of the development of the productive forces in each country. This approach should be familiar to those acquainted with 'neoclassical' trade theory, which makes the assumption of the same 'production function' prevailing in each country, but in Emmanuel's case the 'coefficients of production' are fixed; i.e., no 'factor substitution'. With the additional assumption that 'capital' is perfectly mobile internationally, it appears to follow that the production costs of the means of production will be the same in each country. We say 'appears', because it is not obvious why raw material costs would be the same in each country. But this is a minor point. With these assumptions in hand, unit costs will be lower in countries where the wage is lower unless a lower wage is associated with a correspondingly lower level of productiveness of labour. Emmanuel assumes that productiveness of labour does not vary as much as wage levels, so the generality of his theory is not affected by simply assuming equal productivity of labour in each country. Indeed, Amin proceeds to this assumption.

If 'non-labour costs' are the same across countries, and current (living) labour creates the same value per period of time, the rate of profit will be higher where wages are lower. According to Emmanuel, 'unequal exchange' occurs by the movement of capital in search of the higher profit rates. Commodity prices rise relatively in the high-wage country as capital flees (relatively), and commodity prices fall in the low-wage country. As a consequence of the equalisation of the rate of profit through these price movements, international exchange occurs at rates which are not equal to the labour time embodied in commodities. In particular, the ratio of advanced country prices to backward

ing by correctly defining the component parts of the value of the commodities and the sum of the value-product incorporated in them, and then demonstrating how these component parts form so many different sources of revenue, *after thus deriving the revenues from the value*, he proceeds in the opposite direction – and this remains the predominant conception with him – and turns the revenues from "component parts" into "original sources of all exchangeable values," thereby throwing the doors wide open to vulgar economy' (Marx, 1967, II: 376–377, first emphasis added).

country prices is greater than the ratio of the labour time in advanced country commodities to the labour time in backward country commodities, where 'advanced' and 'backward' are defined purely in terms of the wage level in each country. In this way, through exchange, advanced countries 'appropriate' more labour time in exchange than they generate in production. A 'surplus' is transferred from backward countries, reducing the rate of accumulation there for lack of a sufficient investable surplus.

Even on its own terms, this analysis is rather unsatisfactory. On an empirical level, it suggests that the main tendency would be for foreign investment to flow to backward countries. But this is not the case.[26] This aside, Emmanuel's theory, by stressing the equalisation of the rate of profit, itself predicts that the worst that can happen is that the relative 'surplus' will be the same in advanced and backward countries; i.e., at the worst, the 'surplus' remaining in backward countries is sufficient to match the rate of accumulation of advanced countries. Further, as long as profit rates are not equal, but only tending to equalisation, production in the backward country must grow faster than in the advanced country. So, unless Emmanuel believes that profit rates are actually in equilibrium, the movement of capital to equalise the rates of profit must generate more rapid accumulation in backward than advanced countries. A theory whose mechanism predicts a faster rate of accumulation in backward countries would not seem to be a very powerful tool for explaining unequal development. Amin attempts to resolve this problem.

5 Synthesis of 'Unequal Exchange' and Underconsumptionism: Amin's Presentation

Amin's writings, which are numerous,[27] explicitly integrate the theory of 'unequal exchange' with the underconsumptionist thesis. His work is sometimes hard to follow, because of a tendency on his part to use an eclectic mixture of terms, taken from Marx, neo-Ricardian writings, 'mainstream' neoclassical theory, plus some he introduces himself, whose intellectual kinship is unclear. Overall, his work is neo-Ricardian, by which we mean he treats production as a technical rather than social process, and treats distribution as largely independent of production.

26 From 1957 to 1960, approximately 40 percent of U.S. foreign investment was located in what the Survey of Current Business defines as 'under-developed' countries; by 1967–70, this share had fallen to 33 percent, and was about 27 percent in 1975–6. U.S. Department of Commerce (1972 and 1977, pp. 42, 43).

27 Here we shall refer to Amin 1973 and 1976.

The most important theoretical objection raised to Emmanuel's work from a Marxist viewpoint is that he fails to distinguish between use value and exchange value in his discussion of wages.[28] The objection is a simple one. Workers must consume a certain mass of use values in order to reproduce labour power currently and in future generations. This mass of use values constitutes the standard of living for a worker, and the standard of living for the working class varies enormously among countries. The wage tends to represent the exchange value of those use values. Given the mass of use values (the standard of living), the wage is determined by how efficiently the commodities which workers buy are produced. The greater the productivity of labour, the lower the value of commodities, and the lower the exchange value. As capitalism develops, productivity rises, the value of commodities falls, and the wage which must be paid to cover a given mass of use values (a given standard of living) also falls. Marx called this process the raising of relative surplus value.[29] Since it is in the developed capitalist countries that labour productivity is higher, it is not obvious that a high standard of living of workers in such countries implies that the exchange value of the commodities making up that standard of living is also higher than in backward countries. A simple example can illustrate this. Assume that in country A, the average worker consumes a pound of wheat a day, and in country B two pounds. If wheat production is three times more efficient in country B, the price of wheat will be correspondingly lower, and the wage lower where the standard of living is higher. Thus, it appears that it cannot be established theoretically that the appearance of things (differences in living standards) necessarily implies differences in the exchange value of labour power (the wage).

It is from this argument that Amin seeks to rescue Emmanuel. He seeks his solution in the 'pre-eminence of world values'. He summarises Emmanuel's contribution as follows:

> … the [world economic] system is defined in the abstract by the great mobility of goods and capital and by a relative immobility of labour. This means that commodities are not first of all national commodities and then, exceptionally or marginally international. On the contrary, it means that commodities are primarily world wide.[30]

28 Bettelheim 1972a.

29 Marx 1906, Part IV.

30 Amin, 1973, p. 1.

While there is some ambiguity here – it is not clear what the statement 'commodities are world wide' means – the overall implication seems to be that commodities which are exchanged internationally have an international price. He goes on to argue that international exchange renders concrete (particular) labour to abstract (general, homogeneous) labour. This is certainly true, a characteristic of the alienation of use value from the seller in the act of exchange. From this, he moves to an important conclusion: 'Since all products are international commodities, the same quantity of labour used up in different parts of the world and incorporated in the products, also gives rise to a single world value'.[31] That is to say, all labour for all labour processes ('all products') produces the same value per unit of time. Now, if this is true, Emmanuel's problem is resolved. If a commodity, say corn, has the same value in every country, then differences in living standards do translate directly into differences in the value, and thus, exchange value, of labour power. Amin points this out: 'It is obvious that if the labour-hour in all countries creates the same value, while labour power in one of the countries has a lower value, that is, the wage is lower, the rate of surplus value is higher [in that country]'.[32] Amin provides a numerical example:

> If the labour-day is the same in countries A and B (8 hours for example) and if the real wage of the proletariat is 10 times higher in B (real wage in B equivalent to 10 kilograms of wheat per day as against only one kilogram in A) and if world output of wheat (where wheat productivity is highest) is 10 kilograms in 4 hours, the rate of surplus value in B will be 100% … while it will be 1900% in A … This reasoning does not call for a comparison between the productivities of the two capitalist productions in which A and B specialize: it is even meaningless to do so.[33]

Amin clearly feels he has established the theoretical basis of unequal exchange: if constant capital costs are equated by the movement of capital, and the rate of surplus value varies with variations in wage levels, unequal exchange seems to follow.

Emmanuel's error, as pointed out, was in failing to distinguish use value from exchange value, a common element in neo-Ricardian analysis.[34] Amin's

31 Amin 1973, p. 9.
32 Ibid.
33 Ibid.
34 For a discussion of the neo-Ricardian method see Fine and Harris 1976.

error is more subtle, but equally serious in its consequences – he fails to distinguish between value and exchange value, or value and price, where price is the money form of exchange value.[35] Value is the socially necessary abstract labour time embodied in a commodity. This abstract labour time is crystallised in the commodity in the process of production. Further, the value of a specific commodity is not merely the labour time embodied in it, but the socially necessary abstract labour time embodied in it. The abstraction from concrete labour is a consequence of exchange, which renders specific forms of human labour comparable. The competition among producers enforces a standard abstract labour time to each commodity, a socially imposed standard – socially necessary labour time. The particular labour time involved in the production process organised by a given capitalist may be above or below the socially necessary labour time. Labour time expended under the dominance of capitals of below (above) standard efficiency thus represents less (more) value than that simple quantity of labour time. If production is under capitalist relations, there is a tendency for socially necessary abstract labour time (value) to gravitate toward the specific labour time embodied by the most efficient producer, as the less efficient are driven out of operation.

Exchange value is the abstract labour time which a commodity commands in exchange. Price is the denomination of exchange value in the universally equivalent commodity, money.[36] Values and exchange values diverge for a multitude of reasons: (1) they diverge systematically due to the contradiction between social production and private appropriation which requires the transformation process by which the rate of profit tends to equalise across branches of industry;[37] (2) they diverge with regard to their sum due to failures to realize all value (in which case total value is greater than total exchange value); (3) they diverge commodity-by-commodity due to 'supply and demand' in the short run; and (4) they diverge for any one commodity because all capitalists in an industry do not produce with equal efficiencies, so specific labour times (for one capital or capitals) may be below the prevailing value and others above, and socially necessary labour time is in flux. Thus, the essence of the value-exchange value relationship, and the value-price relationship, is that while there is a general law that relates them (the law of value), they

35 Marx 1970a, p. 66 ff.

36 'Price is the converted form in which the exchange value of commodities appears in the circulation process' (Marx, 1970a: 66).

37 For discussion of this, in which the distinction between value and exchange value is developed, see Shaikh 1977a.

are never equal except momentarily and accidentally.[38] It is a question of a tendency versus equilibrium.

This distinction, between value and exchange value, is the key to understanding what Amin has demonstrated. His statement that commodities are exchanged internationally, in and of itself, establishes only that there is a common price for a given commodity when quantities of the same type of commodity, produced in different countries, meet in a common market. Once quantities of the same commodity – say wheat – meet in a common market, the conditions under which they are produced are irrelevant to the buyer of the commodity. He is concerned only with the particular use value characteristic of the commodity. But this does not negate the fact that the different quantities were produced under different circumstances, whether these circumstances differ as to the social relations of production or the degree of the development of the productive forces within certain social relations.[39] Amin deduces a common value from a momentarily common price. In effect, he is arguing that the value of a commodity is determined by its exchange value, that the incidental equation of exchange value results in the equating of the value produced per unit of time in different work processes. In short, he totally liquidates the process of production, treating production as merely a moment in circulation, whose technical and social characteristics are derivative from exchange. This approach is explicit in his statement that 'commodities are primarily world wide'; i.e., they are not primarily the consequence of concrete labour carried out in a social context of human activity, but are first and foremost exchange values. This is the reverse of Marx's procedure; more importantly, it stands reality on its head. The fact that quantities of a commodity momentarily exchange for equal amounts of labour time, does not imply 'the same quantity of labour used up in different parts of the world ... gives rise to a single world value', it gives rise momentarily to a single world exchange value (and price). It does not imply this because 'the same quantity of labour used up in different parts of the world' refers to concrete labour, the actual human effort expended in production while 'a single world value' refers to abstract labour. That is, in the process of producing commodities, people expend a certain amount of time in particular, concrete tasks. Through interaction with other producers (competition),

38 Marx 1970a, p. 66.

39 Marx writes: 'No matter what the basis on which products are produced, which are thrown into circulation as commodities – whether on the basis of the primitive community, of slave production, of small peasant and petty bourgeois, or the capitalist basis, the character of products as commodities is not altered ...' (Marx, 1971, III: 325).

the products of different producers exchange against money at a common ratio. But the fact that different producers use up different amounts of effort is not altered by the common price.

A simple example demonstrates this. Assume we have two workers filling similar tanks with water from a river; one worker uses a bucket and the other a pump (hand-driven, say); and assume that the second worker, using a pump, can transfer ten times as much water in a working day as the worker with the bucket. When they sell the water in the same market, it will command a certain exchange value per gallon, regardless of whether it has been supplied by bucket or pump. The value of water is determined by some weighted average of the two processes, not by the more efficient alone, and a single price does not imply 'the same quantity of labour used up'. Presumably, Amin would argue that because one worker is more efficient, he will eliminate the other from operation. While this is a tendency, it is a tendency only under certain social relations of production.[40] If production is being carried out under petty-commodity production, there is no reason why the less efficient producer should be driven out of production; the less efficient producer merely has a lower standard of living. In fact, this precisely is why, in all backward countries, one finds low-productivity peasant production of commodities like coffee, sugar, and peanuts, side by side with highly mechanised plantation production of the same commodities. And to the extent that the plantations tend to eliminate peasant production, this is not solely, or even primarily in many cases, due to greater efficiency. We pursue this point below in our discussion of so-called 'primitive accumulation'.

It is incorrect to think that the exchange value of a commodity (water in our example) is determined by the most efficient producer ('where wheat productivity is highest', in Amin's example). First, this denies the existence of above-average profits that result from capitalists seizing upon technical advances before their competitors do.[41] Amin's treatment of this question is essentially neoclassical, for in that analysis it is assumed that all producers operate with the same 'production function'. Second, and related, the role of supply and demand is liquidated, an error which is the result of equating value and exchange value. It is implicitly assumed that the most efficient producer can supply the entire demand for the use value in question. While Nebraska and Kansas may be large, few would argue that these areas actually do or potentially can replace all the wheat producers in the underdeveloped world. But for Amin's argument, this must be the case. Otherwise, the export of US wheat to

40 Brenner 1977 develops this in detail, showing that it is not primarily through exchange that pre-capitalist social relations of production are eliminated.

41 Marx 1971b, Chapters 9 and 10.

Latin America (say) merely results in greater-than-average profits for US wheat producers as they sell their wheat above its specific value, and a drop in price of wheat in Peru, the extent of the drop depending on the relative magnitude of imports to domestic production. This, of course, is what actually occurs.

In this formalistic line of argument, Amin in fact liquidates the law of value as a theoretical tool. In his logical formalism, exchange value is primary, determining all phenomena, and value is purely passive. In contrast to this approach, the law of value is not a theory of pricing, but a mechanism which explains the variation and diversity of the sphere of appearances, of which prices are a part. Amin's formalism notwithstanding, the same commodity does command different exchange values at the same moment in time, differences which are not the result of transportation costs alone. The law of value, which explains them by differences in the productive application of labour power to the means of production. Differences in the productivity of labour are an empirical fact, substantiated by common sense as well as numerous comparative studies. Marxian analysis, the law of value and its operation, predicts such differences and uses them to explain variations in exchange values.

We have sought to show that the fact that there is a daily quotation for most commodities in an institutional setting involving buyers and sellers from different countries does not imply that 'the labour-hour in all countries creates the same value'. That is to say, it does not imply that the labour time required for the production of a specific commodity is the same in different countries. It simply means that such a market institution exists. Further, it does not imply that price quotation applies in every market where the commodity in question is bought and sold. The germ of truth in Amin's analysis is that under capitalist relations of production different levels of efficiency by different capitals tend to give rise to the centralisation of capital as the more efficient capitals assert their productive efficiency through underselling the less efficient capitals. But this is a tendency among capitals (e.g., not among capitalist producers and peasant producers), and is a tendency which is closely related to the process Amin implicitly denies, the law of the uneven development of the productive forces.

Amin is at pains to establish his 'world values' because they provide the basis of surplus extraction in his analysis. At one point, he actually estimates the total surplus extracted from backward countries by this mechanism.[42] As we pointed out, the surplus extraction argument in the form of 'unequal exchange' is incomplete as an explanation of underdevelopment, because of the capital flows to backward countries which it necessarily implies. Amin's solution to

42 Amin 1976, pp. 142–5.

this quandary is underconsumptionism. His use of underconsumptionist theory is in essence the same as Marini's, so we need not analyse it in detail. For Amin, the basic problem in capitalist society is that 'the spontaneous tendency of the system is in fact to lower the level of wages, to maximize the rate of surplus value ...'[43] It may not be obvious why this is a problem, since capitalists produce for the purpose of profit. It is a problem according to Amin, however, because accumulation is limited by realization – if surplus value is too great a portion of net value, value cannot be realized; Marini's position also.

This problem, if not resolved, allegedly has been contained in the developed capitalist countries by rising wages. In Amin's words, '... since the second world war, conditions have emerged at the centre (i.e., developed capitalist countries) for this movement to be controlled through a "social contract" of a social-democratic nature'.[44] Thus, income redistribution has stabilised the tendency of the rate of surplus value to rise. But this is not the case in the 'periphery', 'with expansion being forbidden or very restricted',[45] because of low wages and the corresponding smallness of the market.[46] While his treatment is not too clear, he must be arguing that due to the very restricted size of the home market in backward countries, the size of the investment inflow which will saturate that market and equalise profit rates internationally is relatively small. In its own terms, it is a logically consistent argument: lower wages in the 'periphery' result in higher profit rates; the movement of capital from the centre equalises these profit rates and results in 'unequal exchange' ('surplus extraction'); and because of the smallness of the peripheral market, the actual capital inflow is too small to result in significant accumulation.

We have sought to demonstrate that Amin's work is very much in the 'surplus extraction' or 'dependency' school. Because of his heavy stress on the realization of value as a barrier to accumulation, it might be thought that this

---

43 Amin 1973, p. 31; and Amin 1976, Chapter 2.

44 Amin 1973, p. 31. The 'movement' referred to is either the cyclical process of crisis and boom, or the 'spontaneous' tendency for wages to fall and surplus value to rise; in either case, the meaning of the sentence is the same, since the first is caused by the second in Amin's analysis. He is quite clear that it is realization and nothing else which causes crises. Speaking of the tendency of the rate of profit to fall, he writes, "But although this law manifests itself through the cycle, it is not the *cause* of the cycle, which lies in the combined effect of the evolution of the capacity to consume, which does not increase as does the capacity to produce (owing to the increasing share of income taken by profit), and of the immediate prospect of profitability, which guides investment ..." (Amin 1976, p. 98).

45 Amin 1973, p. 32.

46 He argues that 'peripheral' capitalists squander their surplus value as consumption, so do not generate accumulation.

represents a separate (if, however, related) explanation of underdevelopment. Such is not the case: since all capitalist economies suffer from this problem if any do, underconsumptionism in and of itself cannot explain why some capitalist countries develop and others do not. Surplus extraction is a necessary 'keylink' here. The complementarity of the two theses was demonstrated in the analysis of Marini, and again with Amin.

6 Breaking with Dependency Theory: Cardoso's Critique

A number of the points we have raised in opposition to the surplus extraction thesis and dependency theory in general have been taken up by Cardoso in his recent work (1977). In his earlier work, Cardoso was an underconsumptionist, placing emphasis upon the search for markets as the cause of imperialism.[47] However, he apparently breaks with this, characterising it as 'vulgar' and generating 'a relatively impoverished political analysis'.[48] This is a major criticism, coming as it does from probably the most respected member of the dependency school; and it is particularly telling against Marini (whom he discusses explicitly) and Amin (whom he does not).

More important from a methodological viewpoint, Cardoso points out that early dependency writers in Latin America stressed the role of social relations of production, particularly during the colonial period. As we have pointed out, it is exactly this emphasis which is lacking in subsequent writings. Cardoso, too, sees this as unacceptable analytically – 'the approach ought to be historical, and it therefore starts from the emergence of social formation'.[49] Thus, he rejects the view that liquidates internal causes of backwardness and places all emphasis upon the external.

---

47 Cardoso seems to have believed that Lenin was an underconsumptionist also: 'In Lenin's interpretation the imperialist economies needed external expansion for the realisation of capital accumulation' (Cardoso 1972, p. 90). This is not our interpretation of Lenin, who wrote: 'But what about the foreign market? Do we deny that capitalism needs a foreign market? Of course not. But the question of a foreign market has absolutely nothing to do with the question of realisation, and the attempt to link them into one whole merely expresses … the romantic inability to think logically' (Lenin 1972a, p. 162). The same point is found in *Capital*. In discussing realisation, Marx writes: 'The involvement of foreign commerce in analysing the annually produced value of products can therefore only confuse without contributing any new element of the problem, or of its solution. For this reason it must be entirely discarded' (Marx 1956, p. 286).

48 Cardoso 1977, p. 21.

49 Cardoso 1977, p. 13.

However, as important as Cardoso's critique is, it does not break sufficiently with the method he sees as erroneous. After stressing the necessity of a historical approach which analyses the relations of production, he elaborates:

> Underdevelopment then comes to be seen not merely as a process which is a concomitant of the expansion of mercantile capitalism and recurs under industrial capitalism, but as one which is actually generated by them ... The approach ought also to emphasize the specificity of dependency situations, as against societies in the countries of the economic center.[50]

It would not seem a distortion to interpret this as saying that it is not enough ('not merely') to see underdevelopment as the consequence of external factors, but that one 'ought also' to analyse the social relations of production particular to the backward areas. Such a formulation of one's method makes dependency analysis more sophisticated, but retains its fundamental errors. This approach places external and internal contradictions on the same level of importance. As such, it is an eclectic treatment, wherein one appears to be considering the complexity of causes, but in actuality is not. The thrust of Cardoso's argument is that external causes are primary, but their impact is mediated or assumes different forms as a consequence of internal circumstances. This approach results in a stress upon elements which are absent in the backward country. These absent elements are then raised to the level of explanation, when they are in fact characteristics of backwardness which call for explanation. In the case of Baran and Frank the absent element is the surplus itself; for Marini, Emmanuel,[51] and Amin, it is the absence of higher wages; and in Cardoso's case, in his latest works, it is the absence of the production of the means of production.[52]

The fundamental error in each case is that the authors do not accept that every class society is propelled in its evolution by the contradiction between the forces and the relations of production. This contradiction gives rise to class conflict, the conflict between the appropriating class and the class of direct

---

50 Cardoso 1977, p. 13.

51 Emmanuel, consistent with his approach, treats wage differences as 'initial conditions': 'Once a country has got ahead, through some historical accident, even if this be merely that a harsher climate has given men additional needs, this country starts to make other countries pay for its high wage level through unequal exchange. From that point onward, the impoverishment of one country becomes an increasing function of the enrichment of another ...' (Emmanuel 1972, p. 130).

52 Cardoso, 1977, p. 20.

producers. This generalisation, that class struggle is the motive force of history, applies to all social formations, regardless of whether those formations emerged as a consequence of external influences. Perhaps the clearest case is of slavery in the New World. This was a system wholly 'imposed' or created by external force; it did not exist prior to the spread of mercantile capitalism; indeed, the class of direct producers was forceably created through warfare fostered or exploited by mercantile capital in Africa, and then the captives were transported to the New World. But once the slave society was created, its further evolution was primarily determined by the class struggle internal to it, between slave and master.[53]

Cardoso is correct in stressing the need to analyse the social relations of production in backward countries. But these social relations should be analysed in relation to the contradictory role they play vis-à-vis the forces of production.

7 Summary

While the discussion to this point has been critical, its result has not been negative; we have not merely sought to point out errors, but to point them out in a way which can carry the analysis forward. Stress has been placed on the source of theoretical errors, rather than on the errors themselves, and we are now in a position to sum up the elements which must be present in order to proceed. First, a scientifically sound analysis of backwardness must be based on the concept of mode of production, on a scientific understanding of the exploitation of labour in the social form of labour power, and on an analysis of the contradiction between the forces of production and the social relations of production. In other words, an analysis of the inequality among countries must start from an understanding of the contradictions internal to that country. This is not to exclude external relations. On the contrary, an analysis of the export of capital must necessarily be an important part of any analysis of the uneven development of capitalism in the stage of imperialism. But a scientific understanding of backwardness can neither restrict itself only to an analysis of relations in exchange, nor can it begin with this. Exchange can only be properly understood if it follows from, and forms part of, the analysis of production. Second, to understand the capital-

53 Brenner makes an analogous argument in the case of colonial Virginia (Brenner 1977, pp. 88–90).

ist mode of production, the twofold nature of commodities is key, providing the basis for analysing wage levels, profits and exchange itself. Finally, the latter distinction needs to be carried forward to a distinction between value and exchange value, in order to understand how conditions in the sphere of production manifest themselves in phenomena in exchange, that value rules exchange rather than exchange ruling value.[54] On this basis we can proceed.

7.1 *The Development of Capitalism*

7.1.1 Introduction

In this section we develop the basis for a scientific analysis of the causes of backwardness. First, we show that capitalism develops primarily as a consequence of the emergence of new class relations. We do this briefly, since Brenner (1977) has provided a thorough elaboration of this argument in his critique of Wallerstein and Sweezy. Second, we consider the role of merchant's capital, in order to contrast its effect on backward countries and its role in international exchange to that of industrial capital.

7.1.2 So-Called Primitive Accumulation

To understand the origin of the inequality among countries it is necessary to understand how the capitalist mode of production first developed. This is because capitalism has certain general laws that characterise its development. We analyse some of these laws in order to critique the widespread view that crucial to the emergence of capitalism was the looting and plundering of colonies in the seventeenth and eigthteenth centuries, and the corollary of this proposition that such looting and plundering – in more sophisticated form (surplus extraction) – remains a major basis of the wealth of capitalist countries.

The term 'primitive accumulation', which is found in the works of many Marxists, did not originate with Marx; and it is at the outset of his discussion of this phenomenon that we find Marx at his most sarcastic and caustic,[55] heaping ridicule upon those who argued that the emergence of capitalism was presaged by a period of the accumulation of capital in money or commodity form; further, the part of *Capital* discussing this phenomenon is entitled 'The So-called "Primitive Accumulation"'.[56] While at points Marx could be interpreted as sug-

54 Marx 1970a, pp. 84–5.

55 This primitive accumulation plays in Political Economy about the same part as original sin in theology (Marx 1906, p. 784).

56 Marx 1906, Part VIII.

gesting that European capitalism arose as the result of the exploitation of the resources of the colonial world,[57] it is clear that he did not see this as either a necessary nor a sufficient condition for the development of the capitalist mode of production in Europe. But more important, it does not follow from the laws of development of capitalism that such was the case; though obviously plunder and looting of the overseas pre-capitalist areas was not accidental. Such plunder and looting must be seen as the international extension of a process occurring in the incipient capitalist countries themselves. In Marx's words, 'The so-called primitive accumulation, therefore, is nothing else than the historical process of divorcing the producer from the means of production'.[58]

Thus, contrary to the political economists of the time, Marx recognised that capitalism was a historically specific mode of production, and that its emergence as dominant was the consequence of the dispossession of labour from the land. In recognising this, he swept away the veil of bourgeois apology for the factory system:

> One does not perceive, when looking at the large manufactories and the large firms, that they are originated from the throwing into one of many small centres of production, and have been built up by the expropriation of many small independent producers ... the expropriation and eviction

57 For example: 'Whilst the cotton industry introduced child-slavery in England, it gave in the United States a stimulus to the transformation of the earlier, more or less patriarchal slavery, into a system of commercial exploitation. In fact, the veiled slavery of the wage-earners in Europe needed, for its pedestal, slavery pure and simple in the New World' (Marx 1906, p. 833). Marx mentions plunder of colonies and other non-European areas at a number of points, but primarily as examples of the barbarity and hypocrisy of capitalism. For example he points to 'extirpation, enslavement and entombment in mines of the aboriginal population ... the conquest and looting of the East Indies, the turning of Africa into a warren for the commercial hunting of black-skins ... as the "chief moments of primitive accumulation"' (Marx 1906, p. 823, emphasis added). He also writes, 'The treasures captured outside of Europe by undisguised looting, enslavement, and murder, floated back to the mother-country and were there turned into capital' (Marx 1906, p. 826). But nowhere does he argue that such looting was the basis of capitalist accumulation; on the contrary, even a casual reading shows he stressed the expropriation of the European peasant and artisanal classes as the foundation of capitalist accumulation. He lists the colonial system as only one way that money-capital was accumulated, along with the growth of national debts, agricultural taxation and tariff protection of industry. He saw the plunder of colonies no more crucial than, for example, the 'enchanter's wand' of credit, whereby 'the public debt becomes one of the most powerful levers of primitive accumulation' (Marx 1906, p. 827).

58 Marx 1906, p. 786.

> of a part of the agricultural population not only set free for industrial capital, the labourers, their means of subsistence, and material for labour; it also created the home market.[59]

The destruction of the agricultural labourer and artisan[60] not only created the source of surplus product for capitalists (which under capitalism takes the form of surplus value), but also created the market in which this surplus value would be realized as profit. The control of colonies was neither the basis of pre-capitalist accumulation nor the market in which the products of capitalist enterprise were realized in money form.[61] When Marx writes of capital coming into the world 'dripping from head to foot, from every pore, with blood and dirt', the blood referred to is largely that of the European peasantry and artisan classes.[62] This destruction of pre-capitalist social relations was a social disruption rivalling historical precedent, and in this process were simultaneously created the conditions for capital's existence.[63]

That Marx said these things and held this general position does not make them correct. What is important is the method he used. Using the materialist method, he argued that it is the contradiction between the forces and relations of production which moves society forward; that is, the contradictions internal to a society determine society's development. Thus, the emergence of capitalist social relations was (and is) the consequence of the contradictions within the old mode of production. These contradictions are intensified by external influences – trade with other societies, political domination, plunder, etc. External influences may result in the exploiting class being unable to rule in the old way, and the exploited class being unable to live in the old way; the social relations which result from such a situation emerge out of the contradictions

59 Marx 1906, p. 819.

60 Marx was the first to recognise that capitalism extolls the form of private property by negating its essence:

> The capitalist mode of appropriation, the result of the capitalist mode of production, produces capitalist private property. This is the first negation of individual private property, as found on the labour of the proprietor (Marx, 1974, I: 715).

61 Lenin, in his attack of the Narodnik economists for the view that foreign markets are necessary to capitalist realization, writes, "The mistake [of the Narodnik writers] … is that they bring in the foreign market to explain the realisation of surplus value …. The need for a capitalist country to have a foreign market is not determined at all by the laws of the realisation of the social product" (Lenin, 1972b, p. 65).

62 He is paraphrasing Marie Augier on the development of money (Marx 1906, p. 834).

63 Again, see Lenin's excellent discussion of this for Russia and his biting critique of the position that capitalist development in general requires external exploitation for its accumulation process (Lenin 1972b, Chapter 1).

between these two classes. Merchant's capital, as a specific historical example of external influence, demonstrates this dialectic of external and internal contradictions.

7.1.3 Merchant's Capital and International Exchange

Part of the confusion about the role of colonial domination and surplus extraction from colonies in the development of capitalism derives from a misunderstanding of the role of merchant's capital in the development of capitalism. Basically, merchant's capital was the form of capital without the essence of capital as a social relation. It has the form of capital in that it is self-expanding,[64] but it lacks the essence in that it is not characterised by capitalist relations of production.

> Since merchant's capital is penned in the sphere of circulation, and since its function consists exclusively of promoting the exchange of commodities, it requires no other conditions for its existence ... outside those necessary for the simple circulation of commodities and money ... No matter what the basis on which products are produced ... whether the basis of the primitive community, of slave production, of small peasant and petty bourgeois, or the capitalist basis, the character of the products as commodities is not altered ...[65]

The merchant capitalist derives his profit in the sphere of circulation. While this form of profit making was quite important at a particular historical period, it cannot be so under capitalist relations of production and cannot be an explanation of the inequality among countries in the present epoch of capitalism, a point we develop below. While the merchant capitalist realizes his profit in the sphere of circulation, it derives from a process more complex than that of merely buying cheap and selling dear, this is only the form of the phenomenon. The merchant capitalist is a middle man; he is the intermediary between direct producers. Before the development of capitalism, the merchant capitalist controlled trade between communities. Essential to his realization of profit was the isolation of communities; i.e. monopolising the contact between isolated com-

---

64 'Its form is always M–C–M′. Money, the independent form of exchange value, is the point of departure, and increasing the exchange-value an end in itself ... This M–C–M′ distinguishes it from C–M–C, trade in commodities directly between producers, which has for its ultimate end the exchange of use-values' (Marx 1971, III, p. 222).

65 Marx 1971, p. 222.

munities. This is the antithesis of international trade under capitalism, which is trade among areas integrated into the same system of production and reproduction.

The analysis of the circulation of merchant's capital, and, therefore, of the profit of merchant's capital, is made difficult because merchant's capital emerged and matured prior to the general production of commodities. Merchant's capital emerged, in other words, prior to the development of capitalism – the exploitation of labour in the form of wage labour. As a consequence, we cannot employ the law of value to explain the conditions of exchange and reproduction under merchant's capital, except very late in the era of merchant's capital when industrial capital is replacing it. Surplus value is not the source of profit for merchant's capital, prior to the development of value as a social category; surplus value presupposes value; value presupposes the general production of commodities; and the generalised production of commodities presupposes free wage labour. When communities are under pre-capitalist social relations, and their trade mediated by merchant's capital, there is no tendency for cost-prices to equalise among communities, whatever the social basis of these monetary calculations.[66] The commercial isolation of communities, which merchant monopolies maintain, is not the reason that cost prices do not equalize. Exchange itself does not transform productive relations; it merely establishes a single price in a particular exchange. It is the social relations themselves, their pre-capitalist nature, which prevents such equalisation. Merchant's capital takes advantage of these cost differences which are embedded in pre-capitalist social relations, buying when commodities are exchanged cheaply and selling when they exchange dearly. In addition to differences in social relations, these cost differences may be the consequence of natural variations, such as climate and soil fertility. The limiting cases of such trade involve products so dependent upon the specific circumstances provided by nature that they cannot be produced at all in some communities – e.g., tea, spices, certain minerals, etc.

Merchant's capital expands by virtue of not subjecting the process of production to capital: i.e., it is the antithesis of industrial capital.[67] Merchant's

---

66 For a theoretical discussion of the material basis of economic calculations under different social relations, see Bettelheim (1975). Specifically on economic calculations in the context of feudalism, see Kula (1976: chapters 6 and 7). Kula's book deals with Poland, 1500–1800, for the most part.

67 'The independent and predominant development of capital as merchant's capital is tantamount to the non-subjection of production to capital, and hence to capital developing on the basis of an alien social mode of production which is also independent of it' (Marx, 1971, p. 223).

capital is not a mode of production; it is rather a system of commerce, superimposed upon, or between, modes of production. This reflects the fact that merchant capitalists organise exchange, not production. It is for this reason that the development of merchant's capital does not give rise to the capitalist mode of production, whose essence lies in the buying of labour power and marshalling it on the field of production in large concentrations.[68] While trade between communities, mediated by the merchant capitalist, increases the exchange of products (for external trade), it can do so primarily by reinforcing pre-capitalist relations of production and intensifying their oppressive mechanisms.[69] The development of feudalism in more rigid form than before in Spain and Russia as a consequence of trade is an example of this.[70]

Since merchant's capital obtains profit by buying at one price and selling at another, it follows by definition that an unequal exchange has occurred in such a transaction, and a portion of a surplus product has been appropriated by the merchant capitalist. But this unequal exchange is of a particular type, and its consequences upon backward countries do not primarily result from the appropriated surplus itself, but from the method of appropriation. The backward areas with which merchant's capital dealt were pre-capitalist formations, and merchant's capital was not involved in production. The latter implies that merchant's capital could raise its profits either by increasing the volume of trade, or by forcing harsher terms upon the other party involved in the exchange; it could not raise profits, in general, through greater efficiency, since the only productive activity it was involved in was transportation. The

68 The debate between Sweezy, on the one hand, and Dobb, Takahashi, Hilton and Hill, on the other, on the transition from feudalism to capitalism, is over this issue (see Sweezy et al., 1976). See also Romagnolo 1975. Romagnolo shows that the Trotskyist theory of 'permanent revolution' derives in part from the error of analyzing the rise of capitalism as a result of the spread of commodity exchange. Marx was clear in rejecting exchange as the force generating capitalism. Speaking of the merchant exerting direct control over production, Marx observes, "The system represents everywhere an obstacle to the real capitalist mode of production and goes under with its development. Without revolutionizing the mode of production, [merchant's capital] only worsens the condition of the direct producers, turns them into mere wage-workers and proletarians under conditions worse than those under the immediate control of capital, and appropriates their surplus labour on the basis of the old mode of production" (Marx, 1971, III: 334–335). This shows one aspect of the progressive nature of the capitalist mode of production in contrast to merchant's capital which exploits labour without developing the productive forces. See Brenner's critique of Wallerstein's concept of 'systems of labour control', which the latter implicitly substitutes for the concept of 'mode of production' (Brenner, 1977, pp. 29–33).

69 Laclau 1971; see Sweezy et al. 1976.

70 Kula 1976.

nature of the pre-capitalist formations with which merchant's capital deals sets strict limits to both sources of increased profits. On the one hand, the level of development of the productive forces in pre-capitalist society is low; on the other, the contradiction between the forces and relations of production does not give rise to the continuous and necessary development of the productive forces. Harsher terms in trade or greater volume of trade are satisfied primarily by more intense exploitation of direct producers. This intensification is affected absolutely by the pre-capitalist ruling class, through rigidifying servile social relations of production. To the extent that the pre-capitalist class was historically unable to accomplish this, merchant's capital turned to conquest, looting and plundering, or direct military rule of societies, as in India.[71]

The necessity to raise the surplus product extracted absolutely led to the disastrous impact of merchant's capital upon pre-capitalist (colonial or semicolonial) societies. The actual extraction of surplus, while the motivation for the barbaric rule of merchant's capital, does not explain backwardness. A surplus product of itself is not a source of accumulation and expanded reproduction. It gives rise to these consequences only when it is appropriated within capitalist relations of production, as surplus value. To argue that the loss of surplus product itself is the cause of backwardness is to see accumulation (or, more generally, economic development) as purely a quantitative process.[72] It is also to assume that all the necessary conditions for accumulation were present in pre-capitalist societies prior to the spread of merchant's capital and the world market. The basis for accumulation is a particular set of social relations, not the availability of a surplus product.

In summary, the important effect of merchant's capital in the era of New World Colonialism, its heyday, was the rigidification and mutation of pre-capitalist modes of production, and the duplication of itself in backward countries in the form of comprador classes allied with local pre-capitalist ruling classes. Merchant's capital, due to its nature, did not develop the capitalist mode of production; it did not expropriate the peasantry and generate a class of free wage labourers, but tended to reinforce pre-capitalist social relations, and to extract surplus product through those social relations. 'Outbargaining and cheating' (as well as violence and plunder) are the form of the expansion of merchant's capital, but these forms mask the more fundamental consequences, which were the class developments inherent in them.

71 Baran 1957, p. 144 ff.; Bettelheim 1972a.

72 Marx 1970a, chapter XXV.

7.2 *Capitalism and Uneven Development*

7.2.1 The Law of Value and Exchange

Our purpose in analysing the process of 'primitive accumulation' and merchant's capital has been to demonstrate their role in laying the preconditions for the capitalist mode of production. Taken together, these elements create the possibility for the capitalist mode of production. The development of merchant's capital provides a source of wealth independent of landed property and extends commodity circulation; so-called primitive accumulation generates the expropriated labourer with only his labour power to sell.[73] Their union on an expanding scale is the capitalist mode of production.[74] In its method of appropriation, industrial capital is the antithesis of merchant's capital, and the power and significance of the latter declines as that of the former expands. Merchant's capital derives profit from the monopolisation of trade between isolated communities, and this isolation is shattered by expansion of the capitalist mode of production. The contradiction between industrial and merchant's capital arises from the fact that the latter expands on the basis of an increased mass of use values in circulation regardless of how they are produced, but the former expands through the production of those use values as commodities, commodities which are at every stage capital. While merchant's capital coexisted with pre-capitalist modes, industrial capital, in one form or other, must continually assault the pre-capitalist structures where it encounters them in order to secure the basis of its future source of value, labour power.[75] The attempt to do this does not preclude the creation of 'blocking' forces which reinforce backwardness.[76]

The essential difference between merchant's and industrial capital, described above, gives rise to a second fundamental difference at the next level of abstraction: inherent in the reproduction of merchant's capital is monopoly power, while inherent in the reproduction of industrial capital is competition.[77]

73 "... the capitalist mode of production and accumulation, and therefore capitalist private property, have for their fundamental condition the annihilation of self-earned private property; in other words, the expropriation of the labourer" (Marx, 1974, I: 724).

74 'The historical conditions of [capitalism's] existence are by no means given with the mere circulation of money and commodities. It can only spring into life, only when the owner of the means of production and subsistence meets in the market with the free labourer selling his labour-power' (Marx 1906, p. 189).

75 Referring to colonies, Marx writes, 'Where the capitalist has at his back the power of the mother-country, he tries to clear out of his way by force, the modes of production and appropriation, based on the independent labour of the producer' (Marx 1906, p. 838).

76 Bettelheim 1972a, pp. 289ff.

77 To quote Marx: "... conceptually, competition is nothing other than the inner nature of

Adam Smith's attacks upon the state-protected mercantilist monopolies of his time, on the one hand, and the extolling of the virtues of competition ('the invisible hand'), on the other, were the ideological reflections of this antithesis of merchant monopoly versus industrial competition.

In the production of value under the bourgeois mode of production, the conditions for competition are always present. The necessary conditions for bourgeois production – free wage labour and a market in the means of production – mean that the possibility of capital marshalling the forces of production for an invasion of branches of industry where the rate of profit is low and the advance into those where it is high, which brings about the operation of the fundamental law of capitalist reproduction, the law of value. The law of value does not result in commodities being sold at their values in the sense that prices stand in the same proportion to values in all branches of industry.[78] One of the contradictions of the capitalist mode of production is that while total surplus value determines total profit and changes in value determine changes in price, values and prices are not identical: prices are transformed values. As a result, there is a redistribution of surplus value (therefore, of value) between branches of industry, in which industries with a higher organic composition of capital realize as profit more surplus value than is produced in those branches, and vice-versa for branches with lower than average organic compositions of capital. Inherent in the reproduction of social capital as a whole is the transfer of value; some commodities sell below value and others above value as a result of the movement of capital tending to reduce differences in profit rates in different branches of industry.[79]

Thus, inherent in the law of value is the necessity of the transfer of value, and this results from differing value compositions of capital. This transfer occurs whether the differing value compositions of capital vary because of technical factors or because in some industries the prevailing wage is lower. If in two industries everything is the same except the wage is lower in one, then the movement of capital would result in a tendency for the price in the low wage industry to fall relatively to the price in the high wage industry. Within a mature capitalist society, exchange values are determined on the basis of value by the

capital, its essential character, appearing in and realized as the reciprocal interaction of many capitals ..." (Marx, 1973:414). For an analysis of Marx's theory of competition, see Weeks (1981).

78 Shaikh 1977a.

79 This transfer of value is the basis for the illusion that fixed constant capital (machinery, buildings, etc.) creates value. For a discussion of this 'illusion created by competition' (as Marx called it), see Weeks 1981.

movement of capital to equalise profit rates, where these differences in profit rates are due to technical differences among production processes, particular to each industry, with the same rate of surplus value (exploitation labour) on each.

CHAPTER 10

Class Alliances and Class Struggle in Peru

Elizabeth Dore and John Weeks

The Peruvian regime which came to power in October, 1968, led by President Juan Velasco Alvarado, assumed many of the forms associated with progressive movements. It nationalised with compensation several foreign and national capitals, instituted a sweeping agrarian reform, and initiated industrial and mining communities, whose stated goals were to provide for worker participation in the distribution of profits. The government heralded all of these measures with anti-imperialist rhetoric. It proclaimed that Peru would be neither capitalist nor communist, but would pursue a 'third way', a Peruvian path to economic development. On the one hand, the rhetoric and the forms of these government-created institutions appeared progressive; on the other hand, the state moved to brutally smash strikes and repress peasant land occupations.

The leadership of the working class, the peasantry, and their allies in Peru were faced with deciding whether they should support the government, and if so, what form this support should take. Within the Peruvian left an important debate emerged as to the class nature of the regime, the contradictions between imperial capital and the Peruvian state, and the correct role for Marxist-Leninists. Outside of Peru, progressives were likewise faced with the task of analysing the Peruvian regime in order to determine whether or not it should be supported and to what degree.

In this essay we present some of the elements which are necessary to determine the class nature of the Peruvian regime, and which will aid Marxist-Leninists in deciding whether or not to support the government, and when that support might be appropriate. It was only through discussions with Peruvian comrades that we have been able to develop the analysis which follows and the political conclusions drawn from it.

1 Classes and the Mode of Production

An analysis of Peru, as with any society, must begin by determining the dominant mode of production. That is, it must determine how production is organised – whether goods are produced in pre-capitalist relations of production or if capitalist social relations of production have become dominant. The mode of

 | DOI:10.1163/9789004703193_012

production is determined by how the surplus produced in society is appropriated. In pre-capitalist modes of production, such as the tribute-communal mode and the feudal mode, the masses of people produce their own means of subsistence, and the ruling class directly takes the surplus product, such as surplus corn. Alternatively, peasants may be required to cultivate the rulers' lands part of the month or year. In societies characterised by pre-capitalist social relations of production the surplus product is expropriated in its original and natural form.

Capitalism differs from these pre-capitalist modes of production in that the surplus product of the labourer is no longer appropriated in its natural form. Under capitalism, the worker does not work (say) four hours at home growing the wheat for bread, weaving clothes, etc., perhaps exchanging with other workers, and then reports to a factory to work free for the capitalist. However, what the worker does do under capitalism is *in principle no different from this*. Part of the working day all workers are labouring to produce their needs and the needs of their families. The rest of the working day is *surplus labour time*, which accrues to the capitalist in the form of commodities. This division of the working day is hidden by the payment of a money wage, which *appears* to compensate the worker for the entire day. Hidden also is the fact that one class, the working class, labours under the command of another, the capitalist class, and that the surplus product is appropriated, as in all class societies, from the direct producers by the exploiting class.[1]

From the mode of production derives the class structure of society. If capitalism is the dominant mode of production, the bourgeoisie controls the state and rules in its interests. Although in every society one mode of production is dominant, this does not mean that all other modes are immediately wiped out. The development of capitalism as the dominant mode of production is in every country a long struggle. Even where most of the surplus product of a society is appropriated through capitalist social relations of production, pre-capitalist modes can continue to exist and may become rigidified or transformed. Thus, while some products – primarily food – continue to be produced in pre-capitalist relations of production, the vast majority of the surplus of society is appropriated through capitalist relations of production.

Prior to the coup of 1968, Peru had been ruled for much of the twentieth century by an unstable alliance of capitalist agricultural and mineral exporters, finance capitalists, foreign capitalists and pre-capitalist expropriators. This

1 For a short discussion of capitalist social relations of production, see Marx 1970a, pp. 32–83. For a complete development see Marx 1976c.

alliance was fraught with conflict, for the Peruvian bourgeoisie struggled with its pre-capitalist partners to gain hegemony in the alliance and to ensure that the state adequately protected its interests. Because the ultimate goal of the bourgeoisie was to seize state power for itself and to smash its pre-capitalist allies, the capitalists were driven to try to constantly reduce, both in strength and in extension, the material base of the pre-capitalist allies (pre-capitalist relations of production).

Not only were there struggles between the bourgeoise and the pre-capitalist expropriators, there have also been fierce intra-bourgeois struggles. While capitalism has been the dominant mode of production in Peru for the past several decades, different fractions of the bourgeoisie have sought to control the state in their own particular interests. In keeping with a materialist analysis, first we must demarcate fractions of the Peruvian bourgeoisie according to their material base in production and not according to their political role. A class analysis is a scientific analysis rooted in a consideration of the social relations of production. While the relative strength of the different classes reflects their material base, class-conscious leadership provides the possibility that a class may gain the greatest advantages from its material strength to advance its interests and consolidate its power. The comprador bourgeoisie is 'part of the big native merchant bourgeoisie in the colonies and dependent countries who act as intermediaries between foreign capital and the local market'.[2] This fraction of the local bourgeoisie is wholly situated in the sphere of circulation. Its role is to facilitate the expansion of imperial capital in the oppressed country. Since it is not engaged in production, it has no contradictions with imperial capital. On the contrary, its entire existence depends upon the presence of the imperialists. The national bourgeoisie is made up of those capitalists who invest virtually all of their capital in production processes within the national boundaries and includes the owners of large monopoly capitals as well as the owners of small comparatively weak capitals. In Peru, the capital of the national bourgeoisie is found in all sectors of the economy: industry, manufacturing, fishmeal, mining and metal processing, sugar, etc.

The grand alliance which ruled Peru until 1968 included compradors, certain members of the national bourgeoisie, imperial capitalists, and pre-capitalist expropriators. The unifying force of this uneasy alliance was the common goal of facilitating exports. This conflicted with the interests of the emerging national industrial bourgeoisie whose capital was in manufacturing. Throughout the period 1960–8 the productive base of the grand alliance – extract-

2 Stalin 1975, p. 151.

ive industries and export agriculture – was declining while the manufacturing sector was expanding.[3] The national industrial bourgeoisie made repeated attempts to secure its grasp on state power in order to defend its interests. In 1963 this bourgeoisie in manufacturing was momentarily stronger than the other fractions of the bourgeoisie, and Fernando Belaunde Terry became the President of Peru as a weak representative of the interests of the national industrial bourgeoisie.[4] But the hegemony of this fraction of the bourgeoisie was brief. The members of the grand alliance perceived the threat to their continued control of the state and thus to the policies favouring exports. Through their control of the banking sector, they effectively strangled the industrial fraction of the bourgeoisie by withholding credit. Without removing Belaünde from the Presidency, the grand alliance quickly reassumed control of the state and continued the policy of favouring the extractive industries and export agriculture to the detriment of manufacturing.

The economic crisis beginning in 1967 provided the national industrial bourgeoisie with the possibility for another attempt at state power. Recognising that it was not yet strong enough to gain control through bourgeois elections, this fraction enlisted the armed forces to be both its front man and its force. Once holding the power, the national industrial bourgeoisie moved to eliminate the material base and through this, the power of the Peruvian partners of the grand alliance. Bourgeois democracy with its masquerade of harmonising conflicting interests through congresses and the like had proved inadequate for the national industrial bourgeoisie. Faced with extinction in the economic crisis, it ripped the facade of democracy off of the dictatorship of the bourgeoisie and ruled through the armed forces. Contrary to bourgeois interpretations of Peru which maintain that the military rules 'independently' and is 'above classes', the military rulers of Peru are the loyal agents of the national industrial bourgeoisie.

The coup of 1968 was the culmination of the Peruvian bourgeois revolution. This struggle began in the nineteenth century, but the possibility for its complete success could come only when capitalism developed as the dominant mode of production, when industrial capitalism dominated capitalism in agriculture, and when the material base and the power of the pre-capitalist ruling class was irrevocably weakened.

The national industrial bourgeoisie did not take on the entire grand alliance in its last, successful bid for power. The strongest partner of this alliance,

3 For a more detailed analysis of what follows, see Dore and Weeks 1976a.

4 Molinari and Gorman 1977.

imperial capital (primarily North American capital) was already finding that the grand alliance had outlived its usefulness. Whereas in previous decades the grand alliance had facilitated the introduction of foreign capital in mining, agriculture and banking, and the consequent growth of these sectors; in the 1960s the Peruvian partners of the grand alliance were placing obstacles in the path of further industrialisation. These obstacles were but straw men for imperial capital which could not be constrained from taking advantage of the higher profitability in industry, even if such action meant undermining the material base of its partners. And throughout the 1960s the portion of US foreign investment which went to industry was steadily growing.[5]

The relationship between the national industrial bourgeoisie and imperial capital was fraught with contradictions – a precarious unity of conflicting interests. Imperialism oppresses countries in the political sphere in order to facilitate the penetration of imperial capital and to secure its competitive advantage over the national capitals. While competition is inherent in capitalism, the possibility exists for the competitive struggle between the imperialists and the national bourgeoisie to be converted into a national struggle, with the national bourgeoisie playing an anti-imperialist role. The national bourgeoisie in general attempts to limit the expansion of imperial capital in its country in order to preserve for itself more of the profits produced in Peru.

With the intensification of the contradictions of capital on a world scale, the possibilities for the national bourgeoisie in oppressed countries to play this progressive role have been reduced. In the competitive struggle with imperial capital, the national bourgeoisie is at a great disadvantage. The Peruvian national bourgeoisie is no exception. The modernising or revolutionising of the means of production – machinery and technology – takes place primarily in the advanced industrial countries. This modernising constantly increases the productivity of labour – less and less labour power is needed to produce the same number of commodities. With production requiring less necessary labour time, each worker in the advanced industrial countries tends to produce more and more surplus value which is appropriated as profit by the imperialists – the capitalist class in the advanced industrial countries.[6]

Because of the lower level of the development of capitalism in Peru, the productive processes are not as efficient and more labour power is needed to produce a given number of commodities than is required in the advanced industrial countries. Because of this, the Peruvian national industrial bourgeoisie

5 Dore and Weeks 1976a, p. 64.

6 Dore and Weeks 1976b.

cannot produce as cheaply as the imperial capitalists and is at a potentially fatal disadvantage in the competitive struggle. Its inability to successfully compete with imperial capital compels the national industrial bourgeoisie to attempt to ally with its formidable rivals. Through such an alliance the national industrial bourgeoisie preserves for itself a portion of the production process closely integrated to imperial capital, avoids competing directly with its more efficient partners, and saves itself from destruction.

Of course, like all alliances this one is not static. The national industrial bourgeoisie is constantly trying to own and control more and more production processes within Peru and to appropriate for itself a larger portion of the surplus value produced by the Peruvian working class. The struggle within this unstable alliance has given the particular form of anti-imperialism to the Peruvian state. The national industrial bourgeoisie seeks to re-negotiate the terms of the alliance with imperial capital, but to do this it needs a popular base. Using nationalist rhetoric, it tried from 1968 to 1975 to appeal to the petty bourgeoisie and even to portions of the working class and the peasantry. In its rhetoric the national bourgeoisie cast all of the blame for Peru's economic backwardness on the imperialists. The free use of anti-imperialist rhetoric was intended to convince the Peruvian people that the imperialists were solely responsible for poverty and exploitation in Peru. The national bourgeoisie was and is careful not to implicate capitalism in this rhetoric because, through capitalist social relations of production, it continues to exploit the working class and appropriate profits. It continues to steer clear of any acknowledgement that classes exist at all in Peru and denies that the working class is exploited or the peasantry oppressed by the Peruvian bourgeoisie.

Obviously, the goal of the national bourgeoisie in Peru or elsewhere cannot be to overthrow capitalism. Rather, it hopes to develop and strengthen capitalism in Peru. Because of the advanced level of capitalist development in the imperialist countries, the national bourgeoisie recognises that strengthening capitalism can only be accomplished through an alliance with the strongest and most advanced capitalists of all – the imperialists. The main aspect of this contradictory alliance alters with the changes in the material conditions. While at all times this alliance is characterised by both unity and struggle, the comparative strength of imperial capital, of the national bourgeoisie, and of the proletariat affects the degree to which it is possible for the national bourgeoisie to struggle against imperialism. In periods of economic prosperity and the expansion of profits such as from 1969 to 1973 in Peru, the Peruvian national bourgeoisie utilised anti-imperialist rhetoric, occasionally but infrequently accompanied by concrete actions, in an attempt to extort from the imperial capitalists a larger portion of the profits produced in Peru. This anti-imperialist rhetoric was accompanied by nationalist appeals to the petty bourgeoisie. In these moments of prosperity the bourgeoisie could offer material rewards to the petty bourgeoisie in return for its support. While it promised the same to the working class, the national bourgeoisie was hard pressed to deliver. In the competitive economic struggle the imperial capitalists can raise the productivity of labour, which leads to an increase in relative surplus value. The national capitalists, struggling to re-negotiate the terms of the alliance to secure a bigger piece of the pie, do not have access to the technical innovations which will raise the productivity of labour to the same extent. It has no choice but to resort to more primitive means of extracting more absolute surplus value – lengthening the working day and speeding up production. This heightens the class struggle between the national bourgeoisie and the Peruvian proletariat. Upon seizing power, the Peruvian bourgeoisie made extravagant promises to the working class to enlist its support in the competitive struggle among capitals. The bourgeoisie instituted 'worker participation' in the ownership and management of some companies and profit-sharing plans. But as long as capitalism exists in Peru and the national bourgeoisie is engaged in a bitter struggle over the division of the spoils with the more efficient and stronger imperial capitalists, these promises could be fulfilled only momentarily. Instead, the national bourgeoisie was and is continually driven back to the shop floor to intensify the exploitation of the proletariat and to the countryside to increase the oppression of the peasantry.

While capital was expanding rapidly, the national bourgeoisie was able to pass on enough crumbs to the petty bourgeoisie to maintain the support of this vacillating class. In the period 1968–75 the state was also able to preserve more-or-less intact its nationalist and anti-imperialist facade, aided by the revisionist Peruvian Communist Party and a legion of petty-bourgeois propagandists, such as the former guerrilla leader, Hector Bejar. The economic crisis of 1975 shattered this image. In general, periods of crisis function to resolve the contradictions in the forces of production by great leaps in the processes of concentration and centralisation. The crisis itself momentarily restores the rate of profit by causing the smaller and less efficient capitals to be destroyed while the larger and more efficient capitals expand. In Peru the present crisis threatens the national industrial bourgeoisie with destruction. Rather than being presumptuous in the hopes of securing more advantageous terms in the alliance, the national bourgeoisie is now begging its imperial allies to save it from extinction. The economic crisis has forced the national bourgeoisie to agree to virtually any terms in exchange for IMF, World Bank, and private bank loans. The terms that the imperialist big brothers are imposing are not totally disagreeable to the national bourgeoisie inasmuch as the aim of the terms of the loans is to safeguard a higher rate of profit for capital in Peru. However, in crises all capitals do not share the losses equally, and the Peruvian national bourgeoisie is receiving a bitter lesson in this fact of capitalism. Whatever illusions it may have nurtured in more prosperous times now have been dashed. The first clear indication that the national industrial bourgeoisie could no longer reward its petty-bourgeois sycophants came in February, 1975, when the government answered the demands of the *guardia civil* with bullets.[7] As the crisis deepened, all concessions – both material and ideological – to the petty bourgeoisie were ended as the national bourgeoisie was forced to shed all of its excess baggage in an attempt at self-preservation. To this end in August, 1975, the bourgeoisie changed figureheads. President Juan Velasco Alvarado, a strong advocate of the alliance with the petty bourgeoisie, was replaced by a President more appropriate for the crisis situation – General Francisco Morales Bermúdez.

The assault on the working class which had waxed and waned for six years intensified in 1975. The crisis which heightened the contradictions between the national bourgeoisie and imperial capital drove the national bourgeoisie to further increase the exploitation of the working class. The previous attempts at blunting class struggle and creating false consciousness had to be discarded in favour of more direct and repressive methods of squeezing out surplus value on the shop floor. A new economic policy, the Plan Bartia, adopted in March, 1976, made no effort to hide its goal – the production of the highest profits possible and the preservation of the capitalist class. This could only be accomplished through the increased exploitation of the working class and heightened oppression of the peasantry. To achieve this, money wages have been virtually frozen while the cost of the means of subsistence has risen on average by about 200 percent. From early 1975 to 1977 all strikes have been prohibited and job security for workers has been suspended. Many militant labour union leaders have been arrested, thus weakening the leadership of the class-conscious struggles of the working class. Masses of militant workers have been arrested or have simply disappeared. The vanguard of the proletariat, the Marxist-Leninist parties, have been forced into clandestinity and face severe repression. Intellectuals and lawyers who are allies of the working class have been imprisoned or deported. All periodicals which supported the struggles of the working class and the peasantry have been closed. Censorship of the press is now so complete that all news of strikes, demonstrations, arrests, and all manifestations of the unity, militancy, and class consciousness of the working class and the peasantry is suppressed.

7 Dore and Weeks 1976a, pp. 77–8.

2 Revolutionary Alliances

The bourgeoisie is not the only class which must make alliances in order to secure its control over the state. The leadership of the proletariat applies a concrete analysis of the dominant mode of production and of the material base, strengths and weaknesses, and primary and secondary contradictions of the different classes in society in order to determine with which classes or fractions of a class the proletariat can ally at a particular historical moment in its revolutionary struggle to seize state power. The proletariat needs all possible allies, even if they are but momentary and vacillating in its long struggle to overthrow the dictatorship of the bourgeoisie and replace it with the dictatorship of the proletariat. This general rule is no less true in Peru as elsewhere.

> The more powerful enemy can be vanquished only by exerting the utmost effort, and by the most thorough, careful, attentive, skillful and *obligatory* use of any, even the smallest rift between the enemies, any conflict of interests among the bourgeoisie of the various countries and among the various groups or types of bourgeoisie within the various countries, and also by taking advantage of any, even the smallest, opportunity of winning a mass ally, even though this ally be temporary, vacillating, unstable, unreliable and conditional. Those who do not understand this reveal a failure to understand even the smallest grain of Marxism, of modern scientific socialism *in general*.[8]

The proletariat takes advantage of all possible mass allies 'provided that they *do not restrict* the revolutionary propaganda and agitation of the party of the proletariat, and *do not restrict* the party's work of organising the working class and the labouring masses'.[9] The party of the proletariat reserves the right to strenuously criticise and expose the errors and class nature of its allies while struggling to gain the leadership of all alliances into which it enters. Conditions change and new contradictions emerge in the course of a revolutionary struggle. Allies at one stage in the struggle may turn into bitter enemies at another stage as their fear of, and contradictions with, the proletariat develop. This is true especially as the proletariat gains strength. The proletariat must be prepared for the treachery and desertion of its erstwhile allies as the class struggle intensifies.

---

8 Lenin 1972b, pp. 70–1.

9 Stalin 1975, pp. 100–1.

The party of the proletariat faces a difficult task in pursuing the correct revolutionary strategy. It leads the working class by summing up and concentrating the experience and knowledge of the masses. Through this and the application of the science of Marxism-Leninism, the party develops the scattered experiences of the masses into revolutionary consciousness. Through this process, the party directs the struggle for the overthrow of the bourgeoisie and capitalism. This process of summing up and directing struggle always must involve a careful consideration of concrete historical conditions, not merely application of general theoretical guidelines.

> The principle of using different methods to resolve different contradictions is one which Marxist-Leninists must strictly observe. The dogmatists do not observe this principle; they do not understand that conditions differ in different kinds of revolution and so do not understand that different methods should be used to resolve different contradictions; on the contrary, they invariably adopt what they imagine to be an unalterable formula and arbitrarily apply it everywhere, which only causes setbacks to the revolution or makes a sorry mess of what could have been done well.[10]

All revolutionary theoreticians and leaders have emphasised that the proletarian party must make a careful material and class analysis of the specific conditions of its own revolutionary struggle. The vanguard of the proletariat cannot mechanically adopt strategies which proved successful in other struggles. They were successful because they reflected and responded to the unique characteristics of the development of the forces of production and of the class struggle at that particular moment. The contradictions of capitalism are continually resolved to a higher level. To imagine that each revolutionary situation presents the same material conditions, the same contradictions of capitalism and the same class forces is to ignore lessons learned from successful revolutionary struggles. For example, Stalin criticised Trotsky and the 'left opposition' on China for such dogmatism,

> Notwithstanding the ideological progress of our party, there are still, unfortunately, 'leaders' of a sort in it who sincerely believe that the revolution in China can be directed, so to speak, by telegraph, on the basis of the universally recognised general principles of the Comintern, *disregarding* the national peculiarities of China's economy, political system, culture,

10 Mao Tse-tung 1971, p. 99.

> manners and customs, and traditions. What in fact distinguishes these 'leaders' from real leaders is that they always have in their pockets two or three ready-made formulas, 'suitable' for all countries and 'obligatory' under all conditions. The necessity of taking into account the nationally peculiar and nationally specific features of each country does not exist for them. Nor does the necessity exist for them of co-ordinating the general principles of the Comintern with the national peculiarities of the revolutionary movement in each country, the necessity of adapting these general principles to the national pecularities of the state in each country ...
>
> Hence the attempts to stereotype the leadership for all countries. Hence the attempts mechanically to implant certain general formulas, regardless of the concrete conditions of the movement in different countries. Hence the endless conflicts between the formulas and the revolutionary movement in the different countries, as the main outcome of the leadership of these pseudo-leaders.[11]

A major question which revolutionaries in oppressed countries must resolve is, who are their potential allies at the different stages of the revolutionary struggle? Some revolutionaries raise an alliance with the national bourgeoisie to the level of principle and necessity. Others, such as the Trotskyists, exclude this alliance altogether, in practice leaving the proletariat alone to take on the struggle against imperialism and capitalism. The Marxist-Leninist position is to analyse the concrete material conditions, and from this analysis to decide who potential allies are, even 'though this ally be temporary [and] vacillating'.[12] The peasantry and the petty bourgeoisie are the natural allies of the proletariat because both classes are oppressed under *capitalism*. The unnatural allies of the proletariat include the national bourgeoisie in oppressed countries. 'Unnatural' ally because this is the class which exists through the exploitation of the working class; it is the class which personifies capital; and it is the class which must eventually be overthrown. The possibility for the alliance exists because the entire backward country is oppressed by *imperialism*. Imperial capital represented by the advanced industrial countries uses political, social, cultural, and other superstructural institutions to facilitate its exploitation of the working class in the backward country. All classes in Peru and in other backward countries, except the comprador bourgeoisie, are oppressed by imperialism.

This oppression has caused the national bourgeoisie to play a progressive role at certain historical moments and to enter into momentary alliances with

11 Stalin 1975, pp. 94–5.

12 Lenin 1972b, pp. 70–1.

the proletariat against imperialism. The clearest example of this was in the Chinese revolution. Responding to intervention by the Japanese imperialists, the Chinese national bourgeoisie entered into temporary alliances with the Chinese Communist Party against the dominant feudal ruling class and its imperialist allies in the bourgeois-democratic stage of the Chinese revolution. Stalin, in his insightful writings on the Chinese revolution, declares that the Chinese Communist Party was correct in entering into this alliance, but he warns the Chinese revolutionaries that coming out of this alliance there were,

> two paths for the development of events in China: *either* the national bourgeoisie smashes the proletariat, makes a deal with imperialism and together with it launches a campaign against the revolution in order to end the latter by establishing the rule of capitalism; or the proletariat pushes aside the national bourgeoisie, consolidates its hegemony and assumes the lead of the vast masses of the working people in town and country, in order to overcome the resistance of the national bourgeoisie, secure the complete victory of the bourgeois-democratic revolution, and then gradually convert it into a socialist revolution.[13]

He advised that while the Chinese Communists should always make use of the contradictions between feudalism and imperialism, on the one hand, and the national bourgeoisie, on the other, they should always orient their work towards building and strengthening the proletarian movement. In this way they would convert the anti-imperialist bourgeois-democratic revolution into a socialist revolution; otherwise they would be crushed. Stalin repeatedly warned the Chinese Communist Party against allowing itself to be subordinated to the national bourgeoisie. This would lead to '… a revolution of the top stratum, a revolution of the national merchant bourgeoisie, arising in a struggle against the foreign imperialists, and whose subsequent development is essentially directed against the peasants and workers …'[14]

This alliance between the Chinese national bourgeoisie and the Communist Party was strengthened because feudal social relations of production were predominant in China, and imperialism fostered and preserved feudal forms. Under these conditions, the national bourgeoisie may frequently see it in its own interests to join an anti-imperialist alliance and may play a progressive role. But, as Mao has argued, different material conditions may place the national bourgeoisie firmly in the reactionary camp.

13 Stalin 1975, pp. 22–3.
14 Stalin 1975, pp. 53–4.

> When imperialism launches a war of aggression against a [semi-colonial] country, all its various classes, except for some traitors, can temporarily unite in a national war against imperialism. At such a time, the contradiction between imperialism and the country concerned becomes the principal contradiction, while all the contradictions among the various classes within the country … are temporarily relegated to a secondary and subordinate position …
>
> But in another situation, the contradictions change position. When imperialism carries on its oppression not by war, but by milder means – political, economic and cultural – the ruling classes in semi-colonial countries capitulate to imperialism, and the two form an alliance for the joint oppression of the masses of the people.[15]

It is obvious that Stalin and Mao did not see the national bourgeoisie in oppressed countries as an ally of the proletariat at all times and under all conditions. The dominance of a pre-capitalist mode of production and the re-inforcing by imperialism of feudalism were the primary conditions for the alliance. For 'with the development of the productive forces, the bourgeoisie changes from being a new class playing a progressive role to being an old class playing a reactionary role …'[16]

With the development of capitalism and its expansion on a world scale, the capitalist mode of production has now become dominant in many countries which were formerly predominantly pre-capitalist, such is the case in Peru, and this changes the nature of the contradictions and of the possible revolutionary alliances.

> In capitalist society the two forces in contradiction, the proletariat and the bourgeoisie, form the principal contradiction. The other contradictions, such as those between the remnant feudal class and the bourgeoisie … between the non-monopoly capitalists and the monopoly capitalists … between imperialism and the colonies, are all determined or influenced by this principal contradiction.[17]

The possibilities for the national bourgeoisie in Peru and other oppressed countries to play a progressive role have been restricted in the present period. With

15 Mao Tse-tung 1971, pp. 110–11.
16 Mao Tse-tung 1971, p. 113.
17 Mao Tse-tung 1971, p. 110.

capitalism dominant, no longer can this class personify the assault by capitalism on the dominant pre-capitalist social relations of production. This does not mean that the proletariat in oppressed countries can never ally with its national bourgeoisie against imperialism, only that the possibilities for such an alliance have been reduced. The possibility of an alliance between the national bourgeoisie and the proletariat exists due to imperialism's oppression of backward countries.

For the national bourgeoisie this oppression is most acute in the field of the competitive struggle with imperial capital. While this competitive disadvantage is in the sphere of production, in the inability to produce as cheaply as imperial capital, the form that this assumes in the sphere of circulation is the struggle over markets, loans, and the re-negotiation of debts. Clearly the national bourgeoisie would like to expel the imperialists and be left with the national market to itself. All capitalists seek to eliminate their competitors, particularly the strongest. But the strength of imperial capital and the relative weakness of the national bourgeoisie forces the latter to ally with its formidable rivals, in many cases in order to save itself from destruction. Within this uneasy alliance the material conditions are such as to push the national bourgeoisie to take advantage of favorable circumstances for the limitation of the scope of imperial penetration, and thereby promote its own expansion.

The national bourgeoisie is a *class*, and how it behaves is a *class* question. Analyses of the revolutionary struggle in oppressed countries which do not take into account the concrete historical conditions, the contradictions arising out of the development of capitalism to its present imperialist stage, and the class struggle, hinder rather than advance the communist movements. Many such analyses apply the term 'Third World' to all oppressed countries in order to show that these countries are all alike in their opposition to imperialism. Enver Hoxha declares that such terms obscure more than they reveal.

> All [the] terms, [the 'third-world', the 'non-aligned world' or the 'developing countries'] which refer to the various political forces acting in the world today, cover up and do not bring out the class character of these political forces ... The slogan of 'non-aligned' countries gives the false impression that a group of states which have the possibility of 'opposing' the superpower blocs is being created. It gives the impression that these countries, all of them, without exception, are anti-imperialist, opposed to war, opposed to the dictate of others, that they are 'democratic', and even 'socialist'.[18]

18 Hoxha 1976, pp. 173–5.

Hoxha argues that in order to determine correct revolutionary strategy in oppressed countries, one must start with a scrupulous class analysis. The general conclusion that he reaches is that,

> ... the proletariat, all those who are for the revolution and socialism, must closely link their struggle of the peoples for freedom and independence. This can be done only by resolutely struggling against the bourgeoisie of one's own country, by struggling against imperialism and predatory war.[19]

Revolutionaries in Peru have sought to apply this Marxist-Leninist tradition to unite the working class and its allies in the battle against imperialism. Since 1968, the main aspect of the alliance between the Peruvian national bourgeoisie and imperial capital has been collaboration rather than struggle. Obviously, this has limited the possibilities for the proletariat joining the national bourgeoisie in an anti-imperialist alliance. While the progressive leadership of the anti-imperialist forces have in general supported actions by the state that appeared genuinely anti-imperialist, this leadership has been wary not to give support to measures which (like many of the much touted nationalisations) take the form of opposing imperialism while in essence strengthening the bourgeois alliance and imperialism in Peru.[20]

During the Velasco Presidency in Peru, the position of several Marxist-Leninist parties was to take advantage of the existing bourgeois freedoms to organize a militant and class-conscious workers' movement and to forge links between the proletariat and the peasantry. In this process, Marxist-Leninists revealed the true bourgeois nature of the regime, its close alliance with imperial capital, and its antagonism to the working class and the peasantry. The failure to do this of many so-called 'Marxist-Leninists' such as the revisionist Partido Comunista Peruano (PCP), the Moscow-line Peruvian Communist Party, resulted in weakening the working class and the peasantry. This party's uncritical support for the Velasco regime undermined working-class unity and class consciousness, leaving the proletariat inadequately prepared to resist the assault by the new government of Morales Bermúdez. By failing to make a class analysis, by preaching that the government was leading the anti-imperialist struggle, by admonishing the workers and peasants to refrain from criticising that government, and by discouraging organising and strikes, the PCP disarmed the proletariat and the peasantry.

---

19 Hoxha 1976, p. 176.

20 Dore 1977 and Molinari and Gorman 1977.

A fundamental rule for Marxist-Leninists is that the proletariat not allow itself to become subordinated to the national bourgeoisie, for this can only serve to weaken the working-class movement and aid the bourgeoisie to crush it.

3 The Role of the State in Peru

The role of the Peruvian state and the form that it assumes at any particular historical moment reflects primarily the development of the forces of production and of the class struggle within Peru. When capitalism is emerging and begins to dominate over the pre-capitalist social relations of production, it needs the strong arm of the state to impose its rule. Analysing the genesis of the industrial capitalist, Marx writes,

> … [The] power of the State, the concentrated and organised force of society, … hasten[s], hot-house fashion, the process of transformation of the feudal mode of production into the capitalist mode, and … shorten[s] the transition. Force is the midwife of every old society pregnant with a new one. It is itself an economic power.[21]

The Peruvian national bourgeoisie not only had to crush, once and for all, the power of the pre-capitalist ruling class through destroying the material base and social relations on which its power rested. It also had to stimulate and strengthen capitalism. The active role of the state in facilitating the development of capitalism in agriculture and in hastening the processes of centralisation and concentration of capital in industry was necessary in order to incubate the expansion of capitalist relations of production. While this active encouragement by the state of the expansion of capital is sometimes interpreted as representing a period of state capitalism, as if this were a particular and recent phenomenon in the development of capitalism, in every country where capital reigns, the state has assumed this role at some point. Writing of the state during the early stage of capitalist accumulation, Marx says,

> In the ordinary run of things the labourer can be left to the 'natural laws of production', i.e. to his dependence on capital, a dependence springing from, and guaranteed in perpetuity by the conditions of production them-

21 Marx 1906, p. 824.

> selves. It is otherwise during the historic genesis of capitalist production. The bourgeoisie, at its rise, wants and uses the power of the state to 'regulate' wages, i.e., to force them within the limits suitable for surplus value making, to lengthen the working-day and to keep the labourer himself in the normal degree of dependence. This is an essential element of the so-called primitive accumulation.[22]

In Peru, as in other countries where capitalism is ascending or ascendant, the apparently strong and interventionist state is a historical necessity. The bourgeois state *rises* to facilitate accumulation and provide the conditions for the production and appropriation of surplus value; i.e., the conditions for the exploitation of labour, which, when capitalism is more highly developed, is enforced by capital itself.

While the form that the Peruvian state assumes is primarily dictated by internal contradictions, it is also influenced by the struggle among the imperialist powers. In the present epoch, the leading imperialist countries are the United States and the social-imperialist Soviet Union. The weaker imperialist powers are Germany and Japan. In these countries where capitalism has matured to the monopoly stage, the capitalist classes are driven to compete through the export of capital. Each bourgeoisie must continually export its capital to other countries to exploit the working classes there, in order to counteract the tendency for the rate of profit to fall in the imperialist homeland. This intra-imperialist contention creates rifts within imperialism, which the bourgeoisies in oppressed countries can try to take advantage of.

The Peruvian national industrial bourgeoisie has utilised the competition among the imperialists in an attempt to bargain for more favourable terms in their alliance with imperial – primarily US – capital. President Velasco's familiar slogan, that Peru was neither capitalist nor communist, was in essence a declaration that the Peruvian bourgeoisie would bind itself irrevocably with neither the US imperialists nor the Soviet social-imperialists, but would attempt to maintain its independence – independence to side momentarily with whichever set of capitalists offered a better deal. As the contradictions of capital intensify, and the contention among the imperialists heightens, we can expect the Peruvian national bourgeoisie (and bourgeoisies in other emerging capitalist countries) to attempt to play off one imperialist power against the other in hopes of gaining momentary advantages. Like all advantages, these will accrue to a class – the bourgeoisie. Whether these will also be

22 Marx 1906, p. 809.

advantages for the proletariat depends upon the political line followed by the leadership of that class.

4 Class Analysis and Dependency Theory

Up to this point we have sought to demonstrate the necessity of making a class analysis of Peruvian society and have developed conclusions based on that analysis. The discussion of classes in society is not and never has been monopolised by Marxists. Reformists, revisionists, and even reactionaries have employed the concept of 'class' to analyse society and have even seen the history of mankind as the history of class struggle. What distinguishes Marxist analysis is that it treats the concept of 'class' as derivative from the material base of society, rather than as an autonomous sociological category. Concretely, the development of classes is conditioned by and determined by the development of the social relations of production and the forces of production. An analysis which considers *class* without first considering the mode of production is both unscientific and trivial. It is unscientific because classes 'hang in mid-air', brought *ex machina* into the discussion. It is trivial, because it can never go beyond a mere description of reality.

Herein lies our critique and rejection of dependency theory. All the articles in this issue to an extent break with dependency theory. The analysis in every case begins with the social relations of production, and it is only on this foundation that any consideration of political phenomena is constructed. This is the unifying theme of this issue, a unifying theme much more basic than the fact that the articles happen to all refer to Peru. Our objection to dependency theory is that it seeks to integrate economic and political phenomena without considering the underlying cause of both, the mode of production.

It is worthwhile to briefly state our objection to dependency theory, an analysis which has played a progressive role in the debates over backwardness in Latin America, despite its deficiencies.[23] At the heart of dependency theory is the concept of 'dependence', the domination of one country by another, which is said to 'condition' the development of Latin American countries. However, rigorous definition of this concept has been the despair of dependency theorists themselves,[24] and we do not feel it necessary to repeat these discussions. Relatively clear is the major mechanism by which the development of 'depend-

23 Harding 1976, pp. 3–11.
24 Cardoso 1972.

ent' economies are 'conditioned'. This mechanism is 'surplus extraction' by the 'centre' ('exploiting') country from the 'peripheral' ('exploited') country.[25] 'Surplus extraction' plays in dependency theory the role which exploitation plays in Marxian theory. Opposing the two concepts crystallizes the difference between the two theories: surplus extraction is a phenomenon *between countries*, while exploitation is a phenomenon *between classes*. However, the two are not complementary; that is, it is a fundamental error to imagine that dependency theorists, through the use of the concept 'surplus extraction', have built upon Marx's category of exploitation and extended it from the *class* level to the international level. In fact, what we have is a *substitution* of concepts, a break with Marx, a *replacement* of one concept with another. For it is at the *class level* that *all* 'extraction', appropriation, or expropriation of surplus product occurs, with the categories of community, region, or country merely providing the geographic context of this class appropriation of surplus product.

Surplus product or surplus labour is appropriated by a *class* in production, and this process is technically described by the word *exploitation*. Exploitation is the appropriation of part of the product of one class by another. To understand the origin of this surplus product, we must understand the conditions under which it arises – the social relations of production. However, the dependency theorists initiate their analysis after the barn door has been opened and the horse is in full gallop. By looking at surplus product in its circulation *between countries*, the analysis commences after surplus product has been produced and *after* it has been appropriated. Such a procedure is hopelessly crippled in its analytical power, for the analysis begins after all the major events are over. It is restricted to the realm of *appearances*. All the shortcomings of dependency theory derive from this.

The transfer of surplus product from one geographic area to another – an act of *exchange* – can never explain the poverty of the one and the wealth of the other. The explanation of the poverty of some countries and the wealth of others lies in the nature of production, not in the movement of products (the circulation of commodities). If there is a net flow of surplus product out of a country, this represents the fact that there prevail barriers to reproduction on an expanding scale. Here we must explicitly introduce the capitalist mode of production. The goal of capitalism, of capital as a social relation, is *not* the accumulation of a hoard of commodities nor of money; nor is its goal the amassing of wealth in any particular geographic area. The contradictions of capital require production for greater and greater profit, irrespective of geo-

25 For a more complete discussion of what follows, see Dore and Weeks 1976b, pp. 1–25.

graphic area or commodity produced. If there were no barriers to the expansion of capital in Latin America (and the rate of profit higher there than in the 'centre'), the net flow would be *into* these countries. Capital does not by *design* seek the impoverishment of countries through extracting profits from backward countries for use elsewhere; it seeks everywhere to expand where profits are high, thereby reaping the greatest profit possible. Capital retreats with its prize of surplus value only when it is no longer able to exploit labour for the profits it hoped for. Thus, to explain 'underdevelopment', backwardness, to use the term of Marx and Lenin – we must explain why there are *barriers* to capital's advance. In other words, we must recognize the *progressiveness* of capitalism,[26] recognise its expansion internationally as the unwitting handmaiden of revolutionary development, not, like generations of petty-bourgeois critics, decry its expansion as the source of all evils. As Lenin wrote, 'The development of capitalism in the young countries is greatly *accelerated* by the example and aid of the old countries'.[27] Further the instability and exploitiveness of capitalism in no way amends this. Again, Lenin is clear in attacking petty-bourgeois critics of capitalism, 'their failure to understand the elements of progress *inherent* in this instability makes their theories *reactionary*'.[28]

The ingredients of the explanation of the barriers to capital's expansion – and thus of backwardness – lie in the sphere of production. A brief discussion of these are found in the paper by Weeks (in this issue) derived from our earlier work,[29] itself based on Lenin, among other sources.[30] Basically, it is argued that it is the persistence of pre-capitalist relations of production which are the barrier to the development of capitalism in oppressed countries. These pre-capitalist relations retard productivity growth in the production of wage goods – the means of subsistence. This retardation at some point presents a major problem to capital. Profit derives from the difference between the total time the worker labours in the production of commodities under capitalist relations of production, and the time he must labour to produce the equivalent of his or her subsistence. The latter equivalent can only be reduced by cheapening the production of wage goods (the means of subsistence). This cheapening is blocked by pre-capitalist relations of production.

26 Lenin 1972a, 1972b.
27 Lenin 1972b, p. 490.
28 Lenin 1972b, p. 217.
29 Dore and Weeks 1976b, pp. 25–39.
30 Lenin 1972a, and 1972b.

5 The Struggle In Peru

A fierce class struggle rages in Peru. The coup of 1968 established the dictatorship of the national industrial bourgeoisie, and as such was a historic and progressive milestone for Peruvian society. The working class and the peasantry have made important gains since 1968. They have developed class consciousness and built fighting organisations to lead their struggles against imperialism and capitalism. With the expansion of capitalism, the proletariat has grown in size and organisation. It has rejected the Aprista petty-bourgeois union bureaucrats and heightened the struggle against the revisionist leaders who now dominate many unions. Both as the result of revolutionary leadership and spontaneously, the peasantry and proletariat have fought and exposed the class collabouration of the government-created mass organisations: the Confederación Nacional Agrária (CNA), the pro-government peasant organisation, and the Confederacion de Trabajadores Revolucionários del Perú (CTRP), the government's trade union. The militant and class-conscious organisations are, in contrast, growing, under revolutionary leadership.

As the Peruvian national industrial bourgeoisie struggles to survive in the face of economic crisis, it has intensified the attacks against the proletariat, the peasantry, and the progressive elements of the petty bourgeoisie. The bourgeoisie is currently seeking to roll back gains which the proletariat and peasantry have achieved through decades of struggle. Direct repression includes the jailing of militant leaders of the working class and peasantry, closing progressive newspapers and magazines, and exiling and jailing intellectuals and professionals such as lawyers. Strikes are in practice illegal. Momentarily, the bourgeoisie appears successful; but part of its success is illusory, for it only represents an advancement of the struggle from conditions of relative bourgeois freedom to a period when the mass struggle must take a more clandestine form, due to the end of that relative freedom. In this new stage of the struggle, the leadership of the proletariat is much more advanced than in the past, much more able to win allies in the struggle against imperialism, and much more prepared for the long struggle for the seizure of state power and the struggle for socialism which will follow.

CHAPTER 11

Backwardness, Foreign Capital, and Accumulation in the Manufacturing Sector of Peru, 1954–75

The process of capitalist accumulation is one of crisis and boom, uneven development and the insatiable greed for the surplus labour of one class by another class. In backward countries the essence of capitalist accumulation is no different than in advanced countries. But due to the low development of the forces and relations of production in the former, the manifestations of the basic laws of motion of capitalism may differ from the forms assumed in the advanced countries. A particular aspect which assumes great import in backward countries is the ownership of capital, whether it is local or foreign. Some writers are obsessed with this phenomenon of the world of appearances, and in their obsession never discover that the uneven development that characterises countries of the capitalist world is a consequence of the capitalist mode of production itself, not the result of who owns capital. This obsession with form is the delight of the petty bourgeoisie, which in every country tends to see the thwarting of its pathetic hopes to rise out of its class to be the result of foreign domination and conspiracies, the 'dirty tricks' of imperialists.

The purpose of this paper is to investigate the process of accumulation in the manufacturing sector of Peru, and in so doing, to explore the role of foreign capital in that process. But before we can deal with the process of accumulation in Peru, it is necessary to lay to rest certain myths that plague the analysis of backwardness; namely, the complementary pseudo-scientific theses that capitalist development in backward countries is blocked by (a) the lack of an internal market and (b) the extraction of surplus, which eliminates the source of accumulation. These theses are, of course, the heart of the 'dependency' school of analysis. We deal with the latter in section II, and in section III briefly develop an analysis which places the limits to capitalist development in the sphere of production, the barriers to the *production* of surplus value inherent in a backward economy. In section IV, we analyse Peru, emphasising the role of centralisation, the organic composition of capital and the wage in the process of accumulation in manufacturing. It is out of these factors in accumulation that we interpret the role of foreign capital. In the final section, we consider the present crisis in Peru and revolutionary developments arising from it.

 | DOI:10.1163/9789004703193_013

1 Errors of Arguments Grounded in the Sphere of Circulation

In all societies the ascendency of one class over others derives from the appropriation of surplus labour. It is through this appropriation that class structures are reproduced. Under slavery the appropriation of surplus labour is obvious in form: the slave owner actually owns the labourer himself. The appropriation of surplus labour is so dramatic under the slave mode of production it appears that the slave does not work for himself at all.

Under slavery, as under capitalism, the division of the day between necessary and surplus labour time (discussed below) is hidden. In slavery, the entire working time of the labourer appears as surplus or expropriated labour; under capitalism the opposite obfuscation occurs. 'There [slavery] the property-relation conceals the labour of the slave for himself; here [capitalism] the money-relation conceals the unrequited labour of the wage labourer'.[1] Under feudalism, appropriation of surplus labour is in the form of use values or actual labour time. In capitalism the class ascendency of the bourgeoisie is also the result of the appropriation of surplus labour, but is masked by the wage system, which makes it appear that the labourer is paid the full value of his labour, while in reality he is paid the value of his *labour power*.

> That which comes directly face to face with the possessor of money on the market [the capitalist], is in fact not labour, but the labourer. What the latter sells is his labour power. As soon as his labour actually begins, it has already ceased to belong to him; it can no longer be sold by him. Labour is the substance, and the imminent measure of value, but *has itself no value*.[2]

The rendering into money form of the means of subsistence of the labourer and products taking the social form of commodities *masks*, but in no way changes, the fundamental proposition that under capitalism, like under all modes of production with classes, the ascendency of the ruling class is effected by the appropriation of surplus labour.

Once it is realized that bourgeois production is merely one of the historical forms which the appropriation of surplus labour can take, we can begin to understand the nature of backwardness. The appropriation of surplus labour is a phenomenon of *production*. While it is true that under capitalism the

1 Marx 1970b, p. 505.
2 Marx 1970b, p. 503.

appropriated labour, surplus value, must be realized, i.e., exchanged for money, the appropriation itself occurs in production and is a relationship *between classes*. Marx, in his writings, repeatedly stressed this. Writing of trade between advanced and backward countries, he says, 'The favored country recovers more labour in exchange for less labour, although this difference, this excess is pocketed, as in any exchange between labour and capital, by a *certain class*'.[3]

Thus, in the analysis of backwardness, we must begin with the process of appropriation, a relationship between classes, *not* between countries.[4] This may seem obvious, but, in fact, the most prevalent explanation of backwardness treats the phenomenon as the result of the relations between countries, going as far as to speak of some countries 'exploiting' others. Briefly stated, this position holds that the inequality among nations, or the incompleteness of capitalist development in backward countries, is the result of the extraction of surplus out of one country for the benefit of another country.[5] In the modern epoch of imperialism, when the dominant form of appropriation of surplus labour is no longer looting and plundering, the 'surplus extraction thesis' is tantamount to saying that backwardness is a phenomenon of *circulation*.

Viewing exploitation as a relationship between *countries* involves the bourgeois method of *personifying* countries with the attendant fiction that class conflict is not the motive force of history, but that conflicts between *countries* are. Obviously, class conflicts can take the *form* of conflict between countries, but it is the task of Marxist-Leninists to reveal the underlying class antagonisms that generate such a form.[6]

That in many or even most cases there is a net flow of surplus labour out of backward countries into advanced countries in commodity or money form is, no doubt, the case in the present epoch of capitalism. But as we argue in the next section, this is the *consequence* of backwardness, not its cause. Put another way the net outflow of value from a backward country either through commodity trade or profit repatriation is one of the *forms* which backwardness takes. To elevate this transfer of value to a *cause* of backwardness is to fall into the trap of petty-bourgeois nationalism[7] and identify backwardness with the form capitalism takes, rather than with capitalism itself. While revolutionaries can utilise

3 Marx 1971, p. 168.

4 See Dore and Weeks 1976b, for a longer discussion of what follows.

5 This position is clearly presented in Baran 1957, and Frank 1969b. See particularly Frank 1969b, p. 9; and Baran 1957, pp. 142–3, and the amazing comment about India in Baran 1957, p. 150. See also Kuusinen n.d., pp. 247–8, which Frank cites to buttress his case.

6 See WWFES, 1976.

7 Bettelheim 1972c.

this nationalism in building alliances, they can have no part of its analytical underpinnings; indeed, these underpinnings must be exposed.

Due to ignoring the class nature of exploitation (indeed, the class nature of societies) and never venturing into the sphere of production, the 'surplus extraction thesis' is left with an unresolvable paradox which it can only hope will go unnoticed. If capital in the advanced countries is 'exploiting' the backward countries, then it must follow that profit rates in backward countries are extraordinarily high.[8] But if profit rates are high, why does imperial capital repatriate such a large share of its profits as the 'surplus extraction' thesis maintains rather than reinvesting them? That is, why is the surplus *extracted*?

This paradox disappears once the international transfer of value is seen as a *consequence* of backwardness. In the next part we outline a theory which shows that the nature of backwardness initially provides for high profit rates for imperial capital, but due to the nature of backwardness, these high profits are temporary, and the repatriation of profits is explained by a tendency for profitability to decline as imperial capital seizes upon more and more branches of industry. This analysis, grounded in the sphere of production and stressing the interaction between capitalist and pre-capitalist modes of production, exposes the petty-bourgeois ideology of the reactionary Peruvian regime; this regime seeks to convince the working class and peasantry that their exploitation derives from the exploitation of 'their country' by foreigners, and not from *class* exploitation carried out by the dictatorship of the Peruvian bourgeoisie in association with imperial capital.[9]

2 Backwardness and the Sphere of Production

2.1 *Relative Surplus Value and the Nature of Backwardness*

At the outset, we must define our terms. We define a backward country as a national geographic unit in which pre-capitalist relations of production remain

8 This is asserted explicitly by both Baran and Frank, as well as by dependency theorists such as Marini 1972, and follows theoretically from the nature of imperialism.

9 Bettelheim, in his critique of Emmanuel, writes, 'The [local bourgeoisies in backward countries] are always trying to convince the working masses of their countries that their poverty is due not to the class exploitation of which they are victims, and the existence of production relations that block the development of the productive forces, but to the national "exploitation" of rich and poor, capitalists, peasants, and workers are said to be *all alike victims*' … (Bettelheim 1972a, p. 314).

significant, though not necessarily dominant. Since pre-capitalist relations of production persist longest in agriculture, an important aspect of our definition is that a major part of the means of consumption, the use values which provide for the production and reproduction of labour power, are produced pre-capitalistically.[10] This aspect of backwardness will play a crucial role in our analysis of bourgeois production in backward countries. We shall also use the term 'monopoly', by which we mean a situation in which one capital[11] holds a commanding position in one branch of industry.

All production in all societies, as noted above, is the result of human labour, and the surplus product of a society is that amount of the product of labour which exceeds what is necessary to reproduce the labour force. Under capitalism, products take the form of commodities, and their exchange values are determined by the dead and living labour time embodied in them – prices are transformed values.[12] Profit is the phenomenal form taken by surplus product in bourgeois production, passing through the intermediate form of surplus value. The rate of profit is uniquely determined by the rate of surplus value when commodities sell at their values.

Before proceeding, we need to establish some familiar definitions in Marxian theory. Taking social capital as a whole, the *value* of capitalist production (measuring all quantities in labour time) is,

$A = C + V + S$, where

A is the value of production,
C is constant capital – the means of production and depreciation on fixed capital,
V is variable capital, and
S is surplus value,
$s = S/V$ is the rate of surplus value, and
$p = S/(C + V)$ is the rate of profit[13]

From this, we can write (by dividing the top and bottom of the expression for the rate of profit by V, variable capital),

---

10 Our definition of backwardness is the same as that used elsewhere: Fernandez and Ocampo 1974; and Romagnolo 1975. The discussion which follows is based on the analysis developed in the second part of Dore and Weeks 1976b; Fernandez and Ocampo 1974; Romagnolo 1975; Dore and Weeks 1976b.

11 A 'capital' is what bourgeois economists call a firm.

12 Johansen 1972; Medio 1972; and Baumol 1974.

13 Marx 1970b, pp. 497–500.

$$p = \frac{s}{(\frac{C}{V}+1)}$$

With other things equal, a rise in the organic composition of capital (C/V) leads to a *fall* in the rate of profit, unless compensated by a rise in the rate of surplus value (s, which equals S/V).

All new value created in a production period is the result of living labour put in motion and is equal to variable capital plus surplus value (V + S). The *rate of surplus value* is the ratio of *surplus labour time* (S) to *necessary labour time* (V). Labour power, like all commodities, tends to sell at its value, and therefore the value of the wage represents the labour time necessary to produce this commodity. Ignoring for the moment changes in constant capital, the rate of profit is determined by the rate of surplus value (S/V). Each working day of each worker under capitalist relations of production is divided between necessary labour time (the time the worker labours to produce a mass of products necessary for his reproduction) and surplus labour time (which the capitalist appropriates and realizes as profit). Therefore, the rate of profit can only be raised, given the organic composition of capital, by reducing necessary labour time relatively to surplus labour time. This can be done by extending the working day without compensation (the raising of *absolute* surplus value), or by reducing that portion of the working day required to reproduce the worker (the raising of *relative* surplus value).[14]

In the early stages of capitalist development, absolute surplus value is important;[15] but as capitalism matures, it is the raising of relative surplus value that is the engine of capitalist accumulation. Except briefly, relative surplus value can only be raised through increasing labour productivity in the branches of industry which produce the means of consumption, directly or indirectly; and if commodities are sold at their values, this leads to a fall in the exchange value of the wage, though the use values it can buy may rise. That is, labour - power can be cheapened at the same time that the worker is enjoying a higher standard of living. This merely reflects the twofold nature of commodities (use value and exchange value). In summary, relative surplus value is raised and profit increased by the cheapening of the commodities workers buy, relatively to other commodities. This is the operation of the law of value: prices of commodities are determined by the labour time required in their production. To quote Marx,

14 Marx 1970b, pp. 476–96.
15 Marx 1970b, part III.

> In order to effect a fall in the value of labour power, the increase in the productiveness of labour must seize upon those branches of industry, whose products determine the value of labour power, and consequently either belong to the class of customary means of subsistence, or are capable of supplying the place of those means ... [Further] a fall in the value of labour power is also brought about by an increase in the productiveness of labour, and by a corresponding cheapening of commodities in those industries which supply the instruments of labour and raw material, that form the material elements of the constant capital required for producing the necessaries of life.[16]

Given that the source of profit is surplus labour time, an increase in the productivity of labour in one branch of industry will result in a sustainable increase in the rate of profit in that branch of industry only to the extent that it does so in all branches. An increase in the productivity of labour only affects the rate of profit in a permanent way if it reduces necessary labour time by cheapening the 'necessaries of life' (to use Marx's term). That is, increases in productivity *do not* directly increase the rate of profit in the industry in which they occur except in the short run.

In one industry, increases in productivity lower the value of the commodity produced; that is, they reduce the living labour embodied in the commodity per unit. *Temporarily*, this may raise the rate of profit if capitals can continue to sell the commodity at the existing price, i.e., *above value*. But the process of competition will drive the price of goods down to their values, eliminating the momentary profit.[17] In a fully capitalist society, the advance of the forces of production continually results in the reduction of necessary labour time, since the means of consumption, necessaries of life, are produced capitalistically. It should be noted that even in advanced countries, a portion of necessary labour time is provided pre-capitalistically through the family. As capitalism matures, this portion becomes a barrier to reducing necessary labour time, analogously to the discussion which follows of backward countries. In summary, inherent in capitalist accumulation in advanced societies is the progressive cheapening

16 Marx 1970b, p. 299.

17 Marx 1970b, pp. 300–1. "The object of all development of the productiveness of labour, within the limits of capitalist production, is to shorten that part of the working day, during which the workman must labour for his own benefit, and by that very shortening, to lengthen the other part of the day, during which he is at liberty to work gratis for the capitalist" (Marx, 1970b, p.304).

of commodities and a rising rate of exploitation (S/V). For this reason, the rate of surplus value tends to be highest in the most advanced countries.[18]

In a backward country such as Peru, on the other hand, a large proportion of the means of consumption is produced pre-capitalistically, and this creates a barrier to raising the rate of surplus value. Necessary labour time in a backward country is largely determined outside of the capitalist sector. Since the internal contradictions of pre-capitalist modes of production do not give rise to revolutions in the means of production, there is a tendency for the value of labour power to stagnate, or not to fall as rapidly as the values of capitalistically produced commodities. This is the relationship inherent in backwardness which prevents the full development of capitalism.

3 Profitability and Crises in Backward Countries

Elsewhere it has been argued theoretically that imperial capital tends to be more efficient in the use of labour power than local capital in backward countries.[19] Below we show this empirically for Peru. As a consequence of this greater efficiency, imperial capital can enter backward countries in anticipation of high *initial* profit rates. It secures these super profits through producing much more efficiently than local capital and selling *above value*. This is above value in terms of the living and dead labour embodied in commodities through the more efficient process, but at or below value in terms of the production process of local capitalists. This enables the imperial capitals both to reap super profits and to drive local capital out of operation. In doing this, imperial capitals may establish a temporary monopoly in a branch of industry.

This monopoly position and the super profits it implies cannot persist, however. It is an error of petty-bourgeois reformism and revisionist interpretations of Marx to equate the growth of monopoly with the permanent elimination of competition. In reality, monopoly creates the conditions for *intensified* competition by the extraction of super profits.[20] Revisionists and reformists in their analysis of monopoly, as in all other areas, perpetuate the myth that it is the *form* of capitalism not capitalism *itself* which is the source of society's ills. Their critique of monopoly is that it holds up prices, a theoretical revision of Marx,[21] and empirically false, as we have shown for Peru.[22] Monopolies make

18 Bettelheim 1972c.
19 Dore, Weeks and Bollinger 1975; and Dore and Weeks 1976a.
20 Lenin 1972d.
21 Bullock and Yaffe 1975, section III.
22 Weeks 1976.

their super profits through greater efficiency, achieved by the process of centralisation, not by higher prices. While the barriers to competition in backward countries may be considerable, there will be a tendency for price to be driven down towards value in the temporarily monopolised industry as capital (particularly foreign capital) flows into it to seize upon the super profits. The idea that a monopoly position can be maintained indefinitely contradicts the nature of capital as a social relation, and will be shown to be empirically false for Peru. As renewed competition drives down price in the branch of industry in which imperial capital is reaping super profits, the rate of profit must fall to or below the level that prevailed before imperial capital appeared. This is a necessary result, because the distribution of the working day between necessary and surplus labour time has been *unaffected*; only the *value* of the commodity has changed (by falling).

Thus, we can summarise the process of accumulation in backward countries. Imperial capital enters a branch of industry and reaps super profits by producing more cheaply than local capitals, driving a portion of the latter to ruin. Renewed competition, either from local capital with access to advanced techniques or from other imperial capitals, drives down prices and destroys profitability. At this point, imperial capital leaps to another branch of industry in the backward country to play havoc, following the same cycle of super profits, temporary monopoly, and finally the destruction of profitability. It is this cycle, conditioned by the pre-capitalistic production of the means of subsistence, that accounts for the spurts of rapid accumulation followed by crises that characterise backward countries.

It is the same process that generates growing importation of foodstuffs, in an attempt by capital to drive down the value of labour power through cheaper, imported substitutes. This response to the barrier to the reduction of necessary labour time has been quite important in Peru, and generates its own counteracting barrier to accumulation.

In the next section, we apply this analysis of capitalist accumulation in backward countries to Peru during the post-Second-World-War period. Using it, we can identify the three basic determinants of accumulation in manufacturing: imperial capital, the process of centralisation and concentration, and the value of labour power. In pursuing this approach, we make a clean break with those analysts who attribute the incompleteness of capitalist development in Peru (and elsewhere) to the 'lack of a home market'[23] and 'surplus extraction'.[24] Here

23 Bonilla 1974.

24 Anaya Franco 1974b, pp. 30–1.

we have not dealt with the 'lack of a home market' thesis, but do so elsewhere,[25] showing that it incorporates the errors of the Russian *Narodnik* analysis, so brilliantly critiqued by Lenin.[26]

4 Accumulation in Peruvian Manufacturing

4.1 *Introduction*

Elsewhere, we have considered the nature of Peruvian society,[27] and here we only summarize that discussion. During the period under review, Peruvian society passed through a profound change. Until the coup of 1968, Peruvian society was semi-feudal, though capitalist relations of production were becoming increasingly dominant. By semi-feudal, we mean (a) pre-capitalist relations of production characterised sectors of the economy, and (b) the indigenous bourgeoisie had not established its class dictatorship, but ruled in an alliance with a pre-capitalist landed class. Further, only a portion of the bourgeoisie was in this alliance – that part which was involved in export agriculture and finance. Bollinger (1977) has shown that such an alliance is a characteristic of the initial emergence of the capitalist mode of production in backward countries. Such an alliance is made possible because of the common interests of the exporting bourgeoisie and the pre-capitalist class, and by the nature of finance capital, which is consistent with the extraction of surplus product through pre-capitalist modes of production. The coup of 1968 brought to power the Peruvian industrial bourgeoisie, establishing its class dictatorship. By virtue of this coup, capitalism became the dominant mode of production in that the bourgeoisie had established its dictatorship, but pre-capitalist relations of production persist and remain important in some sectors (primarily agriculture).

Reliable figures for the manufacturing sector of the Peruvian economy do not begin until 1954,[28] but available sources indicate that in 1944–5, there were about 100,000 manufacturing employees in establishments hiring five or more, and slightly less in 1950–1.[29] While this decline in measured employment would

25 Dore and Weeks 1976b.

26 'From what has been said above, it follows automatically that the problem of the home market as a separate, self-sufficient problem not depending on that of the degree of capitalist development does not exist at all. This is why Marx's theory does not anywhere or ever raise this problem separately … The "home market" for capitalism is created by capitalism itself …' (Lenin 1974, p. 69).

27 Dore and Weeks 1976a; and Weeks 1977a.

28 Ministerio de Fomento y Obras Publicas 1956.

29 Banco Central 1957, p. 77.

seem to indicate a period of post-world-war stagnation, a generalisation made by many dependency theorists for Latin America as a whole,[30] it is difficult to take these figures seriously. Independent sources show a continual increase in manufacturing production from 1945 to 1950,[31] and while it is possible that this increase was achieved with *less* employment, this is unlikely a *priori*. It is unlikely a *priori*, because only under unusual conditions can capital extract a greater mass of surplus value from the same or a smaller labour force, and the purpose of capitalist production is to increase the production of surplus value.[32] Our judgment is that in 1950 there were some 150,000 manufacturing employees in all establishments, and these workers accounted for 14 percent of national income.[33]

As shown elsewhere,[34] the period 1945–7, was one of positive but relatively slow growth of manufacturing output compared to the overall trend in production for 1945–74. Taking into account the upward trend value of production growth (in real terms), the manufacturing sector was in long-term *relative* decline until 1957, followed by an upward swing in accumulation thereafter. This upward swing was interrupted by the economic crisis of 1967–9, then arrested again in 1976 by a crisis which threatens to be much more severe.[35]

The trend rate of growth of manufacturing in Peru has been quite high, about 7 to 8 percent per annum over the last twenty years,[36] and this production has been almost entirely for the internal market. In 1971–1973, less than 10 percent of the market value of manufacturing production was exported, and over half of this was, in fact, from the mining sector (processing of non-ferrous metals).[37] Peru provides a clear empirical refutation of the theoretically confused thesis (mentioned above) that industrialisation in backward economies is limited by the size of the home market (Marini, 1972). The explanation for the crisis in manufacturing in 1967–1969 and 1975 to the present lies elsewhere.

---

30 Frank 1969.

31 Sociedad Nacional de Industrias 1963; and Ministerio de Hacienda y Comercio 1958.

32 Marx 1970b, part VII.

33 Banco Central 1966, p. 32.

34 Weeks 1977a.

35 The trends referred to are for the index of industrial production. Strictly speaking, this index is closer to a measure of the *use values* produced than of accumulation, which refers to the accumulation of *value*. Obviously, the accumulation process in general moves with the production of the mass of use values, but one of the fundamental contradictions of capitalism is that the former can fall while the latter rises (Marx 1970b).

36 Weeks 1977a.

37 Ministério de Indústria y Turismo 1975, pp. 27–37.

5 Foreign Capital and Centralisation

Ignoring the dialectical nature of capitalism, petty-bourgeois nationalists stress only those aspects of the spread of foreign capital into Peru which support their analysis that it is the *form* of capital that explains Peru's backwardness. In fact, the entry of imperial capital is both the source of Peru's industrialisation and activates the forces which block the full development of industrialisation.

In Table 11.1 we provide several indices of Peru's process of accumulation in manufacturing for the years 1950–73. The last column gives a rough measure of the importance of imperial capital in the manufacturing sector. Here is calculated the ratio of the inflow of foreign finance into the sector to total investment in fixed capital actually realized during a year. For any one year, this may not be the portion of investment in fixed capital by foreigners, since the foreign funds may not be converted into fixed capital form in the year they enter the country. However, by using the annual averages over a number of years (as done in Table 11.1), we obtain an indication of the importance of foreign capital in the expansion of total fixed capital. The time periods chosen for the table are not arbitrary, but correspond to discontinuous jumps in the ratio of foreign capital to realized domestic investment. In 1958, the ratio was .364, while it had been .269 in 1957, and only once above .3 from 1950 to 1957 (in 1955 it was .307). In 1963, the ratio was over .5 for the first time, an increase from .363 in 1962. Finally, in 1968, the ratio was .729, compared to .576 in 1967.[38] The other columns in Table 11.1 give annual compound growth rates for various indicators for the periods selected. That is, they give the growth rate between two selected years as a constant trend value. To overcome the problem of atypical and extreme year-end values, this growth rate has been calculated on the basis of a three-year 'moving' average.[39]

The general relationship between foreign capital and the growth of production (column 1) is clear. Manufacturing production grew slowest in Peru when foreign capital was *least* important (1950–7). The sudden increase in imperial participation in manufacturing in 1958, which represented a shift out of the *relatively* unprofitable extractive sectors,[40] was associated with a burst of rapid accumulation in 1957–62, continuing at a slightly lower rate during the periods 1962–67 and 1967–73. The last period shows a lower rate of growth as a result of the crisis of 1967–9, which we have analysed elsewhere.[41]

38 Anaya Franco 1974; Ministério de Indústria 1962; and other sources.

39 Suits 1963, pp. 203 ff.

40 Dore and Weeks 1976a.

41 Weeks 1977a.

TABLE 11.1 Output, employment and wage changes and foreign investment in Peruvian manufacturing, 1950–73

Period	Real output	Employment	Real wage producer	Real wage consumer	Ratio, foreign capital inflow to realized domestic investment
1950–57	6.7%	2.3%[a]	2.9%[b]	5.9%	.259
1957–62	9.4%	5.3%	-2.5%	4.0%	.394
1962–67	8.7%	2.8%	2.9%	1.2%	.582
1967–73	8.1%	5.0%	4.6%	7.5%	.799[c]
All years	8.2%	4.0%	2.6%	4.4%	N.A.

[a] See text for explanation.
[b] 1952–1957 only.
[c] 1967–1971 only. This ratio is calculated for 1950–1957, 1958–1962, 1963–1967, and 1968–1971. That is, unlike the growth rates, it does not overlap with the last year of the preceding period.
SOURCES: OUTPUT, MINISTERIO DE HACIENDA Y COMERCIO, 1958: 323–324; SOCIEDAD NACIONAL DE INDUSTRIA, 1963; MINISTERIO DE INDUSTRIA Y TURISMO, 1974; AND BANCO CENTRAL, N.D.; EMPLOYMENT, MINISTERIO DE FOMENTO Y OBRAS PTIBLICAS, 1956–1960, 1961A, AND 1961B; MINISTERIO DE INDUSTRIA, 1962; MINISTERIO DE INDUSTRIA Y COMERCIO, 1966–1970; MINISTERIO DE INDUSTRIAE Y TURISMO, 1974A AND 1975; REAL WAGES, WEEKS, 1977A, WHERE METHOD IS EXPLAINED IN DETAIL AND SOURCES GIVEN; AND INVESTMENT FLOWS, ANAYA FRANCO, 1974B.

In terms of our theoretical discussion, this period, 1957–62, represents the phase of imperial penetration when more efficient, foreign capitals were seizing markets from local capitals and progressively eliminating monopoly positions. For 1954–63 (there are no data on centralisation[42] before 1954), the degree of centralisation in 18 branches of manufacturing decreased by an average of 30 percent (rising in only three of the 18).[43] This was the period in which imperial capital was destroying local monopolies in the sphere of circulation because of their greater efficiency in the sphere of production. During 1963–7, the trend was reversed, with centralisation rising by an average of 3 percent across branches (centralisation increased in 11 of 18 branches). In this second period, the competitive struggle advanced to the point of foreign capitals elim-

42 Marx distinguished between centralisation (fewer competitors) and concentration (larger capitals). Bourgeois economists use the latter term, in effect, to cover both. Clearly the latter process can advance (larger capitals), while the former declines (more competitors).

43 The measure used is the same as in Weeks (1976). The measure is commonly called the 'Herfindahl Index'. The data used are employment by firm. Using employment avoids bias due to inflation. In this index, the share of employment in a branch of industry employed by each firm is squared and summed for all firms. The maximum value of the index is *one* (a single firm employing the entire workforce) and the minimum value approaches zero (Weeks 1976).

inating or marginalising local capitals; indeed, this process, accelerated by the economic crisis of 1967–9, brought on the military coup of 1968, as the national industrial bourgeoisie seized state power to save itself from extinction.[44]

While the process of centralisation is irreversible in the advanced capitalist countries, this is not the case in a backward country (though the process of *concentration* is irreversible). The effect of intra-capitalist competition on eliminating temporary monopolisation is quite clear in Peru. In addition to the overall changes mentioned, by looking at changes in centralisation branch-by-branch, we find that these changes over the periods 1954–63 and 1963–7 are *negatively* related to the *level* of centralisation at the beginning of each period, and that the relationship is significant statistically. That is, in each period, branches of industry with a *high* degree of centralisation tended to become less centralised and vice-versa. The relationship for 1967–73 is more complex. Thus, the growing monopoly position of foreign capital in 1963–7 and the super profits obtained by selling above value created the possibility and necessity of its antithesis, stimulating the inflow of new capital – particularly from Germany and Japan.[45] From 1967 to 1973, the degree of centralisation fell in all 18 branches of manufacturing by an average of 55 percent.

Thus, we must see the process of centralisation in Peru as part of the dialectical process of accumulation. The creation of 'monopolies' – local or foreign – represents one phase in the accumulation process, and the strongest weapon in the destruction of monopolies in Peru and other backward countries is capital itself, its boundless expansion in search of greater profits. To view imperial capital as having the effect of monopolising Peruvian manufacturing, and to speak of 'imperial monopoly capital' as if this were a permanent state of affairs, is to lose the essence of the accumulation process – as well as being empirically false.

Looking at the period 1950–73 with the aid of our theoretical analysis of accumulation in backward countries, we see that it covers the period of entry of imperial capital on a large scale in search of profits through more efficient production than local capitals, into the phase of crisis and stagnation that is a necessary part of that accumulation process (see section III). Rapid accumulation from 1957–62 resulted from foreign capital seizing upon branches of industry ripe for the picking, and in the subsequent years up to about 1967, imperial capital enjoyed its 'golden age' of super profits in Peruvian industry. However, with the resurgence of competition from other imperial capitals,

44 Dore and Weeks 1976a.

45 Anaya Franco 1974.

these super profits began to dwindle, and with them, the rate of accumulation. In 1967–9 occurred the first slump in Peruvian manufacturing in almost two decades, and we interpret this as the coming to fruition of the barriers to extracting surplus value inherent in a backward country.

6 Sources of Accumulation: Organic Composition of Capital

In its most general form, the process of accumulation derives from the appropriation of surplus labour. Under capitalism, this surplus labour is appropriated by the exchange between capital and labour in which the commodity labour power is purchased at its value; that is, the exchange between capital and labour is an exchange of equal values.[46] Through this exchange the capitalist appropriates the use value of labour power, which creates an amount of value in excess of the value of the commodity labour power. In an actual situation, as in Peru, the analysis of the process of accumulation only begins with this abstract model. The actual process of accumulation in Peruvian manufacturing has been conditioned by certain characteristics of backwardness, and the most important are (1) centralisation (discussed above), (2) the particular circumstances affecting the organic composition of capital, and (3) the twofold nature of the wage paid to labourers.

Under bourgeois production, there is a pre-eminent tendency for the organic composition of capital to rise,[47] and there are counteracting tendencies. While it is an empirical question as to which tendency prevails at any moment, the necessary tendency for the organic composition of capital to rise is inherent in the growth of productivity, and follows from the concept of capital itself; i.e., it is not an empirical, but a theoretical proposition. It is the rise in the organic composition of capital that is the source of crisis, since the rate of profit tends to fall as the organic composition of capital rises.

The following discussion presumes that the means of production (intermediate goods and machinery) are produced at lower *values* in the advanced countries, and that these lower values are transformed into lower prices in international trade. This does not require goods to be sold at value (i.e., according to the labour time embodied in them), but for lower values to transform

46 Marx 1970b, pp. 501–7.

47 The organic composition of capital is the ratio of constant to variable capital. The former includes raw materials, intermediate goods, fuels, and the *depreciation* component of fixed capital (machinery and buildings); the latter includes the wage payments to productive workers (Marx 1970b, pp. 289–90).

into lower prices. In Table 11.2 we compute the organic composition of capital in market prices and the share of manufacturing 'inputs' (means of production) which derive from abroad for the period 1955–73. The table demonstrates an important mechanism which has operated in Peruvian manufacturing to counteract the tendency of the organic composition of capital to rise; namely, the possibility of importing a larger proportion of the means of production from the advanced capitalist countries where they are produced more efficiently (have lower *values*). The organic composition of capital moved in a cyclical pattern over the years 1955–73, tending to rise in the late 1950s and middle 1960s. In both cases, the rise was arrested by an increase in the share of imported inputs. That is, the importation of the means of production tended to *lower* the organic composition of capital. This, of course, conflicts with the argument that 'underdeveloped countries' suffer systematically in exchange with 'developed countries'; by this argument the prices of imported machinery rise continuously due to the monopoly power of 'developed countries'. It is beyond the scope of this paper to deal with this argument restricted to the sphere of circulation. Here we only show that the negative relationship between the organic composition of capital and the share of constant capital imported is very close and statistically highly significant. Two-thirds of the variation in the organic composition of capital (67.3 percent) is explained by variations in the share of inputs imported. Statistically, there is less than one possibility in 200 that the relationship is random (or accidental). The estimated relationship indicates that a one percent *rise* in the share of inputs imported leads to a .86 percent *fall* in the organic composition of capital. The relationship was estimated by using the technique of a 'dummy variable' to divide the period into two parts, 1955–66 and 1967–73. The implication of this division is pursued below.

We argued theoretically that the pre-capitalist nature of the production of the means of subsistence is the primary obstacle to accumulation in backward countries and explore this empirically below. From Table 11.2, we see that an important counteracting tendency to the barriers to raising relative surplus value (and thus the rate of exploitation) has been the cheapening of the means of production by their importation. In this way, capital in Peru repeatedly has been able to arrest the rising organic composition of capital and to maintain the rate of profit. In short, the rate of profit is positively related to the rate of surplus value and negatively related to the organic composition of capital; capital has been blocked in its attempt to raise the rate of surplus value and has maintained the rate of profit by reducing the organic composition of capital in *price* terms by importing the means of production.

However, this cheapening of the means of production through importation has not been enjoyed by all capitals, but in part reflects the increased import-

TABLE 11.2 The organic composition of capital and share of inputs imported, peruvian manufacturing, 1955–73

	Organic composition of capital	Share of inputs imported
1955	4.79	N.A.
1956	5.64	19.6%
1957	5.20	17.3%
1958	4.46	21.6%
1959	3.08	28.9%
1960	4.57	26.6%
1961	4.74	26.1%
1962	N.A.	N.A.
1963	4.09	26.8%
1964	N.A.	N.A.
1965	4.57	24.5%
1966	4.68	24.1%
1967	5.81	22.9%
1968	5.37	29.3%
1969	4.82	30.2%
1970	4.73	30.6%
1971	4.45	32.6%
1972	4.23	30.9%
1973	4.36	30.3%

SOURCES: MINISTERIO DE HACIENDA Y COMERCIO, 1958:323–324; SOCIEDAD NACIONAL DE INDUSTRIA, 1962, 1963; MINISTERIO DE INDUSTRIA Y TOURISMO, 1974A, 1974B, 1975; BANCO CENTRAL, N.D., MINISTERIO DE FOMENTO Y OBRAS PUBLICAS, 1956–1960, 1961A AND 1961B, MINISTERIO DE INDUSTRIA Y COMERCIO, 1966–70

ance of foreign capitals. While we have no data on the share of foreign and local inputs used by imperial as opposed to local capital, it would be strange indeed if foreign capital did not import a proportionally larger share of its inputs than national capital.[48] One of the great advantages of foreign capital over local capital is that the production processes of the former are designed to use the cheaper foreign inputs, as well as being intrinsically more efficient.

Considering only the rate of surplus value and the organic composition of capital, this ability to forestall a fall in the rate of profit by the importation of

48 Anaya Franco 1974, pp. 56–69.

cheaper inputs has its limits. As with all temporary resolutions of the contradictions of capital as a social relation, it has forestalled crisis only to advance the contradictions to a higher level. In Table 11.2, we see that the rising trend in the organic composition of capital in price terms from 1965 to 1967, which laid the basis of the crisis in manufacturing (1967–9),[49] was reversed by a sharp increase in the share of inputs imported. But this was achieved at a higher level of *both* the organic composition of capital and the share of inputs imported. In other words, after 1967, the same level of the organic composition of capital was associated with a *higher* import share than prior to 1967 (and the difference is statistically significant). Our interpretation of this is that the same organic composition of capital could be maintained only by a higher level of imports of the means of production. Below, we explain this in terms of the value of labour power.

7 The Productive Advantage of Foreign Capital

Before turning to the value of labour power, we consider the relative efficiency of foreign and local capitals. Throughout this analysis, we have taken it as theoretically established that there is a tendency for imperial capital to be more efficient than local capital. Now we consider this empirically. Unfortunately, we have comparative data only for 1969 and 1973. Also, we cannot compare the results from the two years for the purpose of drawing any conclusions about changes in relative efficiency, because the 1969 data are for the largest 200 companies in the manufacturing sector of Peru, and the 1973 data are from a random sample of all companies.[50]

Table 11.3 gives the result of the comparison for 19 branches of industry at the '2-digit' level (standard United Nations industrial classification).[51] Of the nineteen '2-digit' branches of manufacturing, in only three is average productivity per worker (in soles) greater in local companies than foreign companies (fishmeal, clothing and wood products), and in these branches the difference is not statistically significant. That is, the variation around the two means – for for-

49 Weeks 1977a.

50 INP 1973; Ministerio de Industria y Turismo 1975.

51 The 'one-digit' level is agriculture, mining, manufacturing, etc. The '2-digit' level is the next degree of disaggregation. All manufacturing is divided into 20 subsections (numbered 20 through 39). Each of these 20 can then be further sub-divided into a maximum of 9 branches at the '3-digit' level (see Table 11.4). For example, '2' indicates manufacturing, '21' is all beverages, and 214 is nonalcoholic beverages ('North American Industry Classification System' 2012).

eign and local capitals – is so great that the fact that one mean is larger may be purely an accident of the sample selected. In one sector (transport equipment) no comparison is possible, because no local companies are listed. In nine of the remaining fifteen branches, we can be 90 percent or more confident that the average productivity in foreign firms is in fact higher and not just a statistical accident.

Elsewhere, we have argued that the military coup of 1968 in Peru led to the creation of an alliance between the national industrial bourgeoisie and imperial capital, and that one of the important benefits of this alliance to imperial capital was that the Peruvian state facilitated the restructuring of imperial capital out of relatively less profitable areas and into more profitable ones. This was done by nationalisation with compensation. The statistical analysis in Table 11.3 strongly substantiates this argument. The manufacturing industries in which major nationalisations occurred were food processing (20, specifically sugar refining), paper (27), publishing and printing (28), basic metals (34), and fishmeal (20x). In all of these but one, printing and publishing, foreign companies had no significant productivity advantage over local companies. Foreign capital was significantly more productive for food processing as a *whole*, but it was not in the sub-branch of sugar refining where nationalisations occurred. And printing and publishing, where foreign capital was more efficient, is the exception that proves the rule: in this branch the foreign companies were not nationalised; it was only the local companies, owned by the 'grand bourgeoisie' the coup flung from power, that were nationalised. As shown for mining in this number of *Latin American Perspectives*, the nationalisations were nothing more than the process of centralisation and restructuring of capital, an attempt to overcome the contradictions in the accumulation process as manifested in specific sectors. Thus, they represented an impetus to accumulation by imperial capital.

For 1973, the data on comparative productivity are more detailed, but less comprehensive, covering seven '2-digit' industries and fifteen sub-branches at the '3-digit' level (Table 11.4). In all seven '2-digit' industries, foreign companies have on average higher productivity per worker. Further, we can be 99 percent confident that the difference is real and not accidental in five of the seven. In another, our confidence drops only to 95 percent (basic metals). Only in electrical equipment is the difference not significant. At the more disaggregated level ('3-digit'), local companies have higher productivity than foreign companies in only *one* (a sub-branch of textiles, 233). In eleven of the 15 subbranches, there is a 90 percent or better probability that the difference in average productivity per worker is not accidental. The data for 1973 indicate a much more extensive productive advantage for foreign firms than the data for 1969; i.e., the 1973 data show foreign capital to be of higher productivity in textiles, clothing,

TABLE 11.3 Average productivity in foreign and local companies, 1969

		Ratio, foreign to local firm, average productivity per worker	Significance level of difference in means	No. of companies
20.	Food Processing	2.17	90%	50
20x.	Fishmeal	0.94	N.S.	39
21.	Beverages	2.42	95%	18
23.	Textiles	1.22	N.S.	34
24.	Clothing	0.83	N.S.	16
25.	Wood Products	0.97	N.S.	6
26.	Furniture	1.23	N.S.	9
27.	Paper Products	3.88	N.S.	9
28.	Printing	1.54	95%	14
29.	Leather Products	1.18	90%	6
30.	Rubber Products	6.19	99%	5
31.	Chemicals	2.80	90%	51
33.	Non-metallic Minerals	2.08	99%	34
34.	Basic Metals	2.49	N.S.	9
35.	Metal Products	2.21	95%	15
36.	Machinery (non-elec)	1.81	N.S.	14
37.	Electrical Machinery	1.54	N.S.	17
38.	Transport Equipment	N.A.	N.A.	N.A.
39.	Other Manuf.	1.64	95%	48

Note: A number greater than one in column one indicates average productivity per worker is higher in foreign firms. 'N.S'. means not significant.
SOURCE: INP, 1973

and basic metals, while the 1969 data do not. The nature of the 1973 sample (i.e., its randomness) suggests it to be much more reliable.

Thus, the information in Tables 11.3 and 11.4 strikingly demonstrates the productive advantage of imperial capital. This advantage is largely (but not *exclusively*) due to imperial capitals being larger. In column 3 of Table 11.4, the difference in productivity per worker is adjusted for size of company (measured by number employed). This adjustment is made through regression analysis, in which output per worker is explained as a function of size of company (number employed) and ownership, where the latter takes the form of a 'dummy' variable. In column 3, the so-called 't-statistic' measures the significance of the difference in mean productivity between national and foreign companies *as if* both were on balance the same size. In two of the seven '2-digit' branches, foreign companies remain significantly more productive after we account for size of enterprise (in food processing and nonmetallic metals, 20 and 33). At the more disaggregated '3-digit' level, the larger size of foreign capitals accounts for their productive advantage in all subbranches except non-metallic metals.

TABLE 11.4 Average productivity in foreign and local companies, 1973

	Ratio, foreign to local firm productivity	Significance of level of means		Number of companies
		Simple	Adjusted for size	
20. Food Processing	3.29	99%	99%	124
202. Milk Products	5.04	99%	N.S.	11
205. Grain Milling	1.14	N.S.	N.S.	22
206. Baking	4.44	99%	N.S.	44
209. Other	2.52	98%	N.S.	20
21. Beverages	2.85	99%	N.S.	44
213. Beer	1.16	N.S.	N.S.	8
214. Non-alcoholic	2.78	95%	N.S.	12
23. Textiles	1.70	99%	N.S.	73
231. Piece goods	1.38	N.S.	N.S.	32
233. Cord & Rope	0.77	N.S.	N.S.	9
24. Clothing and Processed Textiles	2.30	99%	N.S.	64
241. Footwear	4.52	99%	95%	20
243. Clothing	1.67	90%	N.S.	34
244. Non-clothing	1.46	N.S.	N.S.	10
33. Non-metallic Minerals	3.67	99%	99%	57
331. Clay	8.74	99%	99%	15
332. Glass	3.18	99%	99%	11
333. Porcelain	2.78	99%	99%	10
339. Other	2.86	99%	N.S.	21
34. Basic Metals	1.87	90%	N.S.	19
37. Electrical Machinery	1.90	N.S.	90%	10

Note: 'N.S.' means 'not significant'.
SOURCE: MINISTERIO DE INDUSTRIA Y TURISMO, 1975

These statistics substantiate our earlier analysis of accumulation in backward countries and for Peru in particular. The rapid accumulation during the period 1957–67, was the result of the entry of foreign capital, seizing upon branches of industry in which it had competitive advantage. As shown in the previous sub-section, this advantage was augmented by the importation of the means of production, which reduced the organic composition of capital. In this part, we have shown the extent of imperial capital's productive advantage and its persistence.

To this point, we have considered the inherent contradiction in the accumulation process – arising from the pre-capitalist production of the means of consumption – only as a theoretical proposition. In the next part, we consider this empirically.

8 The Value of Labour power

The tendency for the production of use values in pre-capitalist agriculture to grow slower than in industry is inherent in backwardness. This tendency has been quite marked in Peru. From 1955 to 1973, gross national product grew at 5.2 percent in constant prices, while agricultural output grew at only 2.4 percent. Further, the difference between the two rates of growth increased after the early 1960s. From 1963 to 1973, GNP grew at 5.2 percent, as before, but agricultural output growth fell to 1.9 percent.[52] This slow growth of agricultural use values is the source of the pressure on profitability in the capitalist sector, as we showed theoretically in section III. If we look back at Table 11.1, we see in columns 3 and 4 the consequence of this in the manufacturing sector. The first column gives the growth rate of the 'producer real wage' or the wage cost to capital (see Dore, this issue). This is the growth rate of the nominal (money or *sol*) wage, divided by an index of manufacturing prices. This measures the real exchange value of the wage to capital. The wage the capitalist must pay determines how much labour power he can obtain from a given advance of variable capital. By raising prices, capital can seek to offset an increase in the wage paid. Thus, a price increase has the effect of devaluing the wage from capital's point of view. For example, if the wage rises by ten percent and the price of what labour produces rises by ten percent, capital, at the end of its circuit, can purchase as much labour power as before with the capital realized in money form.[53]

In Table 11.1, we see that the earliest period (1950–7) was characterised by a rising producer real wage (at 2.9 percent per annum). In the second period, the wage cost to capital actually fell (at 2.5 percent per annum), even though money wages rose. This was also the period of most rapid growth of output and employment. However, in the last two periods, the wage cost to capital rose at an increasing rate. These were periods of rapidly rising manufacturing prices, but money wages rose even faster.

It is to be noted that the wage cost to capital need bear no close relationship to the purchasing power of wages, which is determined by movements in the prices of the means of consumption, largely produced pre-capitalistically in Peru until the 1970s. In general, the purchasing power of wages (the use value of the wage to the worker) rose faster than the wage cost to capital (except for 1962–7). This indicates that manufacturing prices rose faster than agricultural

52 Banco Central, 1966, 1974.

53 Weeks 1977a.

TABLE 11.5 Consumption goods as share of total imports 1950–73

	Consumption goods	Non-durables	Food
1950–1957	23.6%	13.1%	7.0%
1958–1962	21.3%	12.2%	6.4%
1963–1967	19.9%	11.0%	6.4%
1968–1973	14.3%	11.2%	N.A.

SOURCES: BANCO CENTRAL, 1966 AND 1974

prices. Obviously, such a relationship is in the interest of the capitalist class, since it allows for workers' demands for a higher standard of living to be met in part from outside of the capitalist sector. The ability to hold food prices down despite slow growth of output per man during several periods has been the result of both importing wage goods and state policies to depress agricultural prices directly. The latter lies beyond the scope of this paper.[54]

The ability to keep prices of the means of consumption down *relatively* to the prices of manufactures is limited when agriculture is pre-capitalist and the production of agricultural use values grows slowly as a consequence. The relatively slower rise in the prices of the means of consumption in Peru has been achieved through importation of workers' necessities of life. This is shown in Table 11.5, where we give the share of consumption goods in total imports and divide them into non-durable goods and food products. From the early 1950s to the early 1970s, consumer goods fell sharply as a share of imports (from about 24 percent to about 14 percent). However, the share of non-durable consumer goods fell only slightly, and actually *rose* in the last period. And the share of imports consisting of food products remained virtually unchanged from 1958 to 1967 (last year for which we have data), while the total volume of imports was rising dramatically. While in the early 1950s imports represented about 8 percent of total consumption of food, in the mid-1960s this proportion reached over 11 percent.[55]

These imports reflect the necessity to reduce the value of labour power, but the inability to do so through domestic production. This is due to the pre-capitalist nature of food-crop agriculture before 1968, and the problems associated with the so-called 'land reform' subsequently.[56] The necessity to import

54 Portocarrero 1974.

55 Banco Central 1966.

56 Dore and Weeks 1976a.

TABLE 11.6 Thousands of metric tons of selected food crops, domestic production, 1968–74

	Potatoes	Maize	Rice	Wheat
1968	1,526	590	465	N.A.
1969	1,856	584	444	127
1970	1,929	614	587	125
1971	1,968	616	557	122
1972	1,712	589	436	140
1973	1,712	590	440	140
1974	1,743	633	405	147
Annual Increase	2.2%	1.1%	-2.3%	3.0%

SOURCE: INP, 1975B

goods for workers' consumption is shown dramatically by a study which found that the poorest 20 percent of the urban Peruvian population in the early 1970s had the highest import content of their expenditures compared to all other income classes (22 percent, compared to 15 percent for the wealthiest 20 percent of the population).[57] While the state has not released reliable figures on food imports in recent years, all indications are that the problem is growing more acute.[58] Indeed, available data on agricultural production show that the need for more food imports is growing. Table 11.6 gives the domestic output in metric tons of the major staples of the working class diet for the years 1968–74.

Our interpretation is that the 'land reform' in part sought to capitalise agriculture in order to drive down the value of labour power and raise the rate of surplus value in the industrial sectors. While the data in Table 11.6 are only for a few years, these are the crucial ones, and they indicate that success has been limited. The production of potatoes in 1972–4 was *below* the 1970–1 peak by 12 percent; while maize production in 1974 was the highest of the seven years, the average for 1972–4 was the same as for 1969–1; and rice production has fallen absolutely. Only in the production of wheat has there been a substantial increase from 1969–71 to 1972–4 (fourteen percent), but even here the rate of growth of output is slower than the rate of growth of either population or the industrial proletariat.

57 INP 1975, p. 21.
58 Portocarrero 1974.

In bourgeois production, profit derives from the difference between the value of labour power and the value of the commodities which that labour power produces in combination with the means of production. In this part, while we have not directly measured the value of labour power – a task which is probably impossible in practice – we have indicated the stagnation in the production of use values in agriculture. We take this as *prima facie* evidence of slow or zero productivity growth in that sector.

9 Crisis in Manufacturing

Crisis and its attendant characteristics of unemployment, falling wages and the intensification of work are inherent in capitalism. This is true in Peru as in other capitalist countries. This is true regardless of the ownership of capital, deriving from capital itself as a social relation. The significance of foreign ownership in Peru is that imperial capital was the major source of the rapid accumulation in manufacturing from 1957–67. This imperial capital-led accumulation accelerated the dialectical process by which crises became inevitable. The gathering storm of economic crisis in manufacturing is not the result of foreign looting and plundering, but the pre-capitalist nature of agriculture. The source of crisis lies in the stagnation of agriculture, for it is only by cheapening the means of consumption that relative surplus value can be raised. Ultimately, this can only be done by the Peruvian land reform successfully capitalising agriculture.

The present crisis of the Peruvian economy reflects the further maturing of the inherent contradictions in accumulation in backward countries, as developed above. Despite all-time record high exports in 1975, the Peruvian state faced its worst balance of payment deficit in history. Two devaluations (in mid-1975 and mid-1976) represented attempts to correct this massive excess of imports over exports. But these adjustments in the sphere of circulation cannot touch the underlying contradictions arising from the interaction of the value of labour power and the tendency of capitalist production to reduce the value of commodities.[59]

The current repressive steps taken by the bourgeois regime – virtually outlawing strikes, arresting labour militants, militarily suppressing work stoppages – represent the response of the local and imperial capitalist classes to the contradictions they face. Unable to reduce the value of labour power, they seek

59 New 'mini-devaluations' were promised by the Minister of the Economy in September, 1976.

to drive the wage below that value. Temporarily, they may be successful, as in 1967–9, when manufacturing real wages fell. However, short of a prolonged, primarily military assault against the working class (as in Chile), this is a *very* temporary solution. Indeed, a prolonged repression of the working class itself would provide only temporary relief.

Further sustained accumulation in the Peruvian economy and particularly in manufacturing must be achieved by the revolutionising of the agricultural sector. The basis for this was created by the land reform. We can expect more intense efforts by the state to raise productivity in that sector. However, the bourgeoisie faces a growing militancy in the peasantry and can only achieve the necessary productive changes through an intense class struggle. In this class struggle, the bourgeois state cannot, as in 1968, present itself to the peasantry as the crusading enemies of the hated landlord class.[60]

The Peruvian bourgeoisie entered the current crisis with its cloak of anti-imperialism in tatters, the true nature of its military front-man government no longer concealed by a mythical 'independence', and the petty bourgeoisie driven increasingly into the camp of the proletariat and peasantry. The class struggle the bourgeoisie sought to undermine has now emerged in more intense form.

60 Dore and Weeks 1976a.

John Weeks' Academic Publications

Sole Author

Weeks, John 1967, 'Review: New Educational Media in Action: Case Studies for Planners I.II.III by UNESCO; The New Media: Memo to Educational Planners by W. Schramm, P.H. Coombs, F. Kahnert, J. Lyle', *Comparative Education*, 4, 1: 68–9.

Weeks, John 1968, 'A Comment on Peter Kilby: Industrial Relations and Wage Determination', *The Journal of Developing Areas*, 3, 1: 7–18.

Weeks, John 1970, 'Review: Manpower Development in Africa by Robert D. Loken', *ILR Review*, 23, 2: 280–2.

Weeks, John 1970, 'Review: Teaching in Developing nations: A Guide for Educators', *Comparative Education*, 6, 1: 70–1.

Weeks, John 1971, 'Does Employment Matter', *Manpower and Unemployment Research in Africa*, 4, 1: 67–70.

Weeks, John 1971, 'Further Comment on the Kilby/Weeks Debate: An Empirical Rejoinder', *The Journal of Developing Areas*, 5, 2: 165–74.

Weeks, John 1971, 'Review: A Century of Mismatch by Simon Ramo', *Monthly Labour Review*, 94, 3: 83.

Weeks, John 1971, 'Review: The Politics of Tradition: Continuity and Change in Northern Nigeria, 1946–1966', *The Journal of Developing Areas*, 5, 2: 273–4.

Weeks, John 1971, 'The Political Economy of Labour Transfer', *Science & Society*, 35, 4: 463–80.

Weeks, John 1971, 'Wage Policy and the Colonial Legacy-A Comparative Study', *The Journal of Modern African Studies*, 9, 3: 361–87.

Weeks, John 1973, 'An Exploration into the nature of the Problem of Urban Imbalance in Africa', *Manpower and Unemployment Research in Africa*, 6, 2: 9–36.

Weeks, John 1973, 'Introduction', *Manpower and Unemployment Research in Africa*, 6, 2: 3–7.

Weeks, John 1973, 'Review: Foreign Aid and Industrial Development in Pakistan by Irving Brecher, S.A. Abbas', *Monthly Labour Review*, 96, 2: 86–7.

Weeks, John 1974, 'A Brief Note on the Unemployment Crisis in Poor Countries', *Manpower and Unemployment Research in Africa*, 7, 1: 32–8.

Weeks, John 1974, 'Review: Social Change and Economic Development in Nigeria by Ukandi G. Damachi, Hans Dieter Seibel', *International Affairs*, 50, 3: 493.

Weeks, John 1975, 'Review: Labour and Politics in Nigeria 1945–71 by Robin Cohen', *International Affairs*, 51, 1: 115–16.

Weeks, John 1977, 'Backwardness, Foreign Capital, and Accumulation in the Manufacturing Sector of Peru, 1954–1975', *Latin American Perspectives*, 4, 3: 124–45.

Weeks, John 1977, 'The Sphere of Production and the Analysis of Crisis in Capitalism', *Science & Society*, 41, 3: 281–302.

Weeks, John 1979, 'The Process of Accumulation and the "Profit-Squeeze" Hypothesis', *Science & Society*, 43, 3: 259–80.

Weeks, John 1981, 'The Differences Between Materialist Theory and Dependency Theory and Why They Matter', *Latin American Perspectives*, 8, 3/4: 118–23.

Weeks, John 1981, *Capital and Exploitation*, Princeton: Princeton University Press.

Weeks, John 1982, 'A Note on Underconsumptionist Theory and the Labour Theory of Value', *Science & Society*, 46, 1: 60–76.

Weeks, John 1983, 'On the Issue of Capitalist Circulation and the Concepts of Appropriate to its Analysis', *Science & Society*, 47, 2: 214–25.

Weeks, John 1983, 'Review: A Contemporary Critique of Historical Materialism Vol. 1, Power, Property, and the State by Anthony Giddens', *The Annals of the American Academy of Political and Social Science*, 467: 238–39.

Weeks, John 1984, 'Theory, Ideology, and Idolatry', *Economic and Political Weekly*, 19, 48: 2054–6.

Weeks, John 1985, 'Epochs of Capitalism and the Progressiveness of Capital's Expansion', *Science & Society*, 49, 4: 414–36.

Weeks, John 1985, 'Las Elecciones Nicaraguenses De 1984', *Foro Internacional*, 26, 1: 85–106.

Weeks, John 1985, *Limits to Capitalist Development: The Industrialisation of Peru, 1950–1980*, Boulder: Westview.

Weeks, John 1985, *The Economies of Central America*, New York: Holmes & Meier.

Weeks, John 1986, 'An Interpretation of the Central American Crisis', *Latin American Research Review*, 21, 3: 31–53.

Weeks, John 1988, 'The Land Question in Central America', *Economics and Sociology*, 47, 4: 422.

Weeks, John 1988, 'Value and Production in the General Theory', in *J.M. Keynes in Retrospect*, edited by John Hillard, London: Edward Elgar.

Weeks, John 1989, 'Introduction' in *Debt Disaster? Banks, Government, and Multilaterals Confront the Crisis*, edited by John Weeks, New York: New York University Press.

Weeks, John 1989, 'Losers Pay Reparations, or How the Third World lost the Lending war' in *Debt Disaster? Banks, Government, and Multilaterals Confront the Crisis*, edited by John Weeks, New York: New York University Press.

Weeks, John 1989, *A Critique of Neoclassical Macroeconomics*, London & New York: Macmillan.

Weeks, John 1990, 'Abstract Labour and Commodity Production', *Research in Political Economy*, 12, 3–19.

Weeks, John 1990, 'Review: Struggle Against Dependence: Nontraditional Export

Growth in Central America and the Caribbean by Eva Paus', *Journal of Latin American Studies*, 22, 1: 212–14.

Weeks, John 1991, 'Introduction' in *Beyond Superpower Rivalry: Latin America and the Third World*, edited by John Weeks, New York: New York University Press.

Weeks, John 1991, 'Macroeconomic Adjustment and the Fiction of Labour Market Clearing' in *Towards Social Adjustment: labour market issues in structural adjustment*, edited by Guy Standing, Geneva: ILO.

Weeks, John 1991, 'Review: US Protectionism and the World Debt Crisis by Edward John Ray', *Journal of Economic Literature*, 29, 2: 617–18.

Weeks, John 1991, 'Structural Adjustment and Rural Labour Markets in Sierra Leone', *ILO Working Papers*, I. 396/WEP 10–6/WP 101.

Weeks, John 1992, 'Review: A Long-Run Model of Development for Central America by Victor Bulmer-Thomas', *Journal of Latin American Studies*, 24, 3: 713–714.

Weeks, John 1992, 'Review: Feeding the Crisis: US Food Aid and Farm Policy in Central America', *Journal of Latin American Studies*, 24, 1: 218–19.

Weeks, John 1992, 'Review: In the Shadows of the Sun: Caribbean Development Alternatives and US Policy', *Journal of Latin American Studies*, 24, 1: 219–20.

Weeks, John 1992, 'Review: Labour and Politics in Panama: The Torrijos Years by Sharon Phillips Collazos', *The Hispanic American Historical Review*, 72, 4: 629–30.

Weeks, John 1992, 'Review: Modernisation and Stagnation: Latin American Agriculture into the 1990s', *Journal of Latin American Studies*, 24, 3: 708–9.

Weeks, John 1992, 'Review: Perspectives on the Agro-Export Economy in Central America by Wim Pelupessy', *Journal of Latin American Studies*, 24, 3: 714–15.

Weeks, John 1992, 'Second time tragedy: US policy in Panama', *Third World Quarterly*, 13, 1: 184–7.

Weeks, John 1992, *Development Strategy and the Economy of Sierra Leone*, New York: St Martin's.

Weeks, John 1993, 'Review: The Macroeconomics of Populism in Latin America by Rudiger Dornbusch, Sebastian Edwards', *The Economic Journal*, 103, 420: 1325–326.

Weeks, John 1993, 'The Nicaraguan Stabilisation Programme of 1989' in Economic Maladjustment in Central America, edited by Wim Pelupessy and John Weeks, London: Palgrave Macmillan.

Weeks, John 1993, *Development Policy and the Economy of Sierra Leone*, London: Macmillan.

Weeks, John 1994, 'Review: Comparative Development Studies: In Search of the World View', *The Economic Journal*, 104, 426: 1195–6.

Weeks, John 1994, 'Review: The Politics of Trade in Latin American Development by Steven E. Sanderson', *The Journal of Developing Areas*, 26, 3: 780.

Weeks, John 1995, 'A Note on African Growth and Exports', *SOAS Department of Economics Working Papers*, 53.

Weeks, John 1995, 'Introduction' in *Structural Adjustment and the Agricultural Sector in Latin America*, edited by John Weeks, London: Macmillan.

Weeks, John 1995, 'Macroeconomic adjustment and Latin American agriculture since 1980' in *Structural Adjustment and the Agricultural Sector in Latin America*, edited by John Weeks, London: Macmillan.

Weeks, John 1996, 'Regional Cooperation and Southern African Development', *Journal of Southern African Studies*, 22, 1: 99–117.

Weeks, John 1996, 'Review: Monetary Policy in Developing Countries by Sheila Page', *The Economic Journal*, 106, 434: 250–1.

Weeks, John 1996, 'The Manufacturing Sector in Latin America and the New Economic Model' in *The New Economic Model in Latin America and its Impact on Income Distribution and Poverty*, edited by Victor Bulmer-Thomas, Basingstoke: Macmillan.

Weeks, John 1997, 'Employment, Livelihoods, and Macroeconomic Policy for Sub-Saharan Countries' in *Employment Expansion and Macroeconomic Stability under Increasing Globalisation*, edited by Azizur Khan and M. Muqtada, Basingstoke: Macmillan.

Weeks, John 1997, 'Market liberalisation and agricultural performance in Central America', *SOAS Department of Economics Working Papers*, 71.

Weeks, John 1997, 'Open Economy Adjustment and Transition in Vietnam', in *Privatisation, Enterprise Development, and Economic Reform: Experiences of Developing and Transitional Economies*, edited by Paul Cook; Colin Kirkpatrick and Frederick Nixson, Cheltenham: Edward Elgar.

Weeks, John 1997, 'Review: World Food Aid: Experiences of Recipients and Donors by John Shaw, Edward Clay', *Africa: Journal of the International African Institute*, 67, 2: 337–8.

Weeks, John 1998, 'Economic integration in Latin America: Impact on Labour', *ILO Employment and Training Papers*, 18.

Weeks, John 1998, 'Orthodox and Heterodox Policies for Growth in Africa south of the Sahara', *CDPR Discussion Paper*, 0298.

Weeks, John 1999 'The Essence and Appearance of Globalisation: The Rise of Finance Capital' in *Globalisation and the Dilemmas of the State in the South*, edited by Francis Adams; Satya Dev Gupta and Kidane Mengisteab, London: Macmillan.

Weeks, John 1999, 'Stuck in low GEAR? South African Macroeconomic Policy, 1996–1998', *Cambridge Journal of Economics*, 23, 6: 795–811.

Weeks, John 1999, 'Surfing the Troubled Waters of "global turbulence": A Comment', *Historical Materialism*, 5, 1: 211–30.

Weeks, John 1999, 'The Expansion of Capital and Uneven Development on a World Scale', *CDPR Discussion Paper*, 0999.

Weeks, John 1999, 'Trade Liberalisation, Market Deregulation, and Agricultural Performance in Central America', *Journal of Development Studies*, 35, 5: 48–75.

Weeks, John 2000, 'Have Workers in Latin America Gained from Liberalisation and Regional Integration?', *Journal of Developing Societies*, 16, 1: 87–115.

Weeks, John 2000, 'Latin America and the "High Performing Asian Economies": Growth and Debt', *Journal of International Development*, 12, 5: 625–54.

Weeks, John 2000, 'Review: Contemporary Economic Issues: Proceedings of the Eleventh World Congress of the International Economic Association, Tunis: Volume 1: Regional Experience and System Reform. by Justin Yifu Lin; Contemporary Economic Issues: Proceedings of the Eleventh World Congress of the International Economic Association, Tunis: Volume 2: Labour, Food and Poverty. by Yair Mundlak', *The Economic Journal*, 110, 461: F202–F204.

Weeks, John 2001, 'A Tale of Two Transitions: Cuba and Vietnam', in *Globalisation and Third World Socialism*, edited by Claes Brundenius and John Weeks, New York: Palgrave.

Weeks, John 2001, 'Globalize, Globa-lize, Global Lies: Myths of the World Economy in the 1990s', in *Phases of Capitalist Development: Booms, Crises and Globalisations*, edited by Robert Albritton; Makoto Itoh; Richard Westra and Alan Zuege, London: Palgrave.

Weeks, John 2001, 'Growth Variability among and within African Countries: An Aspect of Unsustained Development', SOAS *Department of Economics Working Papers*, 115.

Weeks, John 2002, 'The Efficiency of Small Enterprises in Developing Countries: An Empirical Analysis' in *Small-Scale Enterprises in Developing Countries and Transitional Economies*, edited by Homi Katrak and Roger Strange, Basingstoke: Palgrave.

Weeks, John 2003, 'A Tale of Two Crises: Latin America in the 1980s and the "HPAEs" in the 1990s', in *Development and Structural Change in Asia-Pacific: Globalising Miracles or End of a Model?*, edited by Martin Andersson and Christer Gunnarsson, London: Routledge.

Weeks, John 2003, 'Developing Country Debt and Globalisation' in *Anti-capitalism: A Marxist Introduction*, edited by Alfredo Saad-Filho, London: Pluto Press.

Weeks, John 2003, 'Small Manufacturing Establishments in Developing Countries: An Empirical Analysis', *International Review of Applied Economics*, 17, 4: 339–59.

Weeks, John 2007, 'Exports, Foreign Investment, and Growth in Latin America: Scepticism by Way of Simulation' in *Globalisation and the Myths of Free Trade*, edited by Anwar Shaikh, New York: Routledge.

Weeks, John 2007, 'Inequality Trends in Some Developed OECD Countries', in *Flat world, big gaps: economic liberalisation, globalisation, poverty and inequality*, edited by Jomo K.S. with Jacques Baudot, New York: UN. Department of Economic and Social Affairs.

Weeks, John 2007, 'Moldova's Middle-Income "Mistaken Identity", The Severe Income and Human Development Costs', *International Poverty Centre Country Study*, 11.

Weeks, John 2008, 'A Note on Mundell-Fleming and Developing Countries', *SOAS Department of Economics Working Papers*, 155.

Weeks, John 2008, 'Comparing Policies in Azerbaijan and Zambia', *Development Viewpoint*, 13.

Weeks, John 2008, 'Is a "Resource Curse" Inevitable in Resource-Rich Countries? Comparing Policies in Azerbaijan and Zambia', *Development Viewpoint*, 13.

Weeks, John 2008, 'The Reduction of Fiscal Space in Zambia Due to Dutch Disease and Tight-Money Conditionalities', *International Policy Centre for Inclusive Growth Research Report*, 14.

Weeks, John 2009, 'Miracles and Crisis: Boom, Collapse and Recovery in East and Southeast Asia', in *Confronting global neoliberalism: third world resistance and development strategies*, edited by Richard Westra, Atlanta: Clarity Press.

Weeks, John 2009, 'The Effectiveness of Monetary Policy Reconsidered', *Working Papers Political Economy Research Institute, University of Massachusetts at Amherst*, 202.

Weeks, John 2009, *Impact of the Global Economic Crisis on the Economy of Sierra Leonne*, A Report for UNDP Freetown and Ministry of Finance of Sierra Leone.

Weeks, John 2009, *Macroeconomic Convergence in East, Central and Southern Africa, 1980–2007*, United Nations Economic Commission for Africa.

Weeks, John 2009, *Teoría de la competencia: En Los Neoclásicos y en Marx*, Madrid: Maia Ediciones.

Weeks, John 2010, 'The Freetown Declaration: Countercyclical Policy for Africa', *Working Papers Political Economy Research Institute, University of Massachusetts at Amherst*, 237.

Weeks, John 2010, 'The Theory and Empirical Credibility of the Commodity Money', *SOAS Research on Money and Finance Discussion Papers*, 21.

Weeks, John 2010, *Background Paper on Employment and Poverty in Africa*. Trade and Development Report 2010.

Weeks, John 2010, *Background Paper on Fiscal Policy for Poverty Reduction*. Least Developed Countries Report.

Weeks, John 2010, *Promoting High-level Sustainable Growth to Reduce Unemployment in Africa*. African Union Commission and United Nations Economic Commission for Africa.

Weeks, John 2011, 'A Countercyclical Policy for Africa: Institutional and Economic Feasibility', *International Journal of Public Policy*, 7, 1: 112–33.

Weeks, John 2011, 'Why Did Fiscal Stimulus Work in Sierra Leone in the Crisis?', *Development Viewpoint*, 59.

Weeks, John 2012, 'Dependency theory', in *The Elgar Companion to Marxist Economics*, edited by Ben Fine; Alfredo Saad-Filho and Marco Boffo, London: Edward Elgar.

Weeks, John 2012, 'Macroeconomic Impact of Capital Flows in Sub-Saharan Countries, 1980–2008', *Working Papers Political Economy Research Institute, University of Massachusetts at Amherst*, 290.

Weeks, John 2012, 'Review: The Roller Coast Economy: Financial Crisis, Great Recession, and the Public Opinion by Howard J. Sherman', *Science & Society*, 76, 1: 122–4.

Weeks, John 2012, 'Theory and Empirical Credibility of Commodity Money', *Science & Society*, 76, 1: 66–94.

Weeks, John 2012, *The Irreconcilable Inconsistencies of Neoclassical Macroeconomics: A False Paradigm*, London: Routledge.

Weeks, John 2013, 'A Progressive International Monetary System: Growth enhancing, speculation reducing, and cross-country equity', in *Economics Policies Governance and the New Economics*, edited by Philip Arestis and Malcolm Sawyer, Basingstoke: Palgrave Macmillan.

Weeks, John 2013, 'Open Economy Monetary Policy Reconsidered', *Review of Political Economy*, 25, 1: 57–68.

Weeks, John 2013, 'Quantity Adjustment: The Sine Qua Non of Keynes's Contribution', *Critique*, 41, 2: 171–82.

Weeks, John 2013, 'Review: A Modern Guide to Keynesian Macroeconomics and Economic Policies', *Review of Radical Political Economics*, 42, 2: 240–2.

Weeks, John 2013, *Background Paper on 'Fiscal Space'*. Trade and Development Report 2013.

Weeks, John 2014, 'Euro Cries and Euro Scams: Trade not Debt and Deficits Tell the Tale', *Review of Political Economy*, 26, 2: 171–89.

Weeks, John 2014, 'Macroeconomic Impact of Capital Flight in Sub-Saharan Africa', in *Capital Flight from Africa: Causes Effects and Policy Issues*, edited by S. Ibi Ajayi and Léonce Ndikuma, Oxford: Oxford University Press.

Weeks, John 2014, Review of "Economists and the Powerful: Convenient Theories, Distorted Facts, Ample Rewards" by Norbert Haring, Niall Douglas', *Science & Society*, 78, 2: 249–51.

Weeks, John 2014, *Capital, Exploitation, and Economic Crisis*, London: Routledge.

Weeks, John 2014, *Economics of the 1%: How Mainstream Economics Serves the Rich, Obscures Reality, and Distorts Policy*, London: Anthem Press.

Weeks, John 2015, '2015: A failing fiscal policy' in *The Cracks Begin to Show: A Review of the UK Economy in 2015*, London: Economists for Rational Economic Policies.

Weeks, John 2015, 'Macroeconomic Policies for Full and Productive Employment: Case Studies of Thailand and Viet Nam', *ILO Asia-Pacific Working Paper Series*, available at: https://www.ilo.org/wcmsp5/groups/public/---asia/---robangkok/documents/publication/wcms_402378.pdf

Weeks, John 2016, 'A Growing Record in Fiscal Mismanagement' in *The Gap Widens: Budget 2016 Report*, London: Economists for Rational Economic Policies.

Weeks, John 2016, 'Fiscal Policy: It's the Same Old Story' in *Review of the UK economy Q4 2015*, London: Economists for Rational Economic Policies.

Weeks, John 2016, 'George Osborne's Treasury Estimates of Brexit – & what it tells us about the Tory Party', in *Remain for Change: Building European solidarity for a democratic economic alternative*, London: Economists for Rational Economic Policies.

Weeks, John 2017, 'Understanding Brexit: A Primer on the Split that has now been set into motion', *Dollars & Sense*, May/June.

Weeks, John 2017, 'What Happened to the American Dream?', in *The American Middle Class: An Economic Encyclopedia of Progress and Poverty*, edited by Robert Rycroft, Santa Barbara: Greenwood.

Weeks, John 2018, 'Fifty Years of Radical Economics: Beginnings in Ann Arbor', in 'Memoirs', *Review of Radical Political Economics*, 50, 3: 582–4.

Weeks, John 2019, 'Does the UK really have too much debt?' in *Rethinking Britain: Policy Ideas for the Many*, edited by Sue Konzelmann; Susan Himmelweit; Jeremy Smith and John Weeks, Bristol: Policy Press.

Weeks, John 2019, 'How should we manage inflation?' in *Rethinking Britain: Policy Ideas for the Many*, edited by Sue Konzelmann; Susan Himmelweit; Jeremy Smith and John Weeks, Bristol: Policy Press.

Weeks, John 2019, 'Introduction' in *Rethinking Britain: Policy Ideas for the Many*, edited by Sue Konzelmann; Susan Himmelweit; Jeremy Smith and John Weeks, Bristol: Policy Press.

Weeks, John 2019, 'The macroeconomic role of progressive taxation', in *Rethinking Britain: Policy Ideas for the Many*, edited by Sue Konzelmann; Susan Himmelweit; Jeremy Smith and John Weeks, Bristol: Policy Press.

Weeks, John 2019, 'Using the budget to manage output and employment', in *Rethinking Britain: Policy Ideas for the Many*, edited by Sue Konzelmann; Susan Himmelweit; Jeremy Smith and John Weeks, Bristol: Policy Press.

Weeks, John 2020, *The Debt Delusion: Living Within Our Means and Other Fallacies*, Cambridge: Polity Press.

Co-authored

Stewart, Frances and John Weeks 1975, 'Some employment effects of wage changes in poor countries', *The Journal of Development Studies*, 11, 2: 93–107.

Dore, Elizabeth and John Weeks 1976, 'The Intensification of Assault Against the Working Class in "Revolutionary" Peru', *Latin American Perspectives*, 3, 2: 55–83.

Dore, Elizabeth and John Weeks 1977, 'Class Alliances and Class Struggle in Peru', *Latin American Perspectives*, 4, 3: 4–17.

Dore, Elizabeth and John Weeks 1977, 'Crisis and Accumulation in the Peruvian Mining Industry 1968–1974', *Latin American Perspectives*, 4, 3: 77–102.

Weeks, John and Elizabeth Dore 1979, 'International Exchange and the Causes of Backwardness', *Latin American Perspectives*, 6, 2: 62–87.

Weeks, John and Elizabeth Dore 1979, 'Reply to Samir Amin', *Latin American Perspectives*, 6, 3: 114–16.

Jamal, Vali and John Weeks 1987, 'Rural-urban income trends in sub-Saharan Africa', *ILO Working Papers*, 18.

Jamal, Vali and John Weeks 1988, 'The vanishing rural-urban gap in sub-Saharan Africa', *International labour review*, 127, 3: 271–92.

Jamal, Vali and John Weeks 1988, 'Labour market Analysis and employment planning: rural-urban income trends in sub-Saharan Africa', *World Employment Programme research working paper*, 18, ILO.

Weeks, John and Andrew Zimbalist 1989, 'The failure of intervention in Panama: Humiliation in the Backyard', *Third World Quarterly*, 11, 1: 1–27.

Weeks, John and Phil Gunson 1991, *Panama: Made in the USA*, London: Latin American Bureau.

Zimbalist, Andrew and John Weeks 1991, *Panama at the Crossroads: Economic Development and Political Change in the Twentieth Century*, Berkeley: University of California Press.

Dore, Elizabeth and John Weeks 1992, 'The Red and the Black. The Sandinistas and the Nicaraguan Revolution', *University of London Institute of Latin American Studies Research Papers*, 28.

Mosley, Paul and John Weeks 1993, 'Has Recovery Begun? Africa's Adjustment in the 1980's Revisited', *World Development*, 21, 10: 1583–1606.

Weeks, John and Vali Jamal 1993, *Africa Misunderstood*, London: Macmillan.

Weeks, John and Wim Pelupessy 1993, 'Adjustment in Central America', in Economic Maladjustment in Central America, edited by Wim Pelupessy and John Weeks, London: Palgrave Macmillan.

Weeks, John and Paul Mosley 1994, 'Adjustment in Africa', *Development Policy Review*, 12, 3: 319–27.

Mosley, Paul; Turan Subasat and John Weeks 1995, 'Assessing Adjustment in Africa', *World Development*, 23, 9: 1459–73.

Dore, Elizabeth and John Weeks 1996, 'The changing faces of imperialism', *NACLA Report on the Americas*, 30, 2: 10–16.

Brundenius, Claes and John Weeks 2001, 'Conclusion: Alternative Responses to Globalisation', in *Globalisation and Third World Socialism*, edited by Claes Brundenius and John Weeks, New York: Palgrave.

Brundenius, Claes and John Weeks 2001, 'Globalisation and Third World Socialism', in *Globalisation and Third World Socialism*, edited by Claes Brundenius and John Weeks, New York: Palgrave.

Dagdeviren, Hulya and John Weeks 2001, 'How Much Poverty could HIPC Reduce?', *University of Hertfordshire Business School Working Papers*, available at: https://uhra.herts.ac.uk/bitstream/handle/2299/680/S26.pdf?sequence=1&isAllowed=y

Dagdeviren, Hulya; Rolph van der Hoeven and John Weeks 2002, 'Redistribution Matters: Growth for Poverty Reduction', *Development and Change*, 33, 3: 383–413.

Lübker, Malte; Graham Smith and John Weeks 2002, 'Growth and the Poor: A Comment on Dollar and Kraay', *Journal of International Development*, 14, 5: 555–71.

Weeks, John and Christopher Cramer 2002, 'Conflicts, agriculture and food security', in *The State of Food and Agriculture: Lessons from the Past 50 Years*, Rome: FAO.

Cramer, Christopher; Howard Stein and John Weeks 2006, 'Ownership and Donorship: Analytical Issues and a Tanzanian Case Study', *Journal of Contemporary African Studies*, 24, 3: 415–36.

Weeks, John and Howard Stein 2006, 'The Washington Consensus', in *The Elgar Companion to Development Studies*, edited by David Clark, London: Edward Elgar.

Weeks, John (mission leader); Victoria Chisala; Alemayehu Geda; Hulya Dagdeviren; Terry McKinley; Alfredo Saad-Filho and Carlos Oya 2006, *Economic Policies for Growth, Employment and Poverty Reduction: Case Study of Zambia*. Centre for Development Policy and Research and UNDP.

Weeks, John and Terry McKinley 2006, 'Does Debt Relief Increase Fiscal Space in Zambia? The MDG Implications', *UNDP Poverty Centre Country Study*, 5.

McKinley, Terry and John Weeks 2007, 'A Proposed Strategy for Growth, Employment and Poverty Reduction in Uzbekistan', in *Economic Alternatives for Growth, Employment and Poverty Reduction*, edited by Terry McKinley, London: Palgrave Macmillan.

Weeks, John and Shruti Patel 2007, 'Fiscal Policy', *International Policy Centre for Inclusive Growth Publications*, 1.

Weeks, John; Shruti Patel and Alan Mukumbe 2007, *Effects of the Appreciation of the Kwacha on the Zambian Economy*. UNDP.

Weeks, John and Terry McKinley 2007, 'The Macroeconomic Implications of MDG-based Strategies in Sub-Saharan Africa' in *Economic Alternatives for Growth, Employment and Poverty Reduction*, edited by Terry McKinley, London: Palgrave Macmillan.

Geda, Alemayehu; Abebe Shimeles and John Weeks 2008, 'Growth, Poverty, and inequality in Ethiopia: Which Way for Pro-Poor Growth?', *Journal of International Development*, 21, 7: 947–70.

Weeks, John and Terry McKinley 2009, 'As Implicações Macroeconômicas das Estratégias com Base nos ODM, na África Subsaariana', *International Policy Centre for Inclusive Growth Policy Research Brief*, 4.

Hailu, Degol and John Weeks 2009, 'Can Low-Income Countries Adopt Counter-Cyclical Policies?', *One Pager* 92, International Policy Centre for Inclusive Growth, Bureau for Development Policy. UNDP.

Weeks, John and Degol Hailu 2011, *Background Paper on Macroeconomic Management in Conflict-Affected and Mineral-Rich Developing Countries*. UNDP.

Hailu, Degol and John Weeks 2012, 'Macroeconomic Policies for Resource-Rich Countries' *G-24 Policy Brief*, 71.

Weeks, John and Howard Stein 2012, 'Poverty, Gender, and Insecurity in Africa South of the Sahara' in *Gendered Insecurities: Poverty, Women, and Poverty Reduction Policies in Africa South of the Sahara*, edited by Howard Stein and Amal Hassan Fadlalla, London: Routledge.

Saad-Filho, Alfredo and John Weeks 2013, 'Curses, Diseases and Other Resource Confusions', *Third World Quarterly*, 34, 1: 1–21.

Geda, Alemayehu and John Weeks 2016, 'Short Run Movements in the Kwacha: Analytical Study for the Bank of Zambia'. International Growth Centre, London School of Economics.

Weeks, John and Oswald Mungule 2013, 'Determinants of the Zambian Kwacha', *International Growth Centre Working Paper*, available at: https://www.theigc.org/wp-content/uploads/2015/02/Weeks-Mungule-2013-Working-Paper.pdf

Smith, Jeremy and John Weeks 2017, *Bringing Democratic Choice to Europe's Economic Governance: The EU Treaty Changes We Need and Why We Need Them*, Prime & Rosa Luxemburg Foundation, available at: https://www.rosalux.eu/en/article/653.bringing-democratic-choice-to-europers-economic-governance.html

Geda, Alemayehu; John Weeks and Herryman Moono 2018, 'Impact of macroeconomic reform on labour markets and income in Zambia: Assessing ZAMMOD', Employment Working Paper 245, *ILO*.

References

Alberro, Jose, and Joseph Persky 1979, 'The Simple Analytics of Falling Profit Rates, Okishio's Theorem and Fixed Capital', *Review of Radical Political Economics* 11, 3: 37-44.

Amin, Samir 1973, 'The End of a Debate', African Institute for Economic Development and Planning, Economic Commission for Africa, United Nations.

Amin, Samir 1974, 'Accumulation on a World Scale: A Critique of the Theory of Underdevelopment', *Monthly Review*, 26, 7: 1–12.

Amin, Samir 1976, *Unequal Development*, New York: Monthly Review Press.

Anaya Franco, Eduardo 1974, *Imperialismo, industrialización y transferéncia de tecnología en el Perú*, Lima: Editorial Horizonte Banco Central de Reserva del Perú.

Banco Central de Reserva del Perú 1957 *Renta nacional, 1942–1955*, Lima.

Banco Central de Reserva del Perú 1966 *Cuentas nacionales, 1950–1967*, Lima.

Banco Central de Reserva del Perú 1974 *Cuentas nacionales, 1960–1973*. Lima.

Banco Central de Reserva del Perú n.d. *El desarrollo económico y financiero del Perú*. Lima.

Baran, Paul A. 1957, *The Political Economy of Growth*, New York: Monthly Review Press.

Baran, Paul A. 1975, *Economic Calculations and Forms of Property*, New York: Monthly Review Press.

Baran, Paul A., and Paul Sweezy 1966, *Monopoly Capital*, New York: Monthly Review Press.

Barclay, William, and Mitchell Stengel 1975, 'Surplus and Surplus Value', *Review of Radical Political Economics*, 7, 4: 33–43.

Baumol, William J. 1974, 'The Transformation of Values: What Marx "Really" Meant (An Interpretation)', *Journal of Economic Literature*, XII, 1: 51–62

Bell, Peter F. 1977, 'Marxist Theory, Class Struggle, and the Crisis of Capitalism', in *The Subtle Anatomy of Capitalism*, edited by Jesse Schwartz. Santa Monica: Goodyear.

Bettelheim, Charles 1972a, 'Theoretical Comments by Charles Bettelheim', in Emmanuel 1972.

Bettelheim, Charles 1972b, *Class Struggles in the USSR: First Period (1917–1923)*, Monthly Review Press.

Bettelheim, Charles 1972c, 'The Theory of Imperialism and the Labour Movement', *New Left Review*, 73: 314–18.

Boddy, Radford, and James Crotty 1975, 'Class Conflict and Macro-Policy: The Political Business Cycle', *Review of Radical Political Economics*, 7, 1: 1–19.

Bollinger, William 1977, 'The Bourgeois Revolution in Peru: A Conception of Peruvian History', *Latin American Perspectives* 4, 3: 18–56.

Bonilla, Heraclio 1974, *Guano y burguesía en el Perú*, Lima: Instituto de Estudios Peruanos.

Braverman, Harry 1974, *Labour and Monopoly Capital*, New York: Monthly Review Press.

Brenner, Robert 1977, 'The Origins of Capitalist Development: A Critique of Neo-Smithian Marxism', *New Left Review*, 104.

Broome, John 1973, 'The Sraffa-Leontief Model', Birkbeck College, Department of Economics, Discussion Paper.

Bullock, Paul and David Yaffe 1975, 'Inflation, the Crisis, and the Post-War Boom', *Revolutionary Communist* (London), 2–3, November.

Bukharin, Nikolai I. 1972, *Imperialism and World Economy*, London: Merlin Press

Bukharin, Nikolai I. 1968 *Imperialism and the Accumulation of Capital*, New York: Monthly Review Press.

Cabrales, Antonio 1992, 'Land Reform and Agrarian Change in Chile After the Coup', *Journal of Developing Societies*, 8, 1: 71–80.

Cardoso, Fernando H. 1972, 'Dependent Capitalist Development in Latin America', *New Left Review*, 74 (July–August): 83–95.

Cardoso, Fernando H., 1977, 'The Consumption of Dependency Theory in the United States', *Latin American Research Review*, XII, 3: 7–24.

Cardoso, Fernando H. and Enzo Faletto 1972, *Dependéncia y desarrollo en América Latina*, Mexico City.

Clifton, James 1977, 'Competition and the Evolution of the Capitalist Mode of Production', *Cambridge Journal of Economics*, 1, 2: 137–51.

Christensen, Laurits R., Dianne Cummings, and Dale W. Jorgenson 1975, 'An International Comparison of Growth in Productivity, 1947–1973', *SSRI*, Workshop Series No. 7531, University of Wisconsin, Madison, October.

Colletti, Lucio 1972, *From Rousseau to Lenin*, London: Verso

Dietz, James L. 1979. 'Imperialism and Underdevelopment: A Theoretical Perspective and a Case Study of Puerto Rico', *Review of Radical Political Economics*, 11, 4: 23–36.

Dobb, Maurice 1947, 'On the Relations of Marxian Theory to Soviet Practice', *Science & Society*, 11, 1: 75–92.

Dobb, Maurice 1973, *Political Economy and Capitalism: Some Essays on Economic Transition*, London: Routledge.

Dore, Elizabeth 1977, 'Crisis and Accumulation in the Peruvian Mining Industry, 1968–1974', *Latin American Perspectives* 4 (3): 77–102.

Dore, Elizabeth 1981, 'Crisis and Accumulation in the Peruvian Mining Industry', PhD thesis, New York: Columbia University.

Dore, Elizabeth, John Weeks and William Bollinger 1975, 'The National Bourgeoisie and Revolutionary Struggle', unpublished manuscript.

Dore, Elizabeth and John Weeks 1976a, 'The Intensification of the Assault Against the

Working Class in 'Revolutionary' Peru', *Latin American Perspectives* 3 (Spring), 55–83.

Dore, Elizabeth and John Weeks 1976b, 'The Causes of Backwardness and the Uneven Development of Capitalism', unpublished manuscript.

Dore, Elizabeth and John Weeks 1977, 'Capital, Class Struggle and Wages in the Context of Backwardness', paper presented to Third World Strikes Seminar, Institute of Social Studies, The Hague (September 12–16).

Dore, Elizabeth, and John Weeks 1978, 'International Exchange and the Causes of Backwardness,' *Latin American Perspectives*, 6, 2: 81–4.

Dorfman, Robert, Paul Samuelson and Robert M. Solow 1958, *Linear Programming and Economic Analysis*, New York: McGraw-Hill.

Emmanuel, Arghiri 1972, *Unequal Exchange: A study in the imperialism of trade*, New Left Books, London.

Engels, Frederick 1962, *Anti-Dühring*, London: Lawrence and Wishart.

Fernandez, Raul A. and Jose F. Ocampo 1974, 'The Latin American Revolution: a Theory of Imperialism, Not Dependence', *Latin American Perspectives*, 1, 1: 30–61

Fine, Ben 1975, 'The Circulation of Capital, Ideology and Crisis', *Bulletin of the Conference of Socialist Economists*, IV, 3 (October).

Fine, Ben 1980, *Economic Theory and Ideology*, London: Edward Arnold.

Fine, Ben 1982, 'The World Economy and Inflation Theory: An Interpretation and Critique', in *Issues in Political Economy*, edited by Francis Green and Petter Nore. London: Macmillan.

Fine, Ben 1991, 'Competition', in Tom Bottomore (ed.) *A Dictionary of Marxist Thought*. Oxford: Blackwell.

Fine, Ben and John Weeks 1980, 'Recent Criticism of the Law of the Tendency of the Rate of Profit to Fall', unpublished manuscript.

Fine, Ben and Laurence Harris 1975, 'The British Economy Since March, 1974', *Bulletin of the Conference of Socialist Economists*, IV, 3 (October).

Fine, Ben and Laurence Harris 1976, 'Controversial Issues in Marxist Economic Theory', *Socialist Register*, 141–78.

Fine, Ben and Laurence Harris 1979, *Re-Reading Capital*, Atlantic Highlands, N.J.: Humanities Press.

Frank, Andre Gunder 1969, *Capitalism and Underdevelopment in Latin America: Historical Studies of Chile and Brazil*, New York: Monthly Review Press.

Gerschenkron, Alexander 1962, *Economic Backwardness in Historical Perspective*, Cambridge, MA: Harvard University Press

Gerstein, Ira 1976, 'Production, Circulation, and Value', *Economy and Society*, 5, 3: 243–91.

Glyn, Andrew, and Bob Sutcliffe 1972, *British Capitalism, Workers, and the Profit Squeeze*, Harmondsworth: Penguin

Gough, Ian 1975, 'State Expenditure in Advanced Capitalism', *New Left Review*, 92: 53–92.

Gough, Ian 1972, 'Marx's Theory of Productive and Unproductive Labour', *New Left Review*, 76: 47–72.

Griffin, Keith 1989, 'Gerschenkron Reconsidered', *Social Science History*, 13, 1: 99–126.

Harding, Timothy F. 1976, 'Dependency, Nationalism and the State in Latin America', *Latin American Perspectives* III (Fall), 3–11.

Harcourt, Geoffrey C. 1973, *Some Cambridge Controversies in the Theory of Capital*, Cambridge: Cambridge University Press.

Harris, Laurence 1983, 'Periodization of Capitalism', in *A Dictionary of Marxist Thought*, edited by Tom Bottomore, Oxford: Blackwell.

Hilferding, Rudolf 1981, *Finance Capital: A Study of the Latest Phase of Capitalist Development*, London: Routledge.

Himmelweit, Susan 1974, 'The Continuing Saga of the Falling Rate of Profit. A Reply to Mario Cogoy', *Bulletin of the Conference of Socialist Economists*, 9 (Autumn).

Himmelweit, Susan, and Simon Mohun 1978, 'The Anomalies of Capital', *Capital and Class*, 6: 67–105

Hobson, J.A. 1938, *Imperialism: A Study*, London: George Allen and Unwin.

Hodgson, G. 1974, 'The Theory of the Falling Rate of Profit', *New Left Review*, 84: 55–82.

Hoxha, Enver 1976, 'Report submitted to the Seventh Congress of the Party of Labour of Albania, Tirana', The '8 Nentori' Publishing House.

INP (Instituto Nacional de Planificación) 1973, *La concentración de la producción manufacturera en el Perú*, Lima.

INP (Instituto Nacional de Planificacióon) 1975, *Devaluación*, Lima.

Itoh, Makoto 1977, 'The Inflational Crisis of Capitalism', *Capital and Class*, 4, 1: 21–54.

Itoh, Makoto 1978, 'The Formation of Marx's Theory of Crisis', *Science & Society*, XLII (2): 129–55.

Itoh, Makoto 1980, *Value and Crisis*, London: Pluto Press.

Itoh, Makoto 1988, *The Basic Theory of Capitalism: The Forms and Substance of the Capitalist Economy*, London: Macmillan.

Johansen, Leif 1972, 'Labour Theory of Value and Marginal Utilities', in *A Critique of Economic Theory*, edited by E.K. Hunt and J.G. Schwartz, London: Penguin.

Jones, J. 1997, 'Investment Patterns Across Countries', *Journal of Economic Growth*, 2, 1: 35–50.

Kay, Cristobal 1989, *Latin American Theories of Underdevelopment*, London: Routledge.

Kemp, Tom 1967, *Theories of Imperialism*, London.

Kidron, M. 1970, *Western Capitalism Since the War*, London: Pelican Books.

Krugman, Paul R. 1987, 'Pricing to Market When the Exchange Rate Changes', *NBER Working Paper*, 51.

Kula, Witold 1976, *An Economic Theory of Feudalism*, London: New Left Books.

Kuusinen, O.W. et al. n. d., *Fundamentals of Marxism-Leninism*, Moscow: Foreign Languages Publishing House.

Lenin, V.I. 1972a, 'A Characterisation of Economic Romanticism', *Collected Works*, Vol. 2, pp. 129–226, Moscow: Progress Publishers.

Lenin, V.I. 1972b, 'The Development of Capitalism in Russia', *Collected Works*, Vol. 3, pp. 25–607, Moscow: Progress Publishers.

Lenin, V.I. 1972c, *On the so-Called 'Market Question'*, *Collected Works*, Vol. 1, Moscow: Progress Publishers.

Lenin, V.I. 1972d, 'Introduction', in N. Bukharin, *Imperialism and World Economy*, London: Merlin Press.

Lenin, V.I. 1981, *Imperialism: The Highest Stage of Capitalism*, New York: International Publishers.

Laclau, Ernesto 1971, 'Imperialism in Latin America', *New Left Review*, 67, 1: 24–42.

Luxemburg, Rosa 1968, *The Accumulation of Capital*, New York: Monthly Review Press.

Luxemburg, Rosa and Nikolai I. Bukharin 1972, *The Accumulation of Capital: An Anti-Critique; Imperialism and the Accumulation of Capital* (ed. Kenneth J. Tarbuck), New York: Monthly Review Press.

Mao Tse-tung 1971, 'On Contradiction', *Selected Readings*, pp. 85–133, Peking: Foreign Languages Press.

Mandel, Ernest 1975, *Late Capitalism*, London: Verso.

Mandel, Ernest 1987, *A Marxist Theory of the Business Cycle*, London: Verso.

Marglin, Stephen, and Juliet Schor 1988, *The Golden Age of Capitalism*, Oxford: Clarendon Press.

Marini, Ruy Mauro 1972, 'Dialectica de la dependéncia', *Sociedad y Desarrollo* (January–March).

Marx, Karl 1906, *Capital: A Critique of Political Economy*, Vol. I. New York: The Modern Library.

Marx, Karl 1956, *Capital: A Critique of Political Economy*, Vol. II. London: Progress Publishers.

Marx, Karl 1968, *Theories of Surplus Value*, Vol. II, Moscow: Progress Publishers.

Marx, Karl 1969, *Theories of Surplus Value*, Vol. I, Moscow: Progress Publishers.

Marx, Karl 1970a, *A Contribution to the Critique of Political Economy*, Moscow: Progress Publishers

Marx, Karl 1970b, *Capital: A Critical Analysis of Capitalist Production*, Vol. I, London and Moscow: Lawrence & Wishart and Progress Publishers.

Marx, Karl 1971, *Capital, Vol. III, The Process of Production as a Whole*, International Publishers, available online: https://www.marxists.org/archive/marx/works/download/pdf/Capital-Volume-III.pdf.

Marx, Karl 1972a, *Capital*, Vol. III, London and Moscow: Lawrence & Wishart and Progress Publishers.

Marx, Karl 1972b, *Capital: A Critique of Political Economy*, Vol. 1, London and Moscow: Progress Publishers, available online: https://www.marxists.org/archive/marx/works/download/pdf/Capital-Volume-I.pdf.

Marx, Karl 1973, *Grundrisse: Foundations of the Critique of Political Economy* (*Rough Draft*), translated by Martin Nicolaus, available online at: https://www.marxists.org/archive/marx/works/download/pdf/grundrisse.pdf.

Marx, Karl 1976a, *A Contribution to the Critique of Political Economy*, New York: International Publishers.

Marx, Karl 1976b, *The Poverty of Philosophy*, in *Collected Works*, Vol. 6., New York: International Publishers.

Marx, Karl 1976c, *Capital: A Critique of Political Economy*, Vol. 1, translated by Ben Fowkes, London: Penguin.

Marx, Karl 1991, 'The Economic Manuscripts of 1861–1864', in *Marx-Engels Collected Works*, Volume 33. London: Lawrence and Wishart.

Marx, Karl 1993, *Capital*, Vol. II, Harmondsworth: Penguin.

Marx, Karl and Friedrich Engels 1965, *Selected Correspondence*, Moscow: Progress.

Mattick, Paul Sr. 1971, 'Value Theory and Capitalist Crisis', *Marxism Today*, 15, 6: 175–83.

Medio, Alfredo 1972, 'Profits and Surplus Value: Appearance and Reality in Capitalist Production', in E.K. Hunt and J.G. Schwartz (eds.), A *Critique of Economic Theory*, London: Penguin.

Ministério de Fomento y Obras Públicas 1956 *Estadística indústria 1954*, Lima.

Ministério de Fomento y Obras Públicas 1957 *Estadística indústria, 1955*, Lima

Ministério de Fomento y Obras Públicas 1958 *Estadística indústria, 1956*, Lima

Ministério de Fomento y Obras Públicas 1959 *Estadística indústria, 1957*, Lima

Ministério de Fomento y Obras Públicas 1960 *Estadística indústria, 1958*, Lima

Ministério de Fomento y Obras Públicas 1961a *Estadística indústria, 1959*, Lima

Ministério de Fomento y Obras Públicas 1961b *Estadística indústria, 1960*, Lima

Ministério de Hacienda y Comércio 1958, *Boletín estadístico*, Lima.

Ministério de Indústria 1962, *Estadística indústria, 1961*, Lima.

Ministério de Indústria y Comércio 1966 *Estadística indústria, 1965*, Lima.

Ministério de Indústria y Comércio 1967, *Estadística indústria, 1966*, Lima

Ministério de Indústria y Comércio 1969a, *Estadística indústria, 1967*, Lima.

Ministério de Indústria y Comércio 1969b, *Estadística indústria, 1969*, Lima.

Ministério de Indústria y Comércio 1970, *Estadística indústria, 1968*, Lima.

Ministério de Indústria y Turismo 1974, *Estadística indústria, 1972*, Lima

Ministério de Indústria y Turismo 1975, *Estadística indústria, 1973*, Lima.

Molinari, Baltazar Caravedo and Stephen Gorman 1977, 'The State and the Bourgeoisie in the Peruvian Fishmeal Industry', *Latin American Perspectives* 4, 3: 103–23.

Monthly Review Editors 1975, 'The Economic Crisis in Historical Perspective', 26, 10 (March)

North American Industry Classification System 2012, *United States Census Bureau*, https://www.census.gov/eos/www/naics/

Okishio, Nobuo 1961, 'Technical Changes and the Rate of Profit', *Kobe University Economic Review*, 7, 1: 86–99.

Persky, Joseph, and Jose Alberro 1978, *Technical Innovation and the Dynamics of the Profit Rate*, Chicago: University of Illinois Press.

Portocarrero, Felipe 1974 'La economía peruana en 1973', *Apuntes* (Universidad del Pacífico, Lima), II, 3.

Pritchett, Lant 1997a, 'Remarkably Stable Cross-Country Growth Patterns: Evidence and Implications', *Population and Development Review*, 91–115.

Pritchett, Lant 1997b, 'Where Has All the Education Gone?', *The World Bank Economic Review*, 11, 3: 367–91.

Pritchett, Lant 1997c, 'Divergence Big Time', *Journal of Economic Perspectives* 11, 3: 3–17.

Purdy, D. 1973, 'Theory of Permanent Arms Economy – A Critique and an Alternative', *Bulletin of the Conference of Socialist Economists* (Spring).

Roemer, John E. 1977, 'Technical Change and the Tendency of the Rate of Profit to Fall', *Journal of Economic Theory*, 16, 2: 403–424.

Roemer, John E. 1979, 'Continuing Controversy on the Falling Rate of Profit: Fixed Capital and Other Issues', *Cambridge Journal of Economics*, 3, 4: 379–398.

Romagnalo, David 1975, 'The So-called "Law" of Uneven and Combined Development', *Latin American Perspectives*, II (Spring), 7–31.

Romagnolo, L. 1975 *A Critique of Trotskyism*, Solidarity.

Rowthorn, Robert 1974, 'Vulgar Economy', *New Left Review* 86.

Roy, M.N. 1922, *India in Transition*, Geneva: G. Allen & Unwin.

Shaikh, Anwar 1977, 'Marx's Theory of Value and the Transformation Problem', *Science & Society*, 41, 3: 347–66.

Shaikh, Anwar 1978a, 'An Introduction to the History of Crisis Theories', in *US Capitalism in Crisis*, edited by Joshua Goldstein and Ross Tieman, 219–41. New York: Economics Education Project.

Shaikh, Anwar 1978b, 'Political Economy and Capitalism: Notes on Dobb's Theory of Crisis', *Cambridge Journal of Economics*, 2, 3: 233–51.

Shaikh, Anwar 1980, 'On the Laws of International Exchange', in: E.J. Nell (ed.) *Growth, Profits and Property*. Cambridge: Cambridge University Press.

Sherman, Howard J. 1979, 'A Marxist Theory of the Business Cycle', *Review of Radical Political Economics*, 11, 1: 1–23.

Sismondi, Jean-Charles-Leonard Simonde de 1951, *Nouveaux Principes d'economie Politique*, E. Plan.

Sociedad Nacional de Indústrias 1963, *La indústria manufacturera del Perú*, Lima.

Suits, Daniel 1963, *Statistics*, Chicago: Rand McNally & Company.

Stalin, Joseph 1975, *On Chinese Revolution*, Calcutta: Suren Dutt.

Stedman-Jones, Gareth 1991, 'Utopian Socialism', in *A Dictionary of Marxist Thought*, 504–7, Blackwell Publishers.

Suskewicz, J. 1979, 'Basic Sectors and Regional Income Multipliers: A Survey and Extension', *Review of Regional Studies*, 9, 2: 45–51.

Sweezy, Paul 1968, *Theory of Capitalist Development*, New York: Monthly Review Press.

Sweezy, Paul et al. 1976, *The Transition from Feudalism to Capitalism: A Symposium*, London: Verso

Takahashi, H. Kohachiro. 1976, 'A Contribution to the Discussion', in Sweezy et al 1976.

Taylor, John G. 1981, *From Modernization to Modes of Production: A Critique of the Sociologies of Development and Underdevelopment*, London: Routledge.

Taylor, John G. 1983, 'Colonialism', in T. Bottomore (ed.) *A Dictionary of Marxist Thought*. Oxford: Blackwell.

United Nations 1986, *World Economic and Social Survey*, United Nations Secretariat, New York.

United Nations 1991, *World Economic and Social Survey*, United Nations Secretariat, New York.

United Nations Conference on Trade and Development 1997, *Trade and Development Report 1997*, UNCTAD, Geneva.

United Nations 1998, *World Economic and Social Survey*, United Nations Secretariat, New York.

U.S. Department of Commerce 1972, 'Survey of Current Business'.

U.S. Department of Commerce 1977, 'Survey of Current Business'.

Van Parijs, Philippe 1980, 'The Falling-Rate-of-Profit Theory of Crisis: A Rational Reconstruction by Way of Obituary', *Review of Radical Political Economics*, 12, 1: 1-16.

Warren, Bill 1973, 'Imperialism and Capitalist Industrialisation,' *New Left Review* 81.

Warren, Bill 1980, *Imperialism: Pioneer of Capitalism*, London: Verso.

Weeks, John 1975, 'Relative Surplus Value and the Limits to Capitalist Accumulation in Backward Countries', unpublished manuscript, Madison, Wisconsin.

Weeks, John 1976, 'Price Changes, Centralization, and the Social Productivity of Labour: Peru, 1967–1973', unpublished manuscript, Madison, Wisconsin.

Weeks, John 1977a, 'Crisis and Accumulation in the Peruvian Economy, 1967–1975', *Review of Radical Political Economics*, 8, 4: 56–72

Weeks, John 1977b, 'The Sphere of Production and the Analysis of Crisis in Capitalism', *Science & Society*, 41, 3: 296–311.

Weeks, John 1979, 'The Process of Accumulation and the "Profit Squeeze" Hypothesis', *Science and Society*, 43, 3: 245–70.

Weeks, John 1981, *Capital and Exploitation*, Princeton, NJ: Princeton University Press.

Weeks, John 1982a, 'A Note on Underconsumptionist Theory and the Labor Theory of Value', *Science & Society*, 46, 1: 60–76

Weeks, John 1982b, 'The Differences between Materialist Theory and Dependency Theory and Why They Matter', in *Dependency and Marxism: Toward a Resolution of the Debate*, edited by Ronald H. Chilcote, Westview, Boulder, Colorado.

Weeks, John 1983, 'On the Issue of Capitalist Circulation and the Concepts Appropriate to Its Analysis', *Science & Society*, 47, 2: 214–25

Weeks, John 1984, *The Limits to Capitalist Development: The Industrialization of Peru, 1950–1980*. Boulder, CT: Westview Press.

Weeks, John 1985, 'Epochs of Capitalism and the Progressiveness of Capital's Expansion', *Science and Society*, XLIX: 414–436

Weeks, John 1989, *A Critique of Neoclassical Macroeconomics*, Macmillan, London

Weeks, John 1990, 'Abstract Labour and Commodity Production', *Research in Political Economy*, 12, (edited by Paul Zarembka), Cambridge MA: Emerald Publishing.

Weeks, John 1994a, 'Fallacies of Competition: Myths and Maladjustment in the "Third World"', An Inaugural Lecture delivered on 13 October 1993, London: SOAS.

Weeks, John 1994b, 'A More Detailed Critique of Neo-Classical Competition', *Economic and Labour Relations Review*, 5, 1: 143–56.

Weeks, John 2003, 'Capital and Exploitation', in *Marx's Theory of History*, edited by Terrell Carver, London: Macmillan.

Wood, Ellen Meiksins 1981, 'Marxism and the Problem of Historical Specificity', *New Left Review*, 127: 27–51.

Wright, Erik Olin 1977, 'Alternative Perspectives in Marxist Theory of Accumulation and Crisis', in *The Subtle Anatomy of Capitalism*, edited by Jesse Schwartz, 217. Santa Monica.

Wright, Eric Olin 1987, 'Capitalist Accumulation and Crisis', *New Left Review*, 162: 5–37.

WWFES (World-wide Federation of Ethiopian Students) 1976, 'More on the National Question and the Revolution in Ethiopia', *Struggle*, III, 3.

Yaffe, David S. 1973, 'The Marxian Theory of Crisis, Capital, and the State', *Economy and Society*, II, 2: 186–232.

Index

Printed in the United States
by Baker & Taylor Publisher Services